The A to Z of Dinosaurs:

An Essential Guide to the Paleontology, Biology, and History of the Terrible Lizards

By Maria Kaj

Darwin

For more information:

Visit my blog at kajmeister.com

Table of Contents

Chapter Contents by Theme

The Table of Contents shows chapters according to the alphabet to allow for browsing. However, if you wish to search for chapters grouped by topic, you can look by theme:

What Makes a Dinosaur?
Antorbital Fenestra, Clade, Hip, Variety

Paleontology Theories and Debates
Blood, Godzilla, Living Relatives, the North Pole, Origin, Yucatan

Newfangled Technology
Blood, Living Relatives, X-Rays

Individual Dinosaur Species
Diplodocus, Iguanodon, Godzilla, *Parasaurolophus, Quetzalcoatlus, T. rex, Zuul*

Body Parts
Antorbital Fenestra, Blood, Fossil, Hip, *Parasaurolophus,* Skin

Darwin and Friends
Extinction, Origin, Renaissance

Birds Are Dinosaurs
Living Relatives, Origin, *Quetzalcoatlus,* Renaissance, Skin, Wings

History of Paleontology
Iguanodon, Mary Anning, Unscrupulous

Pop Culture and Dinosaurs
Godzilla, *Jurassic Park,* Zuul

The End of the Dinosaurs
Extinction, K-Pg Boundary, Yucatan

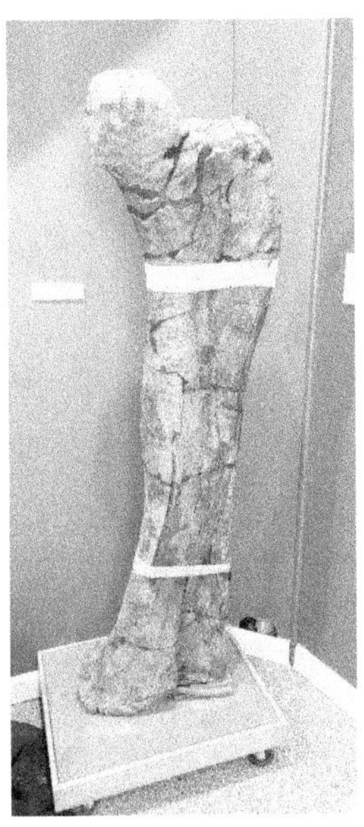

Fig 1. Sauropod Femur

Introduction

This is a dinosaur book for geeks. I mean that in the nicest way. If you are one of those people stopped in their tracks by a dinosaur skeleton—a real one, not a stuffed animal—then this is for you. If your heart beats a little faster when you get to That Section of the natural history museum, you know what I'm talking about. Maybe your screen saver looks something like this...

Fig 2. *Tyrannosaurus* makes a great background image on your phone!

This ain't no kiddie book, though. There will be no frolicking ceratopsians or gamboling gallimimuses, no pictures of cavemen being chased by a *T. rex*. There are plenty of alphabet-themed dinosaur picture books for your toddler out there, if you are looking for a cuddly *Allosaurus*. This is not one of those. This book is for adults.

But it's not particularly for paleontologists, either, who are lucky enough to go into a profession that gets to think about these magnificent creatures for a living. Okay, paleontology is backbreaking work, a painstaking endurance test of a profession, which can take years to deliver a useful result. But, it's DINOSAURS! Of course, I don't mind, paleontologists, if you read this. You may enjoy seeing your life's work idolized.

If you are, nevertheless, a younger person reading this book, then good for you. This book is perfectly acceptable to dinosaur enthusiasts of all ages. It helps if you can say "triceratops" without stumbling. Or, if you are a person young at heart, who simply has a passion for paleontological wandering, even better! Get ready to dig deep into dinosaur details, to walk the path of the ancient, terrible lizards. This book will prove that you don't have to be a scientist to understand science.

Why Read this Book

As a dino enthusiast myself, one of the things that has always bugged me about books on dinosaurs is that they are either for young children or for graduate paleontology students. In other words, either too simplistic or too technical. Either they sport pictures of stegosaurs with glowing, colored bulbs painted like a Lite-Brite set, or they spill Latin and academic jargon across the pages with all the charm of a list of Recommended Daily Amounts of fiber. This book will land somewhere in between.

What *The A to Z of Dinosaurs* will do is tell you the main things you might want to know about dinosaurs, but in a fun and accessible way. Even though it's science, it can still be captivating. I am a historian, a nonfiction storyteller, so my goal is to tell true stories about dinosaurs. How did they get that way? Whose idea was it to investigate them? Why are they so big? Why aren't they here anymore? We are curious people; we want to know things. We just don't want to know more than we need to know to quench our thirst for knowledge.

Unlike a child's picture book, we will get into the weeds a bit. We'll talk about the Saurischians and the Ornithischians and their hip joints—don't worry, it's all in Chapter "H." There will be some scientific language and reference to paleontology research. Now, though it is fun to get a three-year-old to say "antorbital fenestra," your average three-year-old is probably not going to care about the foramen blood index. You might, though, if it convinces you that dinosaurs were warm-blooded, which solves an age-old debate about their activity levels.

At the same time, this is not a textbook. One of the frustrating things for me about dinosaur books for adults is how quickly they begin spouting lists of dinosaur names and the titles of geology formations and so on. While I do have a favorite dinosaur and can name quite a few, I get stuck reading too many words in Latin. Here, topics will be presented in ordinary language as much as possible. For instance, if we're going to talk about the EPB, the Extant Phylogenetic Bracket (Chapter "L"), it is because Living Relative comparisons are a master key to unlocking the secrets of extinct animals. But you won't need to remember what EPB means. There will be no quizzes or tests. You can learn plenty without feeling like you have to memorize anything.

What's Included in This Book

As we start this journey of 26 views on dinosaurs, you'll notice right away that A does not even refer to a kind of dinosaur. I promised! This is not a child's alphabet book, not a book about 26 different dinosaurs. There will be a few named after a single dinosaur but even those will quickly delve into history and body chemistry. Thus, Chapter "A" is not about *Apatosaurus*, *Albertosaurus*, or even *Ankylosaurus*. Instead "A" is about the Antorbital Fenestra, which turns out to be a very important physical characteristic that defined dinosaurs.

So, even before we get into the ant-orbit-a-whatchamacallit, it's important to know that these chapters will wrestle with questions *about* dinosaurs, such as:

- What made a dinosaur a dinosaur?

- Where did the dinosaurs come from? And where did they go?

- What did they look like?

- How did they behave?

- And, most of all, how do we know?

In other words, I'm going to talk about the things that dinosaurs did. Their habits. Their loves and losses… well, maybe not that. But the dinosaur *ouvre*, so to speak, their "body of work." (Body … get it? Yes, no pun will be spared in our learning about paleontology. You have been warned.)

Since they lived 200 million years ago, give or take a few million, it is not always easy to make intelligent guesses about what they were like. However, you would be surprised at what those clever scientists who study bones can figure out just from the bones.

We'll also talk a lot about stereotypes and about the history of dinosaur discoveries. What they knew when they dug them up was not very much, and they made a lot of wrong guesses. Two hundred years and thousands of dinosaur bone specimens later, scientists know a lot more. But how our knowledge changed is an important part of understanding.

That understanding isn't 100% complete, either. It's been estimated that all the dinosaur bones ever discovered represent perhaps 1% of dinosaurs that lived. There is a lot we still don't know; some of it may change after this book goes to print. That's part of the fun, too.

If this was a biology class or a paleontology textbook, the topics would be organized fairly rigidly. Environment, eating habits, breeding habits, origin, extinction, and so on. You would encounter each major type of dinosaur systematically, learning hundreds of those Greek and Latin words. Such books are great for reference but not super fun to read or browse through unless you're trying to earn college credit. The goal of *The A to Z of Dinosaurs* is to cover these things in an unconventional way. Browsing through the topics a bit randomly by letter means these ideas may sneak up on you and, therefore, be a little more memorable.

There is also a Chapter Contents by Theme after the alphabetical Table of Contents. If you are particularly interested in dinosaur body parts, for instance, you can dig into Blood ("B"), Skin ("S"), or Hips ("H"). If you want to look at controversial theories, study what's known about their extinction, or browse through the history of ideas about paleontology, you can do that by theme. Plus, to help you navigate a little better, whenever a topic notes something covered elsewhere, a letter in parenthesis will tell you where ("X"). And, if you really need to know exactly where a particular topic is, there is an index, so knock yourself out![1]

This way, you can browse through this set of topics in whatever order or manner that you want. Read a bit while you're standing in line at the store or at the doctor's office. Wherever and whenever you want, because it doesn't require you to learn in any particular order. It's a buffet. Sample at will!

Why I Wrote this Book

I confess it. I'm not a paleontologist, even though I now know how to write *Parasaurolophus cyrtocristatus* properly. I also am not a commercial fossil hunter, a fossil collector, or even a scientist. I just love dinosaurs.

My infatuation started not as a child, but in college. I found myself one semester with a couple hours to kill between classes. I just wanted to think about something different for a while from English

---

[1] The print version of the book includes two varieties of the index with page numbers: one for ancient reptiles (dinosaurs etc.) and one for people, places, and ideas. The eBook version includes the same two lists but without page numbers, both searchable.

Good researchers know that you can "read" a book by flipping through the index, so I didn't want eBook users to be at a disadvantage. Smart cookie researchers also read the footnotes sometimes, so congratulations for arriving here and earning the designation of "smart cookie!"

Lit and Accounting, my majors. Plus, it was too far to walk back to my dorm, and the library was always too noisy. So I wandered into a large lecture hall that turned out to be covering Paleontology 2E, Introduction to Dinosaurs. It was at Berkeley, which I didn't know until later was one of the best places in the world to study dinosaurs.

Berkeley loves large lecture halls for undergraduates, so I was able to slide into a seat in the back and listen without getting noticed. I was quickly hooked. I went to every class, even bought the cheap, loose-leaf version of a textbook they were using, though I was happy to skip the exams. But, two years later, when I needed a two-unit filler class between studying the Victorian novel and amortizing bond interest, I thought myself uber-clever to take a subject I already knew. Paleo 2E redux! Then, I found myself signing up for another paleontology class on mammals. Honestly, if I hadn't had to graduate, I might have ended up with a Paleo minor.

Later, every time my family's vacation would swing near a natural history museum, I'd persuade us to fit it in and linger over the dinosaur skeletons, pointing out the hip joints. I showed off to my kids, and it is, indeed, fun to teach a three-year-old to say "antorbital fenestra." Every trip, if there was something called "dinosaur" nearby, we would have to go.

To me, even the cheesy stuff was fascinating, such as all the inaccurate dinosaur statues people put on their front lawns or on their gas station signs. Just so you know, if you're ever on a road trip going through Blandings, Utah, the Dinosaur Museum has an excellent collection of inaccurate dinosaur depictions shown on movie posters and in newspaper articles. My wife, who by then had learned her lesson, took the opportunity to do the laundry and have a milkshake, while I happily snapped photos of posters for *Gorgo* and that famous French classic, *Les Monsters de L'Apocalypse.*

Fast-forward to 2020. While writing a blog during the COVID lockdown, I stumbled across an April blogging event called the "A to Z challenge." The goal is to write 26 posts on a topic of your choice. I'd written a book about the Olympics, so I chose that as my first topic (and my first *A to Z* book). Since then, I've also covered the History of Accounting, the Renaissance, and the Silk Road.

Dinosaurs was the theme of my 2024 entry and proved, as always, quite challenging. It is not easy to (a) write thousands of words, every day, for nearly a month; (b) create a set of topics that fit all the letters, including J, X, Q, and Z; and (c) cover what anyone ought to know about a subject in 26 days. That last part is not a requirement of the blogging challenge, but it's a requirement for me. This book, which is a compilation of that work, is designed to cover the gamut and to do the topic of dinosaurs justice.

I have, since starting to write a blog, taken a turn back in school to earn a Master's in History so that I could brush up on my research chops. This has made it easier for me to provide the latest scientific research, which I have used to put more flesh on the bones of these topics. I have also added nearly a hundred photos and illustrations, because when it comes to science, sometimes you need to see it, like this cool photo I took of dinosaur footprints at the Dinosaur Ridge Trail in Morrison, CO.

Fig 3. Prepare to walk the path of dinosaurs.

I hope my example proves to you how far you can go in understanding a nerdy topic without having to go to school yourself. And I hope it inspires you to go off and find some dinosaurs for yourself. Start in Colorado. Or Wyoming, Montana, Utah, or Alberta.

In the meantime, the buffet is now open for sampling!

Two Words about Language

How to Translate Scientific Passages

While you and I don't need to be scientists to understand paleontology, it does help if you can translate paleo-speak into plain English. This book will avoid academic scientific language whenever possible, but sometimes you need to know technical terms. Also, I will cover some of the cutting-edge paleontology debates, and you may want to get more information on your own. Many research articles are publicly available. However, reading them can be a little difficult, even in sources supposedly for the general public, like *Scientific American* or *LiveScience*.

Think of scientific language as similar to learning any other language. Use what you know and examine the context carefully. If you were ordering the *plato especial* in a Mexican restaurant, you could figure it out based on observing pictures, thinking about the context, and using what you already know. Reading science is a form of translating.

Let's try an example. Here's a passage I came across when researching my favorite dinosaur, the *Parasaurolophus* ("P"):

> A neurological method for assessment of nasal cavity
> homologies in extant archosaurs is extended to
> lambeosaurine hadrosaurids (Dinosauria: Ornithischia) to
> test functional hypotheses associated with their
> hypertrophied nasal passages and highly derived cranial

crests. The olfactory system and associated cranial nerve pathways that have consistent relationships to soft tissue divisions of the nasal cavity are reconstructed in lambeosaurines on the basis of new paleoneurological data and a comparative phylogenetic approach. The new model of the lambeosaurine olfactory system and nasal cavity shows that a significant portion of nasal cavity proper was located outside the crest cavities and that the primary olfactory region was located rostromedial to the orbits.[2]

I know. Your eyes are crossing. So are mine. But there are ways to read this stuff. I learned this trick when teaching students how to handle the scientific reading passages on the SAT. What you do is replace every unknown term with "blah blah blah" or a word like "something." Substitute ordinary words for those you don't know. Look for the words you do know and see if there's enough context to get to the basic idea quickly, without having to interrupt yourself and look up a bunch of words, which is a buzzkill. Substitute words, make guesses, and try to puzzle it out. Here's my "translation":

> A special something way of testing nose hole (thingies) in a group of animals is applied to a new L-type of dinosaur, so that we, the scientists, can test our scientific guess about how their extra-something nose holes and head crests worked. The special system and related nerve paths, which are like soft divider things in the nose holes, are created in our new L-type dinosaurs on the basis of some new data we found. Plus, we compared them to others in a separate way that we already knew about.

> This new model of our L-type dinosaur guys and their nose holes shows that most of the part of their noses was actually not on their fancy head crests, also that the main nose thing—oh, olfactory must mean nose—the main nose function was actually somewhere near the orbits, which is eyes!

---

[2] David C. Evans, "Nasal Cavity Homologies and Cranial Crest Function in Lambeosaurine Dinosaurs," *Paleobiology* 32, no. 1 (2006): 109. http://www.jstor.org/stable/4096820.

In other words, this means that L-type dinosaurs didn't smell with their head crests. They had these bony head crests popping out of their faces, but they didn't use them for smelling at all. Can't they just say that? Again, I will avoid sentences as dense as the ones in research papers, but just in case you stumble upon some, you know what to do!

Of course, if you really are going to study paleontology or biology, then you may need to learn to write using the academic stuff, as well as practice dropping *Lambeosaurine hadrosaurids* into conversations at cocktail parties and such. In the meantime, translate with context. Oh, and if those L-types didn't smell with those head crests, what were they for? That answer will be in Chapter "P."

How to Name a Dinosaur

Speaking of *Lambeosaurine hadrosaurids*…do dinosaurs have one name or two or what? The two-pronged dinosaur names come from a system called the International Code for Zoological Nomenclature— back to the polysyllabic scientific world, whoopee! The ICZN code is a shared agreement among biologists for naming animals, a system which dates back to the late 19th century. At the time, scientists kept inventing their own naming systems (Merton's rules, Strickland's codes), and things got very confusing. They had to pick just one.

Naming a new dinosaur is a pretty political process because prestige goes along with any discovery. There are lots of juicy scandals involved. Whenever you read something like "*Kajmeisterus marianus* was recently reclassified because the phylogenetic bracket was deemed insufficient…" you know that groups of scientists have been fighting online in a metaphorical wrestling cage match for months, arguing over whether a tooth defined a whole new animal or was just a piece of a boring-old, already-known one.

When new names are created, the namer gets out a Greek or Latin dictionary, sometimes both. For instance, the name *Tyrannosaurus rex* has a Greek first name and a Latin last name. That dude studied a lot of classical languages!

All names included in the ICZN are given two parts. This is similar to how people have first names and last names (sometimes called a Christian name and a family or surname). Only with dinosaurs, the surname comes first, because the name of the larger group comes first. That name is called the genus.

The genus embraces a group of animals that have similar characteristics. If you know that humans are *Homo sapiens*, that means *Homo* is a genus because there were several versions of humans before our current species category of sapiens. They had names like *Homo neanderthalis*, *Homo erectus*, etc. (If you hated anthropology and this is giving you PTSD, my apologies.) My point is that the first part of the name—the genus—is always capitalized.

The second part of the name—the species—refers to a single type. Species might make you think of specific. Only one type. There might have been many individual animals of that species born to dinosaur mothers across the centuries, but there is only one type that has that genus-species combination. The species part of the ICZN name is never capitalized.

To get really technical about it, there are style rules, too. When you name the full animal, you use italics: *Tyrannosaurus rex*. You can abbreviate the genus, but never capitalize the second part: *T. rex*. My spell check software finds this so confusing, but *T. rex* is correct!

You can also refer to the genus as if it were an individual: "A *Tyrannosaurus* walked into a bar and asked for a straw." Or, you can refer to the group without capitals or italics, as in "The tyrannosaurs came after the stegosaurs." You don't need to worry about the styles unless you plan to write something yourself, but now you know why I'm writing *T. rex* and not T. Rex. It's like those scientists had different rules for everything! But now you can read and write those names with confidence.

Forward, dear reader, into the breach of scientific terms! Let's start with "A."

A is for Antorbital Fenestra

Dinosaurs had an extra hole in their head.

Not in the sense that they were dummies or had tiny brains, or that *T. rex* used the Yiddish expression *I need this like another hole in the head!* But dinosaurs had literally more holes in their head than other types of animals, more than turtles, crocodiles, or mammals. The extra hole in the head was one of the things that made them dinosaurs. The hole wasn't the only defining characteristic of a dinosaur and, as with simple classification groupings, it was not evident in 100% of all dinosaurs. Shh—don't tell them.

One of the ways to begin understanding dinosaurs is to know what makes them dinosaurs. We could do that by describing their place among all the other classification groups or by listing every type of dinosaur, but that would entail spouting a blizzard of names. And names don't always tell you what they *are*. Instead of using a dinosaur roll call, then, let's start with what makes a dinosaur a dinosaur.

And let's start from the top.

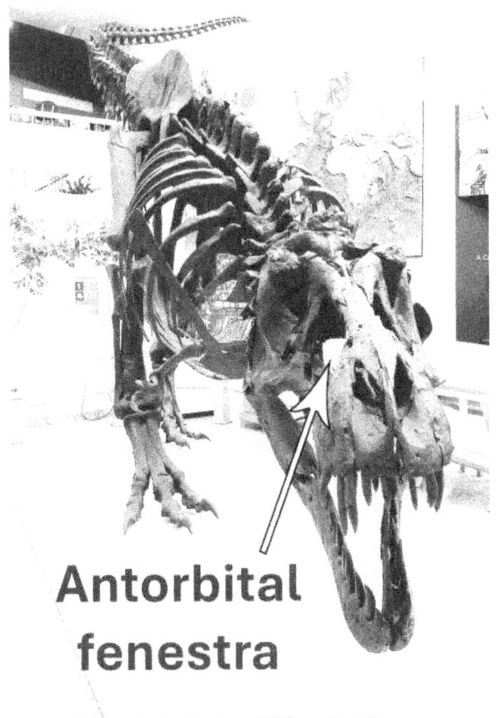

Fig 4. Dinosaurs had several holes in their head in addition
to their eyes, nose, and mouth.

Defining How to Throw People out of the Window

Even though we can sometimes take short cuts reading scientific language, it can be helpful to learn a few terms. Paleontology is certainly full of them. Getting comfortable with the Latin or Greek roots can also help you remember the meaning of names and make better guesses at new words. If you know that *paleontology* means the "study of the ancient world," then you can guess at paleobiology, paleography, and paleozoic.

Antorbital fenestra is a particularly fun one, too.

ant (before) + *orbital* (eye socket) + *fenestra* (window)

So, the antorbital fenestra means there is an extra hole, or window, in the skull of an animal. *Fenestra,* that Latin word for window, is so great. In German, it's *Fenster,* in Spanish, *ventana.* One of my favorite words is "defenestrate," as in "The loan shark threatened to defenestrate the guy who couldn't pay his debt." It's sort of what happens to Alan Rickman in *Die Hard.*

Dinosaurs were land creatures, so they had eyes and noses for breathing air. Most also had an extra hole in their skull between the eye socket and the nose opening. The eye socket is the orbit, and the nose opening is the naris, which is enough Latin for this paragraph. Other animals might have noses or nostrils, but not an extra hole. For example, fish have nostrils even though they don't breathe air because they need a sense of smell. Lots of side journeys beckon when we start looking at skull holes!

It turns out that all of the earliest dinosaurs had this opening, and it is what distinguished them from other reptiles, such as crocodiles. Later in the evolutionary timeline of the dinosaurs, the hole closed up for some types. That idea of evolutionary timeline will crop up a lot (Chapters "E," "O," and "V"). Dinosaurs make Darwin's theories a lot easier to understand.

For now, as far as dinosaur heads were concerned, just remember Alan Rickman.

Holey Ids!

What other creatures have an extra front window in their heads? Fish don't. Turtles don't. Humans don't. Mammals, as a whole, don't. That's how we can use this window-in-the-head thing to group similar animals together. It's a handy method because it's based on bones, and bones might be the only thing still remaining 200 million years later.

Figure 5 below shows examples of the different types of skulls, with their different holes. Most creatures in the animal kingdom have eyes and nostrils. The earliest of reptiles that emerged from the sea and separated from fish had those eyes and those nostrils. Those early land crawlers were similar to modern turtles. Turtles have no extra holes; biologists call them *anapsids* (*apsid* means "skull holes," *an* means "none").

Some early reptiles then developed an extra hole behind their eye and were called *synpasids* (one hole). Later down the evolutionary chain, the synapsids developed into mammals. Mammals weren't just known for their extra skull hole, but also because their eggs grew inside their bodies, they gave milk, and they had hair or fur. The hole behind and below a mammal's eye allowed muscles to attach that opened the jawbone wider than a turtle's for a stronger bite. Apes, dogs, and humans—along with some early types of reptiles—have those holes behind their eyes, called *temporal fenestrae*.

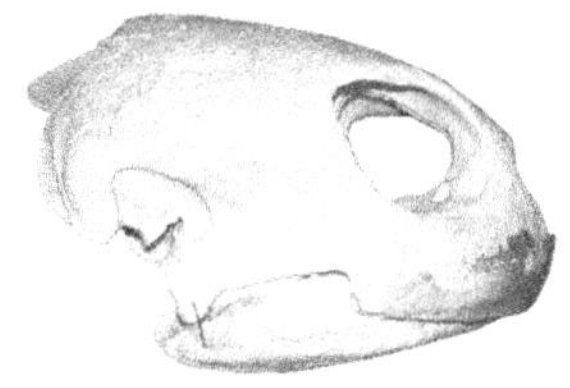

Sea turtle: Anapsid (no-hole)

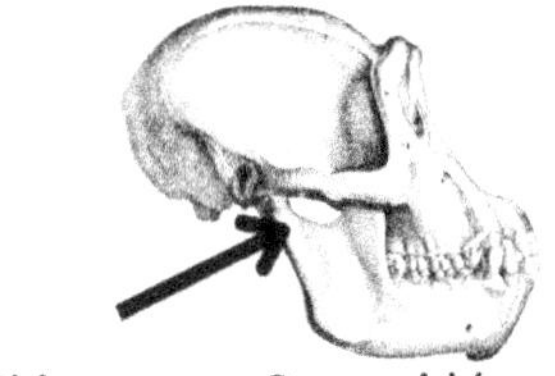

Chimpanzee: Synapsid (one-hole)

Crocodile: Diapsid (two-hole)

Fig 5. Comparative skulls of non-dinosaur relatives.

Other kinds of ancient and modern reptiles also developed two sets of holes behind their eye sockets. Crocodiles and lizards did, as did the dinosaurs. Just as mammals have a stronger bite than turtles, crocodiles have a bite even stronger than mammals. Crocodiles can chomp 3700 lbs per square inch—think of bench-pressing a jeep. The dinosaurs were diapsids *and* had antorbital fenestrae (the extra "e" means plural), so they had the most holey heads of all. Which is why, when an ancient sea turtle saw a *Tyrannosaurus* coming, it said *Holey Dinosaur!*

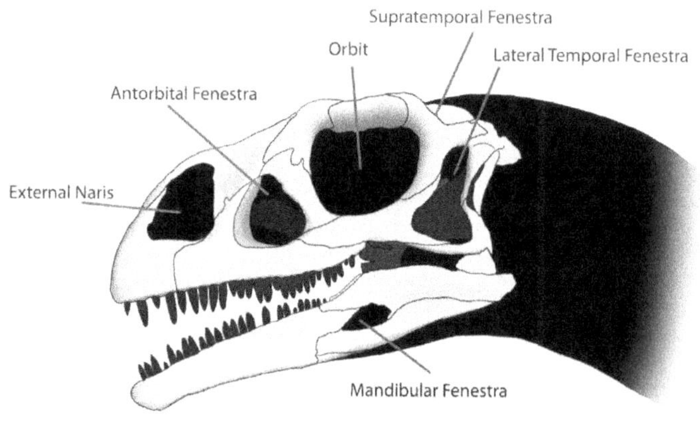

Fig 6. Skull of early dinosaur (*Massospondylus*) showing both temporal and antorbital fenestrae.

What exactly were all those extra holes for? Was it only for their bite? It's one of those things that requires speculation, since a paleontologist can't exactly ask a *Triceratops* these days. But if one thing is for sure, it's that paleontologists love to make good guesses. In fact, it's kind of their superpower.

For one thing, many dinosaurs got really big, which meant they had massive heads. If you've ever seen a *Tyrannosaurus* head, you know that it's some four to six feet long. Almost as big as humans—humans, yum, down in a single bite! That big head full of bone would be awfully heavy. The more holes in the skull, the lighter the heads would be. Just having a little less bone to carry around was helpful.

Second, some scientists think that dinosaurs might have had air sacs in their head like other creatures. Birds do, for instance. Carrying around a head full of air was lighter. Cooler, too, because if you recall, 200 million years ago, the earth was very swampy and humid. Plenty of dinosaurs were vegetarians, so they might not require massive jaws for biting through flesh, but they were huge, so they could use anything that would make their heads lighter.

Last, if it's true that mammal ancestors developed holes for a better bite, and reptile ancestors developed even more holes for jaw muscles to attach, then the dinosaur holes would have had the best bite of them all. A *T. rex* had jaw muscles that could have crushed a car. Their head was so strong and so movable that it could act like arms, which is why modern Trexperts—I just made that word up—think they didn't even need their arms (see "T"). Suffice it to say, after 185 million years of dinosaur rule, the biggest of the meat-eaters was practically all head and teeth.

Who needs arms, when you have all those extra windows in your skull?

A is also for Ankle

Aside from head holes, there was another important characteristic of dinosaur bones that separated dinosaurs from other reptiles of their day. This one had to do with their feet. They were dinosaurs all the way down! This difference had to do with their ankle bones.

A really useful way to understand this ankle bone difference is to compare them with crocodiles. Crocodiles—did you know that crocs are 250 million years old? And that some ancient types were 50 feet long? You probably do know that crocodiles can move exceptionally quickly in the water and even on land for short distances. To paraphrase crocodile scientist Gregory Erickson, there are no mediocre crocodile experts. Those who study crocodiles are either highly skilled or only have one arm.[3]

---

[3] Bill Schutt, "'If You Can Bench Press a Car You Are Good To Go': Inside the Incredible Bite Force of Crocodiles," LiveScience, July 30, 2024. https://www.livescience.com/animals/alligators-crocodiles/if-you-can-

Crocodile, in this case, refers to the big branch on the animal family tree. I'll explain the tree soon ("C"), but *Crocodilia* is both order and a genus—a big branch and a little branch. Crocodilia includes all the cousins of the genus, such as the alligators, caimans, and so on. People from Egypt in 4000 BCE, as well as in Florida, 2024 CE, are all familiar with the family tree of crocodiles. Crocodiles can zip rapidly through the water. However, they can't run on land because they can't really lift their belly off the ground for any length of time. What limited their speed was in their ankles.

**Crocodile ankle joint,
side-orientation, more stable**

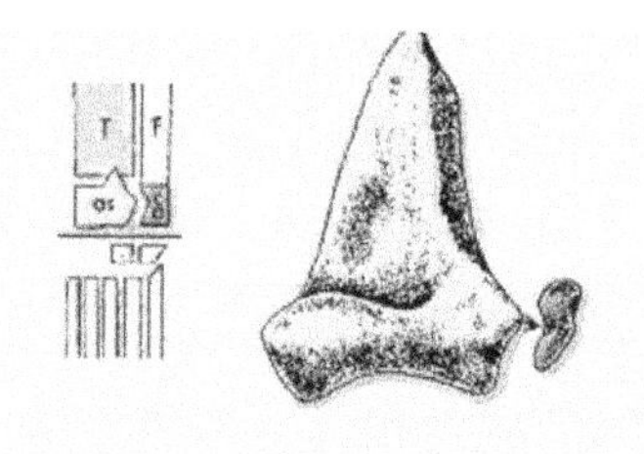

**Dinosaur/Mammal hinge
ankle, less stable but
allows running**

Fig 7. Ankle joints of crocodiles vs. dinosaurs. The flexing side joint of a crocodile promotes stability, not speed. The hinged ankle joint allows dinosaurs to walk upright and even run.

bench-press-a-car-you-are-good-to-go-inside-the-incredible-bite-force-of-crocodiles

Crocodile ankle joints position their feet out to the side for maximum flexibility, as the top example of Figure 7 shows. That joint's advantage was stability and versatility. You can't topple over a crocodile, and it can change direction faster than you can say *Alligator mississippensis*.

Dinosaurs, on the other hand, had a simple hinge joint that positioned their ankle directly below their leg. Once they also evolved a hip socket, they could stand upright. Standing upright allowed dinosaurs to grow much bigger. While you could have toppled a dinosaur more easily than a crocodile, they developed heavy-duty bones to counteract your attempt at dinosaur-toppling. Then, they could chase you down—you chose poorly.

Archosaurs and Definitions

Thus far in our quest to define dinosaurs, we have found two characteristics that separated dinosaurs from their reptilian cousins: head holes and ankle bones. It's worth a pause to think about how these definitions work in ways that are distinct from the ways dinosaurs are often described.

Dinosaurs should not be defined by traits that only belong to some. They should not be defined by how they are named, how they were first discovered, or based on what people once thought. And yet, all of those are ways that dinosaur-o-pedias sometimes answer the definitional question "What is a dinosaur?" For example, one source says dinosaurs had hollow bones, curved necks, and "some were likely warm-blooded."[4] First of all, that's not all true of even most dinosaurs (?*T. rex* didn't have a curved neck!). More importantly, "likely" is not exactly definitive. That description doesn't really tell you what they all were like.

Another definition might tell you when they lived—"230 my ago"—"my" being shorthand for "million years." However, when is not what. A third source might tell you who discovered them. Yet

---

[4] Prehistoricsaurus, "What Are Dinosaurs?" *Prehistoric Saursus,* 2024.https://prehistoricsaurus.com/basics/what-are-dinosaurs/. Accessed November 26, 2024.

even if people like Richard Owen and William Buckland were important to dinosaur history (see "I"), their names don't tell you what dinosaurs are.

We could try to be more exact, to give the narrowest, most all-encompassing definition of dinosaurs. We could say that they are the animals who had the Most Recent Common Ancestor (MRCA) of both triceratops and birds, and all their descendants. But that's like defining humans as people who descended from Adam and Eve, or from *Australopithecus* if you don't want to bring up religion. Either way, that still doesn't tell you what a human is.

Overall, a good way to define dinosaurs is to use a little of both approaches, to combine their branch on the family tree with their physical traits. That early branch on the reptilian family tree is called the *archosaurs* (*arch* meaning both "ruling" and "first," while *saur* meaning "lizards"—i.e., ruling lizards). Archosaurs are reptiles with four limbs, at least two skull openings, and developed embryos in an egg sac called an amniote. The amniote is what allows an egg to survive outside of water, thus allowing animals to spread across land.

The archosaur group includes all the creatures usually shown on the cover of a child's dinosaur picture book: meat-eating dinosaurs, plant-eating dinosaurs, flying pterodactyls, swimming ichthyosaurs, and giant crocodiles. Not everything on that list is a dinosaur, but *Archosaurs!* just doesn't have the same ring to a two-year-old. Meanwhile "terrible lizard" sounds more interesting than "first lizard."

What allowed the dinosaurs to branch off that segment of the archosaur family tree is the traits we've already described and more. Their ankles helped their legs to evolve upright. They developed hip joints to walk far above the ground, a change so important that it earns its own chapter ("H"). It doesn't take a lot of imagination to realize that a creature walking upright, with strong hips and ankles, has the edge over the creatures that slithered or crawled. Upright does not necessarily mean bipedal, even though dinosaurs developed that successful adaptation much earlier than kangaroos or cavemen did. Being upright or bipedal allows for speed and vision, two distinct advantages.

One paleontologist, Sterling Nesbitt, took this one step further in 2011. Nesbitt created a list of about a dozen features—mostly bone-related—shared by all the four-limbed, multi-holed, amniotic-using, upright-walking ancient reptiles. In addition to the antorbital fenestra, hip-socket configuration, and vertical ankle bones, Nesbitt added definitions related to neck vertebrae, shin bones, and arm bone proportions. All of these, he argued, separated all dinosaurs from non-dinosaurs.[5] That list is so full of technical bone words that I'm going to give it the special scientific treatment known as putting it in a footnote. You can follow the note and flip through Nesbitt's list if you like. It will give you plenty of practice in reading scientific language. However, one thing is definite, even if you don't read it.

It's all about the bones.

---

[5] Sterling Nesbitt, "The Early Evolution of Archosaurs: Relationships and the Origin of Major Clades," *Bulletin of the American Museum of Natural History*, 352 (April 2011): 1-292. https://bioone.org/journals/bulletin-of-the-american-museum-of-natural-history/volume-2011/issue-352/352.1/The-Early-Evolution-of-Archosaurs--Relationships-and-the-Origin/10.1206/352.1.full

B is for Blood

There are several scientific debates about dinosaurs, many of which will be addressed in this book. How did they emerge to dominate the planet? Why did they disappear? How should they be organized? Is Godzilla a dinosaur? And so on—the next few chapters will be full of these paleontology donnybrooks.

However, one of the biggest long-standing debates is whether dinosaurs were cold-blooded or warm-blooded. Modern reptiles are cold-blooded, sunning themselves on rocks all day in order to have the energy to run around. In contrast, modern birds and mammals are warm-blooded, producing energy from what they eat and from their activity. Dinosaurs *are* reptiles, so it was long thought that they were slow, sluggish, and required sunlight as energy. Being cold-blooded would restrict where they lived, how they moved, and what they could do. Being warm-blooded would allow for more variation in behavior, habitat, and diet—everything!

The crazy question is: how could scientists even know anything about a dinosaur's internal heat production, i.e., their metabolism? That's not part of their bones.

Or is it?

What's Blood Got to Do with It

Hot blood begets hot thoughts, and hot thoughts beget hot deeds…

Shakespeare, *Troilus and Cressida*

This "hot-blooded" topic is one place where precise, scientific terminology can be helpful. You don't have to use the word *ectothermic* for cold-blooded and *endothermic* for warm-blooded, but those are shorter words. Plus, you could impress your friends! Think of *ecto* as "out" and *endo* as "in," referring to whether you get your temperature, your *therm*, from outside or inside.

If you are an ectotherm, your metabolism doesn't generate enough heat from your body's own processes for you to move around, so you need a little boost from the sun or external heat sources. If you're endothermic, then you produce energy from what you eat. Except on Thanksgiving, when you have to lie down, especially if you drink a lot of water with your stuffing and gravy.

Like gravy, though, the plot thickens. (Yup, I have no shame.) Another way to classify animals and their metabolisms is based on whether their body temperature varies or not. *Homeothermic* animals maintain a body temperature within a narrow band. *Homeo* here mean "the same." For humans, that temperature hovers near that famous 98.6. Homeotherms have mechanisms for raising or lower temperature like sweating or shivering.

Poikilothermic animals (*poiki* means "spotted" or "different") have body temperatures that are broad in range so that they can match their environment, whether cold or hot. To change their body temperature, poikilotherms must move to a different place with a different temperature. Reptiles, amphibians, and fish have to go where it's warmer to warm up, since they are poikilothermic ectotherms. (Mentioning such fancy facts might amaze your grandfather). That means their temperatures fluctuate, and they need warm environments to gather enough energy to move. On the other hand, they don't need as much food as a similar-sized endotherm.

There are reptiles, amphibians, and fish which are poikilothermic *endo*therms, such as large turtles or deep-sea fish. Their body temperatures match their environment, but they can still generate their own internal heat source. That way, deep-sea fish don't need to be close to a warm water source or the sun.

Mammals and birds are homeothermic endotherms. Their body temperature ranges are narrow. Their temperatures don't decrease when the temperature drops, so they don't need to move toward heat sources to warm up. Instead, their metabolisms generate enough heat from food for them remain active. On the flip side, they have to move around a lot because they need a lot more food. They breathe quickly and eat a lot, but they're also active all day, chasing food.

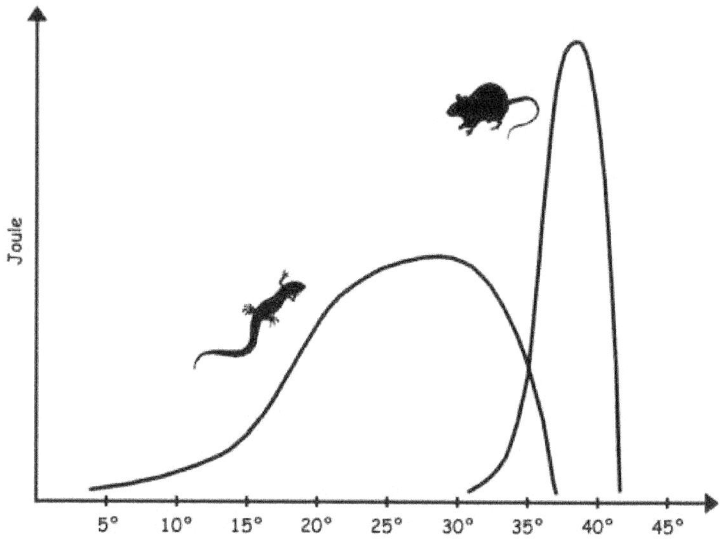

Fig 8. The trade-offs between body temperature (X-axis) and activity level (Y-axis), comparing a lizard (poikilothermic ectotherm) to a mouse (homeothermic endotherm).

Figuring out where dinosaurs fit on that graph has been a long-standing debate. The opinions on whether dinosaurs were warm or cold blooded have bounced around more than that mouse in the past two centuries. To a degree, the opinions have come full circle, although it's been a long, strange trip.

In the Old Slow Dino Days

People used to think paleontologists were slow and stupid. They didn't get much exercise, being cooped up with the bones and all, and didn't eat a lot of fiber, which gave them diseases like gout and piles (have fun looking that up). Mainly, they sat around yearning for fame and sunning themselves. This was in the 19th century when paleontologists were drawn with their tails trailing on the ground… well, something like that. I might be confusing paleontologists with the dinosaurs themselves. It was a bit confusing.

The first discovered dinosaur bone in history was the thigh bone of a giant reptile, called a *Megalosaurus*, back in 1676. But as late as 1840, the list of recognized dinosaurs could still be counted on Charles Darwin's fingers and toes. The naturalists—a catch-all term that included biologists, paleontologists, and geologists—did not agree on how agile and active the creatures were.

Some thought the dinosaurs must be slow and spend their time half-submerged in swamps. Between their giant size, the discovered bones, and the humid conditions, scientists concluded that these giant reptiles must be plodders. Illustrations, like those of American illustrator Charles R. Knight, placed the big boys in the water. If the tail was drawn, it dragged on the ground behind its body, like a lizard.

Fig 9. Knight's picture of the brontosaurus for the influential 1897 publication *American Century*.

Not everyone agreed on this early view, however. Even Knight himself wondered whether some of the giant reptiles might have moved quickly, under the right conditions. While he painted many dinosaurs lumbering and dragging their tails, he also famously painted two carnivorous dinosaurs battling for supremacy. Knight's colleague, paleontologist Edwin Cope, called the creatures *laelaps*, after the mythical Greek dog that never caught what it was hunting. (Cope's story is told in "U.") Cope speculated that some meat-eaters might have moved like kangaroos, jumping around while using a tail for balance.

Fig 10. *Leaping laelaps* by Charles R. Knight, also featured in *American Century*.

How could there have been such two different views—leaping meat-eaters and plodding vegetarians? It was called "pluralistic," a recognition of variation among the four-legged and the two-legged.[6] There was also disagreement in the scientific community and not enough fossil evidence to resolve differences.

---

[6] Warren D. Allmon, "The Pre-Modern History of the Post-Modern Dinosaur: Phases and Causes in Post-Darwining Dinosaur Art," *Earth Sciences History* 25, no. 1 (2006): 55. http://www.jstor.org/stable/24137352.

In a study of how attitudes about dinosaurs have changed over the past century, Warren Allmon points out that not only did paleontologists' views shift, but the view of biology and evolution itself evolved over the century. When Darwin began formulating his theories in the 1820s, only a few ancient bones had been discovered. Naturalists of the day could barely think of these as "real" creatures, let alone envision how the animals moved.

Fifty years later, by the time Knight was mixing his color palette, more skeletons had been discovered, and Darwin's thoughts about natural selection and animal adaptation had gained a lot of ground. Giant sets of teeth were not immediately associated with slow swamp dwellers. Even if they believed these were cold-blooded reptiles, predators must surely be agile and active.

However, at the beginning of the 20th century, the interpretation of Darwin's ideas shifted to emphasize "survival of the fittest." The interpretation was not simply that animals adapted, but that the strongest was the best. It was an idea that gained ground in politics, economics, and science. Evolution was no longer simply adapting but instead about progression. It was called *orthogenesis*, the idea that change was about improvement. This justified everything from the Industrial Revolution to eugenics. Since dinosaurs were no longer around, the new paleontology view was that they died off because they were unsuccessful. Mammals won because they were better; apes and their descendant humans won because they were the best.

Allmon describes this view as "ponderous monsters ascendant."[7] In other words, naturalists decided dinosaurs must be stupid and slow. Even the meat-eaters, like *T. rex*, were lumbering. According to one paleontologist: "The momentum of its huge body involved seemingly slow movements, difficult to start and difficult to shift or to stop. Such movements are wildly different from the agile swiftness which we naturally associate with a beast of prey."[8]

For the first half of the 20th century, then, slow and plodding dinosaurs stalked the dioramas of natural history museums. Hanging out in the swamps solidified the idea that, like modern reptiles, these ancient reptiles were hampered by their cold-blooded natures. Even if a carnivore found a burst of energy to chase down a wayward baby brontosaurus, the notion was that a meat-eater would have to rest

---

[7] Allmon, "Pre-Modern,"18.
[8] Allmon, "Pre-Modern," 19.

after feeding, like lions or pythons that feed big but not often. However, that view has now changed again.[9]

Magic Metabolic Markers

The conundrum of the *T. rex* has been one that paleobiologists struggled with for decades. How could a huge, bipedal predator be cold-blooded and slow? To solve the mystery in decades past, scientists looked at mineral contents in fossil bones, using bone fragments like "paleo thermometers." However, they didn't know if fossilization itself—the bone turning to stone—changed the chemistry. They knew that process was imperfect.

The latest ideas about dinosaur metabolism rely on other types of bone markers that don't change as when bone becomes fossil. Two studies in recent decades make a good case that not all reptiles are created equal.

The first one considers how blood flow moves nutrients around in dinosaur bodies.[10] Even bones have small holes for arteries. Some, called *foramina*, transport essential nutrients through the blood to the muscles and organs. The size of these holes can tell you the strength of an animal's blood pressure. Scientists plotted hole size and blood pressure for different combinations of animals to create a *foramen index*, which allows for comparison. Even though they could never measure a dinosaur's blood pressure, the size of their foramen holes can be used as a proxy.

---

[9] In the last few decades, an assessment of accuracy of dinosaur paintings as become part of paleoanalysis. Consider, for instance, that there is a wiki specifically devoted just to addressing what was wrong in specific paintings of dinosaurs. https://en.wikipedia.org/wiki/Wikipedia:WikiProject_Dinosaurs/Image_review

[10] Seymour, Roger S., Sarah L. Smith, Craig R. White, Donald M. Henderson, and Daniela Schwarz-Wings, "Blood Flow to Long Bones Indicates Activity Metabolism in Mammals, Reptiles and Dinosaurs," *Proceedings: Biological Sciences* 279, no. 1728 (2012): 453. http://www.jstor.org/stable/41412000.

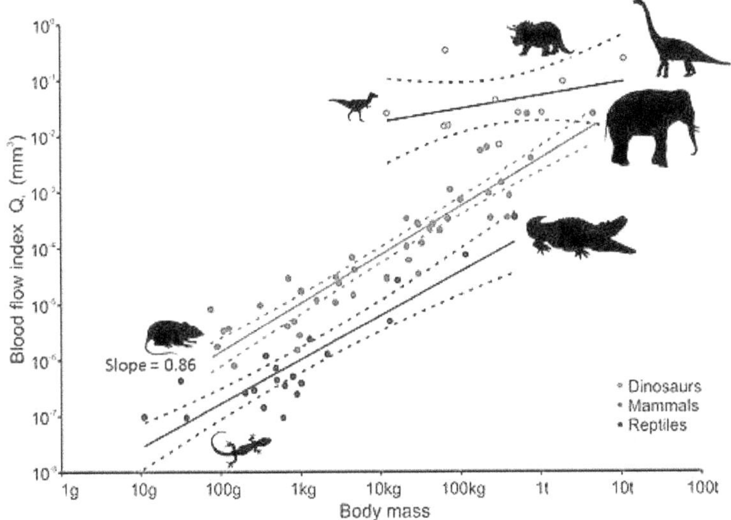

Fig 11. The foramen blood flow index suggests some dinosaur metabolisms were high, like those of large mammals.

Figure 11 suggests that the foramen index for large dinosaurs indicated high aerobic activity, possibly even higher than most mammals. The giants, whether giant plant-eaters or giant meat-eaters, would need high blood pressure, according to this model.

The foramen index idea didn't apply as easily to small dinosaurs, since animals low on the index might include both warm-blooded mice and cold-blooded lizards. Another paleobiologist had a different idea. Jasmina Wiemann noticed that metabolic waste might show up in bones as well.[11] Breathing oxygen triggers a chemical reaction, which affects a body's fat's storage and sugar content. Creatures with high metabolisms use fat and sugars differently from those with low metabolism, leaving different waste products. Those chemical waste products turn out to be very stable, enough to leave evidence of bone fragments that might be 150 million years old.

---

[11] J. Wiemann, I. Menéndez, and J.M. Crawford, *et al*, "Fossil Biomolecules Reveal an Avian Metabolism in the Ancestral Dinosaur." *Nature* (2022): 522–526. https://doi.org/10.1038/s41586-022-04770-6

Wiemann looked at different groups of ancient reptiles: giant sea creatures (plesiosaurs), flying reptiles (pterosaurs), and dinosaurs (allosaurs). She compared them with modern birds, reptiles, and mammals, where metabolic waste markers are readily available. Her comparison of those markers showed that most dinosaurs had high metabolic rates and were warm-blooded, especially the early dinosaurs of the Triassic and Jurassic. This included big predators but some large plant-eaters, too.

Some dinosaurs, like the velociraptors, had zippy metabolisms, almost as high as modern birds. Giant herbivores like *Brachiosaurus* had both efficient digestive systems and high metabolisms. The problem that brachiosaurs had was not that their big bodies required the buoyancy of water to move around, but that their big bodies may have required water to cool them off.

But Wiemann found that later in the dinosaurs' centuries of dominance, some shifted back to having lower metabolic rates. She noted that *Triceratops* had a low metabolic rate even though some of its ancestors had high rates. *Triceratops* developed body armor, horns, and a hard-to-attack shape. Is that because it lost its high metabolism? Maybe, once it became more invincible at slow speeds, it sacrificed a high metabolism in favor of something that didn't require as much food. Otherwise, it would take a lot of leaves to move that three-horned head quickly for hours. There are always physical trade-offs.

Overall, the most recent data suggests that some dinosaurs were warm-blooded, while others were not. The results have turned the clock back for paleontologists, ultimately returning them to the diversity that Knight had painted in the first place. Some were warm-blooded, and some were cold-blooded. It turns out that there was room for all kinds of dinosaurs—even on the inside.

C is for Clade

We saw in Chapter "A" that discussing dinosaurs quickly leads to the idea of a family tree. That tree structure and its organization scheme are important ideas, since they explain how dinosaurs did what they did.

For example, skulls were different on different branches of the tree, depending on muscles needed for biting. Ankle bones were side-oriented in crocodiles and hinged in dinosaurs. Once dinosaurs were off the ground and carrying weight, they needed different hip joints ("H").

Again and again, understanding dinosaurs starts with the tree that shows how animals differ from one another. That tree structure is known as a clade, an idea developed in the late 20th century that changed the design of the tree. Which changed everything.

The Past Is Not What It Used To Be

If you took biology or any kind of living-thing-ology back before the rise of clades, you might have studied animal family trees based on Linnaean taxonomy. Taxonomy is a fancy word that just means an organizing system, the way that you group things. It can be difficult to think about scientifically, so consider systems you use for personal reasons. Perhaps you have a taxonomy for your spice rack: Alphabetical? By cuisine type? By size? You might have a taxonomy for music categories: Rock, Rap, Metal, and so on.

The famous taxonomy used in biology for many years was created by this Swedish guy, Carolus Linnaeus. Maybe you learned the mnemonic "King Philip Came Over For Green Sugar" or something like it. I still remember it from seventh grade Invertebrate Zoology: Kingdom Phylum Class Order Family Genus Species.

You may be wondering why my seventh grade had a class in invertebrate zoology, of all things, and I did at the time. I think the teacher just wanted us to impress our parents with a complicated name for Biology. We did cut up starfish and worms. And we learned KPCOFGS. I could always remember it if I thought about how humans are classified. Kingdom: Animal; Phylum: Vertebrate; Class: Mammals; Order: Primates; Family: Man; Genus: *Homo*; Species: *sapiens*. Here's an example for another recognizable animal.

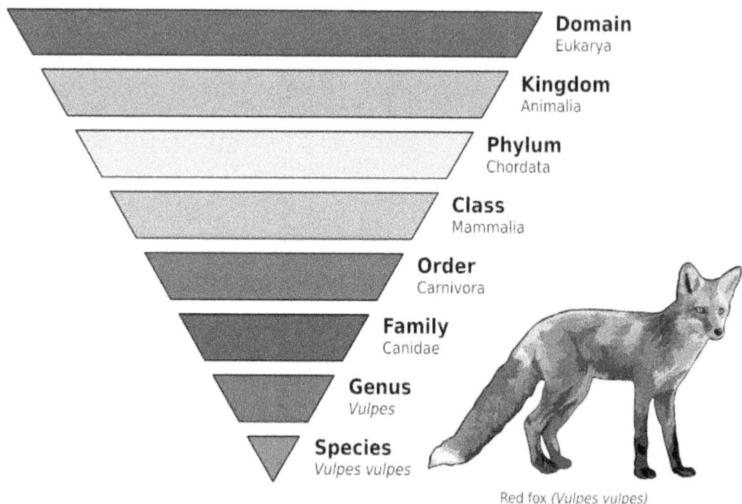

Fig 12. Funnel view of KPCOFGS (Linnaean) biological classification.

The Linnaean system—I keep having to look up how to spell that, his name was not organized very well!—worked for a while, given that the Swedish guy didn't have computers, DNA, or other scientists to pester him. His idea was to group like things together, and it's not hard to imagine him thinking that feathered things are different from scaly things which are different from furry, placenta-based, air-breathing tool users.

Linnaeus was one of the first guys to group humans with apes and other primates. Even if people objected to being compared with monkeys, it's easier to think of humans being more like monkeys than being like foxes, starfish, or bumble-bees.

Over time, though, scientists began to catalog a lot more animals, not just modern living ones but past ones, too. The organizing system needed a lot more categories and, frankly, levels. KPCOFGS just didn't cut it. In particular, the differences between Order and Genus—between primates and human beings—or even between carnivorous mammals and foxes—are just too great. The system of taxonomy, the "order of things," needed to be expanded to a lot more levels.

The new system relies heavily on the idea of trees and branches. That's not a new idea; the Linnaean system can be arranged as a tree with branches, too.

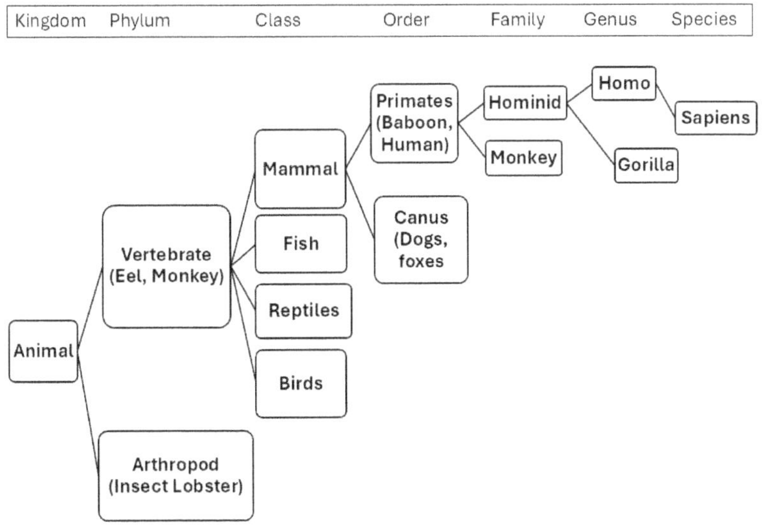

Fig 13. The KPCOFGS system shown in a tree structure.

The tree structure, whether it's shown growing upward, downward, or sideways, has one key feature. Things on separate branches are in different groups, but they emerged from a group that was broader, where things were alike.

Following Branches on the Tree of Life

The idea of the common ancestor is the common starting point for the new system, too. The new system is called *cladistics*, which is a logical name since *clade* means "branch." (I guess *branchistics* didn't have enough of a ring to it.) In this view that builds around common ancestors, everything on the same tree branch has the same common trait as the ancestor.

The Linnaean system grouped things by shared characteristics but ignored the idea of a mandatory common ancestor. Separating birds from reptiles, for example, ignores the idea that birds evolved from dinosaurs. If that's a spoiler alert, surprise! We'll talk about the relationship between birds and dinosaurs throughout several chapters ("R," "W"). The whole idea of reptiles, in a way, violates cladistics because it excludes birds. Reptiles may seem like a natural group, but unless you include birds, reptiles is not a clade—i.e., it does not have its own unique branch excluding birds.

The way things are alike on the branch is also noted. Turtles and mice, for example, both came from a common ancestor that developed lungs, whereas fish and jellyfish do not. Dinosaurs and apes both have amniotic eggs, so they are more similar to each other than to turtles.

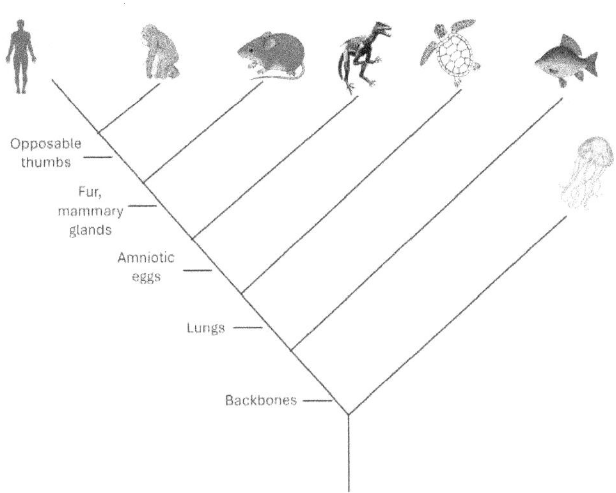

Fig 14. Simple tree structure (clade) emphasizing traits from common ancestors.

The clade view differs from KPCOFGS because it focuses on how traits split groups from each other. But instead of looking at traits in animals that only exist today, all creatures throughout biological history can be placed on this system. The key is to get the trees and branches in the right order, to find the correct common ancestor. Anything that can be viewed as all-inclusive on a branch is a clade. As today's biology textbooks will remind you, you can't group things together from different branches. No matter what, once your system splits turtles from jellyfish, then you can't group them together in a clade diagram.

The more you examine these clades, the more you see how grouping works. Humans are a little like mice, tree shrews, and foxes. As Figure 14 shows, they are even a little like dinosaurs, certainly more like dinosaurs than like fish. But they're still a lot more like chimpanzees.

How Clades Came to Be the Standard

Cladistics emerged from the combination of an improved understanding of Darwin's ideas of natural selection and advances in technology. When the idea of survival of the fittest began to dominate biology in the early 20th century ("B"), evolution was suddenly seen as "progressive." Progressive evolution meant animals marching forward in an ever-improving ascendancy. That progressive idea dictated that everything on the animal family tree had to "lead" somewhere: i.e., to humans.

Nowadays, that notion is viewed as not only inaccurate but harmful, since it implies the need to purify species and other nonsense. As researchers have learned more about species and developed tools to modify genes, it's also clear that genes make trade-offs. When certain traits are "perfected," others get worse. Industrial tomatoes, for example, have been genetically improved to have tougher skin for transportation. They don't bruise easily but now taste like cardboard.

Evolution doesn't care about tomatoes, so biologists—including paleobiologists—have improved their understanding of how adaptations work. Clades have become a standard way of modeling biological family trees based on adaptations, with an emphasis on ancestors and descendants.

Birds might be the only animals with feathers today, but they no longer get their own major branch like mammals. Reptiles also don't have their own branch. Instead, paleontologists realized that bird skeletons had several similarities to dinosaur skeletons. Feathers turned out to be an adaptation, like fur, but feathers and flight are less a unique and defining characteristic than hip joints, ankle joints, and arm lengths.

What clades did was emphasize the physical trait over the behavior. For instance, several different animal branches developed flight. Bats, pterodactyls, and birds all fly (see "W"). But bats don't lay eggs, and pterodactyls don't have hip bones like birds. They all emerged on different branches of the original tree based on the design of their bodies, even though all three developed adaptations in their hands and arms that led to wings that led to flight. Pterodactyls split off from dinosaurs early in the tree. They both can be traced to a common ancestor that they shared with crocodiles, all three being archosaurs. But that's about all they have in common. As another paleontologist, Kristi Curry Rogers, put it elegantly, pterodactyls and birds have "different ways of being the same."[12]

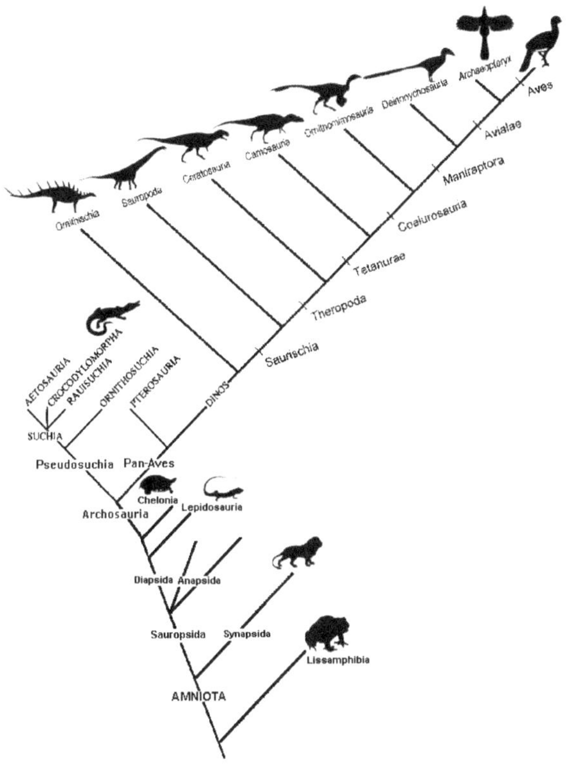

Fig 15. A portion of the dinosaur clade showing where birds fit on the tree.

The idea of traits adapting over time allowed scientists to expand the things included on the tree. A tree that only includes modern animals will be much smaller than if it has to encompass everything that ever lived. How could that be possible? One answer is that the data set in 1897 was pretty small. Fifty years later, the data set of traits of all animals that ever lived began to get huge.

---

[12] Rogers, Kristi Curry, *Rediscovering the Age of Dinosaurs*, Great Course guidebook (Chantilly, VA: The Teaching Company, 2022), 64.

Enter computers. Having a way to keep track of all that data allows you to include tons of animals, extinct and modern, and capture every little bit of data about their bones. The more fossils you find, the more studies you can do that draws conclusions about things like blood through fossil bone. Those studies expand the branches even more. Ultimately, you can gather enough data to tell Linnaeus that birds are not on a different branch on the dinosaur tree—they're just a recent adaptation of a particular dinosaur group. This is why birds are not just descendants from dinosaurs. They are actually dinosaurs.

Clades Evolve

There are two final points worth making about clades. First, when someone is describing a clade, they don't have to include all the branches. Often, the clade might start with an endpoint—say *Diplodocus*—and just trace its common ancestor. It's not a requirement to show all the branches or even most of them.

The second point is that having lots of data doesn't mean the clade is perfect as is. Clades will continue to shift over time. For instance, forever—meaning, since I was in college—dinosaurs have been split into two groups, called Saurischians and Ornithischians, based on their hip bones ("H"). So the clade with two dinosaur branches has been used for over a century, ever since those words were defined in 1888.

However, there is a knock-down, drag-out fight going on right now over this two-branch structure of the dinosaur clade. One set of paleontologists—Baron, Norman and Barrett—claimed in 2017 that there should be a third group, that saurischians are a level "above" the ornithischians.[13] Other researchers claim we should keep the original split of two groups but reorganize the tree to put some of the ornithischians in where the saurischians used to be. You might stumble across sentences such as "Phylogenetic position of

---

[13] M. Baron, D. Norman, & P. Barrett, "A New Hypothesis of Dinosaur Relationships and Early Dinosaur Evolution, *Nature* no. 543 (2017): 501–506. https://doi.org/10.1038/nature21700

saurischians in different topologies," which means the science-y folks don't agree where the saurischians ought to go.[14]

Think back to that music example. Everybody knows you can split Classical from Rock music. But within Rock, do you split Classic Rock from Metal? Plus, what counts as Classic Rock now—does that include Sheryl Crow or the Foo Fighters along with Led Zeppelin? Does Rap have its own group, or is it a sub-category of something else like R&B? If it's a sub-category, then did both Classic Rock and Rap "evolve" out of the Blues? Where did the tree start? I know you've had some of these arguments. If you've ever debated who influenced who or how to organize your music collection, then you understand the subtle controversies of taxonomy.

And you could build your own clade.

___

[14] "Saurischia," Wikipedia, last modified November 20. 2024. https://en.wikipedia.org/wiki/Saurischia

D is for Diplodocus

This chapter is, at last, all about one single dinosaur. He was quite famous, for several reasons. In the first place, *Diplodocus* was one of the oldest dinosaurs discovered. That word—"oldest"—is kind of imprecise, though. Were they the bones of a 120-year-old? Was he from the Triassic, the earliest dino-era? Nope. *Diplodocus* was among the first dinosaurs to be found by the dinosaur hunters in the late 19th century. So Dippy—that's what that first skeleton came to be known as: Dippy—was famous because he was one of the first found. Then, he became more famous for a different reason. Dippy was copied.

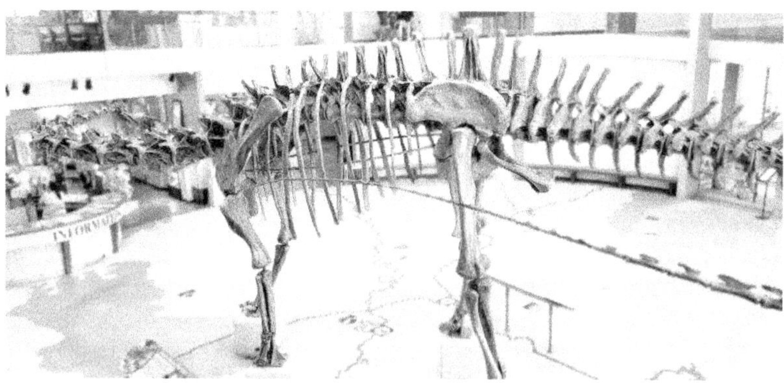

Fig 16. "Dippy" filling the lobby and checking out the Information Desk at the Utah Dinosaur Museum.

Diplodocus, the Original

Diplodocus was one of the "big" dinosaurs, the *sauropods* (*pod*=foot, "lizard foot"). The sauropods had their own branch on the tree, which contained several smaller branches. These huge, long-necked, long-tailed reptiles were vegetarian, and the adults were generally too big for meat-eaters to tackle. The group included the tall *Brachiosaurus*, three stories high, as well as the massive *Titanosaurus*, which could grow to 40 meters (or 45 yards) long, nearly half a football field.

The *Diplodocus* was a bit smaller, at "only" 25 meters, though he had one of the longest tails, thin and whip-like. He weighed about as much as four elephants, so he stood on four sturdy legs and balanced his long neck with that long tail. (There was a Monty Python character named Anne Elk who said, if you remember *ahem* Anne Elk, dinosaurs were thin to start with, then much, much thicker, then thin again. *ahem*.)[15]

diplo (double) + *docus* (beam)

The tail of *Diplodocus* was its stand-out feature and helped generate its name. The name "double-beamed" refers to the way that its vertebrae—the combination of back and tail bones—had two parts sticking out the bottom (Figure 17). Science-y people call them "chevron-shaped," though they look like skis to me. It's believed that these skis gave the tail better stability, which allowed it to extend that much farther across that football field. Reminds me of those segmented Leviathan ships that attack New York in *The Avengers,* but that would be far too long a word in Latin.

---

[15] Yes, Anne was talking about Brontosauruses, but it's a similar idea. "Monty Python Theory on Brontosauruses by Anne Elk (miss)," *YouTube,* uploaded by Yoshiko Negrete, 2015. https://www.dailymotion.com/video/x2oh8ia. Accessed November 26, 2024.

Fig 17. Close-up of *Diplodocus* "chevron" vertebrae (bottom), which look like skis.

Plaster Casts for Dinosaur Diplomacy

Of all the dinosaurs ever unearthed, Dippy's history is one of the most curious. In the 1870s, there was a booming passion for paleontology, fueled in part by a competition now known as the Bone Wars. That story will be told in detail in Chapter "U," but, in brief, paleontologists Edward Cope and O.C. Marsh competed to discover the first, the biggest, and the latest finds. Cope and Marsh's finds generated public fascination with ancient reptiles, which led to others jumping into the fray as well.

Around 1898, Andrew Carnegie, the prominent steel magnate (or wealthy robber baron, depending on your history textbook), read a news story about *Diplodocus* bones discovered in Wyoming. Supposedly, Carnegie barked to somebody, "Go buy that for us!" He financed a major expedition, which began searching in Colorado. They did, indeed, find the bones to construct the majority of an entire skeleton. Then they found a second one, a bit smaller, but mostly intact. This particular species was then named *Diplodocus carnegie.*

Carnegie paid to have the two sets of bones shipped back to Pittsburgh, his hometown. He built a museum to house the entire skeleton. It was not the first, but it was, and still is, the most complete version of *Diplodocus* discovered. He then did something even more remarkable. He paid to have multiple copies of the bones made out of plaster, and he sent them to natural history museums around the world: London, Berlin, Paris, Vienna, Bologna, St. Petersburg, Buenos Aires, Madrid, and Mexico City. Many of these are still displayed today.

Carnegie's kooky idea was that if nations all realized they had a mutual interest in science, they would find more in common with each other than not. Perhaps the idea wasn't that kooky. The Olympics, which were launched in 1896, attempted to achieve a similar ideal, a view that peace could emerge from sport. So this was also peace—but coming from dinosaur bones.

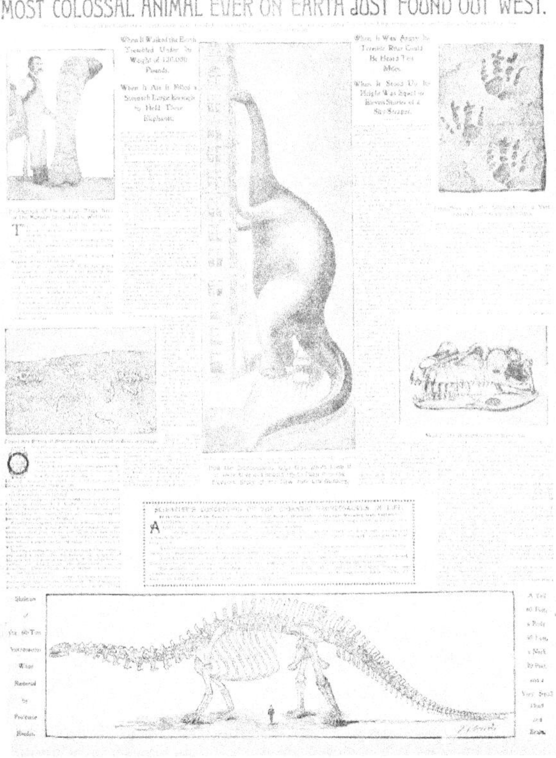

Fig 18. The discovery of the *Diplodocus* skeletons made dinosaurs an everyday topic. This artist even imagined that a 25-meter-long dinosaur might peer into a fifth-story window. Maybe Dippy smelled cookies.

"Dinosaur diplomacy" garnered a huge amount of publicity. The skeleton bound for the Carnegie Museum in Pittsburgh generated a lot of buzz and became an instant hit, along with all of its clones. The museum came to be known as "the house that Dippy built." The idea of dinosaurs burst into popularity, at least until the Depression and the two world wars gave people more pressing things to think about.

DippyGate

But Dippy's story doesn't quite end there. The 1898 discovery of *Diplodocus* was of great fascination to Queen Victoria's eldest son, Edward VII. Eddie was a big supporter of the British Museum. While visiting Carnegie's ancestral home, which happened to be up in Scotland near the Prince's ancestral home, Eddie saw drawings of the dinosaur. Carnegie and the Prince of Wales dreamed up the original plaster cast idea, and eventually the British copy was prominently displayed at the British Museum of Natural History. That statue was dedicated in 1905, two years earlier than when the Yankee Dippy debuted in Pittsburgh, because Carnegie's museum had to be retrofitted to fit that long tail. So the British skeleton, technically, came first.

The British Dippy—also called Dippy as well, a true clone—was a fan favorite for nearly a century. During World War II, the Brits even put the plaster skeleton in the museum's basement so that it wouldn't get destroyed when the Germans bombed London.

However, the museum decided in 2017 to re-theme itself. They dumped Dippy and, instead, filled the hallway with a blue whale skeleton—a boring but "real" whale skeleton rather than one with plaster bones. The decision-makers asserted that they much preferred real bones and, after all, the British Dippy was not the original.

The idea of "real bones" is one worth debating, though. A great many museum displays around the world are replicas rather than the original bones, not just *Diplodocus,* but many others. Plus, skeletons often are strengthened with plaster, metal, and other foreign objects that pin together frail fossils. The originals may also be too valuable to be put on public display without a lot of security. After all, they are irreplaceable. Most of all, as the Fossil chapter will explain, fossils are not technically the "original" bones.

Nevertheless, the British Museum curators took out the *Diplodocus*, and Dippy-lovers across the country protested in droves. Thirty thousand people signed a petition, with many in the media calling it "DippyGate." But the decision-makers didn't budge. Perhaps they also didn't like arranging their displays around something donated by an American robber baron. The whale is probably there to stay.

Meanwhile, the plaster Dippy toured around Britain: Dorset, Birmingham, Ulster, Norwich, Kelvingrove, Glasgow, and Wales. The Welsh word for museum is *amgueddfa*, but there doesn't appear to be a Welsh word for *Diplodocus*. Yet.

E is for Extinction

The pop cultural perspective on extinction is filled with visions of failure. The extinction of the dinosaurs is frequently viewed through this lens. But consider the lengthy reign of dinosaurs on Earth. Dinosaurs spent more than 160 million years ruling Earth's terrestrial ecosystems. And technically, when you consider those modern dinosaurs flying around today, it means that dinosaurs have been around for more than 230 million years.[16]

Kristi Curry Rogers, *Dinosaurs.*

Dinosaurs are often used as a synonym for old, dead, and extinct. Gas-guzzling cars are dinosaurs. Blackberries and iPods are dinosaurs. Baby Boomers are dinosaurs with modern devices.

The metaphor is unfair. After all, dinosaurs did thrive and spread across the globe for longer than any other type of creature. Fish in the "Age of Fish" dominated for only about 60 million years. Mammals have only been the dominant order for 65 million years. Dinosaurs are extinct, but it took a rather dramatic way to take them out. If you think about it, crocodiles were around at the time of the dinos, and still are … so… maybe we're really living in the Age of Crocodiles. And let's not forget bacteria.

Anyway, before we get overwrought about dinosaurs disappearing and all worked up at the idea of species vanishing, we should be clear about how extinction actually works.

---

[16] Rogers, *Dinosaurs,* "Lecture Three: Extinction."

Extinction is a process, and it's happening all the time.

Two Flavors of Extinction

First, there are different kinds of extinction as well as different causes for extinction. The two main kinds of extinction to discuss here are:

- Background Extinction

- Mass Extinction

Extinction is not always an indicator of a global catastrophe. Species go extinct all the time, and they always have. When it's a single species that fails to adapt, that falls into the category of Background Extinction. The species loses its habitat or food source, which could be from climate change or other factors, such as the successful adaptation of predators or invasive competing species. For instance, the saber-toothed tiger was a dominant feline predator throughout the Ice Age when early humans emerged 100,000 years ago.

Fig 19. The saber-toothed tiger was a dominant predator until the ice started to melt.

But once the glaciers started receding, and the frozen tundra began turning to forest and grassland, the tigers didn't fare as well. Some were hunted by ancestral humans, but many simply could not adapt to the world that was changing around them. The saber-toothed tiger is one of many species that could not manage a gradual change of climate.

Climate change has been a recurring theme on our planet, with loss of species recurring due to ice ages, warm-ups, earthquakes, and other natural forces. Every time such large-scale changes occur, species go extinct. It's not necessarily true that the world gets less hospitable for every creature. Some animals did fare better during the icier ages.

In relatively recent history, species such as the dodo and passenger pigeon went extinct. The dodos were thriving on the predator-less island of Mauritius until humans showed up. Humans became successful predators, along with bringing their own invasive species that hurt the dodo's food supply. Passenger pigeons lived in huge flocks in the United States. They were pests, often devastating agriculture. Killing them for sport was considered eliminating a nuisance. The pigeons numbered in the millions and lived in groups; they went quickly, in part, because huge flocks were easy to wipe out.

Over Earth's entire history, most species extinctions have not been caused by humans. Giant beetles, 50-foot crocodiles, and tiny horses are all also now extinct due to all the usual suspects: change of habitat, lack of adaptation, etc. Something else out-competed them. I don't know about you, but I don't want to be competing with a saber-toothed tiger. Or a giant beetle. This is not to say we should ignore all species extinction that is human-caused. It's just that background extinction, the one-off elimination of a single species, is only one type.

The other type, the type we should worry about, is mass extinction. Mass extinction occurs when an event happens that is so cataclysmic that it wipes out multiple species or a huge portion of living species. So far in Earth's history, there have been several mass extinction events, which paleontologists and geologists have nicknamed the Big Five.

The Big Five Extinctions

To understand the Big Five, we need to understand geological time structure. Fortunately, geologists are organized people. They've split the history of the Earth into time periods. Unfortunately, these stretches of time have complicated and hard-to-pronounce names: Ordovician, Permian, Cretaceous, etc.

The source of these names vary. For example, the Ordovices were a Welsh tribe near where some geologists were looking at rocks from 500 my ago. The Permian period was named for the Russian area of Perm, while the Cretaceous was named for the French word for chalk, *cretace*. Those 19th-century geologists were organized, but they went crazy when it came to names, because the terms are not always consistent. Plus, someone made a rule that once a name was picked for a time period, no backsies. Once a label was attached, we're stuck with it, even if it's confusing.

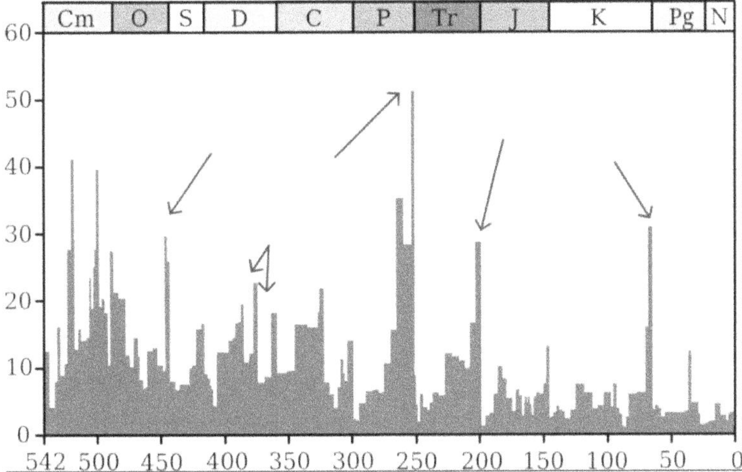

Fig 20. The Big Five, key mass extinctions that mark the end of geologic periods. The final three arrows point to extinctions that influenced the evolution of dinosaurs at the beginning of the Triassic, beginning of the Jurassic, and end of the Cretaceous.

When discussing dinosaurs, we really only need to focus on four periods: Permian, Triassic, Jurassic, and Cretaceous. These are labeled on the diagrams as P, Tr, J, and K. A detailed geological timeline with all the labels is in the Appendix, if you want to know what all of them are named.

These time periods are not of equal lengths. There is a hierarchy of time length, with eons being the longest, then eras, periods, epochs, and ages. However, though periods are longer than epochs, that doesn't mean they are marked out evenly. It's not like years, which are made up of 365 days, or centuries, which are 100 years. The Triassic period started 250 my ago and was 50 my long; the Jurassic, 55 my long; and the Cretaceous, 80 my. Why the difference?

The reason is that the dividing lines between periods are based on cataclysmic events. That's where the Big Five come from. Each of the periods below ended with a huge die-off of species, a mass extinction.

Time period of Extinction Event	How many million years ago?	Cause of Extinction	How many species were lost?
End of the Ordovician	440	Huge cooling and warming periods. Massive changes in ocean chemistry. As the single super-continent Pangaea begins to split up, there are earthquakes, volcanoes, and die-offs in sea life.	86%
End of the Devonian	360	Rapid growth and spread of land plants intensify periods of rapid and severe global cooling.	75%
End of the Permian	250	Big increase in volcanic activity (e.g., Siberia)—sulfur, carbon dioxide, and acid rain change the biosphere.	96%
End of the Triassic	200	Underwater volcanoes! So many volcanoes, especially in the newly formed and growing Atlantic ocean.	80%
End of the Cretaceous	65	Asteroid impact in Yucatan, but also maybe volcanoes (see Chapter "Y").	76%

Fig 21. Information about the Big Five Extinctions.

Mass extinctions don't happen in a week. Even the asteroid that landed 65 my ago took a long time to devastate the ruling species. Scientists debate how long is long, but a thousand years isn't that long when we're talking about a geological layer.

One scientist, James Lawrence Powell, even argues in a fascinating book that asteroid impacts may have happened multiple times, not just at the end of the Cretaceous. In *Night Comes to the Cretaceous*, Powell points out that our solar system itself is on the move, traveling in an orbit that takes it in and out of the spiraling Milky Way Galaxy. (I'd picture it as up and down, though that doesn't make any sense in space.)

Every time Sol and its eight followers go through the heavy traffic of the galaxy, full of star and planetary debris, the chance of bombardment goes up. Powell notes that this journey through rush hour of the Milky Way happens every 20 million years, give or take. It may have influenced some of the climates and mass extinctions that happened. This is a fascinating and terrifying idea, but don't worry— that's way off in the future. Humans may cause their own extinction much sooner, or… wait, I guess there is worry there.

The debate over how dinosaurs died off is a lively one, and we'll delve more into the debates between relative causation of asteroids and volcanoes later ("K," "Y"). But the biggest extinction so far, where nearly all life (96%) was extinguished, was at the end of the Permian. An especially intense outburst of volcanic activity took place, spewing acid rain, sulfur, and carbon dioxide into the atmosphere. Lava masses flowed over a great portion of what is now Siberia. The volcanoes may have been caused by movement of the continents, other asteroids, or shifts in temperature, but whatever the cause, the result for marine and land life at the time was nearly catastrophic.

Prior to that time, most animals were marine creatures. A few of those did survive. But after the lava hardened, over thousands of years, the proto-dinosaurs and proto-mammals emerged and began to diversify. Paleontology conventional wisdom for a long time was that dinosaurs took over first, in the Triassic period, and that mammals did not come along until much later. Fossil finds in recent decades now show that there were many kinds of smaller mammals and smaller dinosaurs that emerged together. Each of those two groups reflected about one-third of the creatures in the Triassic. It was not until the Jurassic that the dinosaurs out-competed and came to dominate most of the available animals.

Across all of these periods of mass extinction, there was continuous background extinction. Early mammal ancestors dwindled to a few as the plant-eating stegosaurs and meat-eating allosaurs became dominant. But even the stegosaurs were gone by the end of the Jurassic. So if you see a painting of a *Tyrannosaurus rex* attacking a *Stegosaurus*, you may now claim with confidence that the two species lived millions of years apart. In fact, *T. rex* is closer to us in our geological time than to that of *Stegosaurus*.

Extinction Is a Process

Modern headlines are full of news about species going extinct and pleas to save this or that animal. Let's be clear: it's bad if humans hunt a species to extinction. It's bad if humans wipe out a habitat that drives a species to extinction. We should avoid killing all the buffalo. Genocide—the elimination of an entire population—is bad. Don't misunderstand the point here.

However, caution is needed. Extinction as a concept is a little like death. It's a natural process. We can't save all species from extinction, nor should we. We really don't want immortality, not for ourselves nor for other creatures. Only focusing on extinction is similar to when the media makes a big deal about layoffs but rarely mentions hiring. There is a natural turnover in employment, and there is also natural turnover in species.

New species are discovered all the time. Some of the "new" enter the fossil record, creatures that lived a long time ago that we just now unearth. But new and living species are also discovered. Sometimes the species was good at hiding, and, at other times, they are a brand-new adaptation. In 2023, for example, a new gecko was discovered in South America, one which spits gooey venom—a handy thing to have. Each year, between a few dozen to a few hundred new species are discovered and entered into the database of creatures.

Ongoing species adaptation tends to offset background extinction. We should not necessarily worry about background extinction of every species. What we need to worry about is mass extinction. And that fear is very real.

We do see data that a high percentage of species are right now being pushed out of their habitats. We know that human intervention is killing off habitats. Some of those habitats are vital to us. We need bees, for instance. It's just that we don't need to worry about every announced extinction of every species. Extinction of one species sometimes creates opportunity for another. The dinosaurs flourished because other species disappeared. The mammals flourished when the dinosaurs disappeared.

This discussion of discovering new old creatures brings up another topic. It involves what seems like a contradiction. That is, how can scientists discover new extinct creatures? That is what fossils are all about.

F is for Fossil

Personally, I was never a big fossil person as a kid. Those school field trips where you end up staring at a 10,000-year-old picture of a leaf? Hardly worth the effort. It was only later that I boarded the dinosaur fossil train. An imprint of 200-million-year-old feather? Now you're talking.

We wouldn't know anything about the prehistoric world without fossils, whether imprints of leaves or of feathers. Everything we know about dinosaurs comes from what they left in the rock. Fossils tell us what *Tyrannosaurus* ate, how *Diplodocus* withstood attack, how *Parasaurolophus* laid eggs, or where *Brachiosaurus* walked. In order for us to see what life was like before humans, we need the geological artifacts and the scientific archives; we need fossils.

And they're not really even bones.

The Theseus Paradox

First, a little Greek history. Trust me, this side excursion will make sense in a minute. Theseus, an ancient warrior, sailed out of Greece to the island of Crete. He slew the minotaur in the labyrinth and performed several other heroic feats before returning home. Upon his triumphant return, they named the city of Athens after Theseus.

They put his ship on display as a monument for everyone to marvel. After a long time, the wood began to rot, so a plank was replaced here, then another, then the sails, then the mast. All of the wood and fabric in the ship was ultimately replaced.

Which prompts a key question: was it still Theseus's ship?

Fig 22. A Theseus-type ship in a Greek museum.

Is the ship the blueprint of the shape? Is it the physical parts that make up the ship? Or the idea of a "sailing thing"? And what if the replaced parts changed how the ship looked?

We can deliberate all day, but this is essentially a Greek zen koan, a puzzle with no solution. A 17th-century philosopher, Thomas Hollywood, took it one step further. He wondered, if you gathered up all the discarded planks from the original ship and built another ship, was that Theseus's ship as well?

If you're thinking this has nothing to do with fossils, think again! Consider the replicas of *Diplodocus*, plaster casts, and original bones. Fossil bones are very much like Theseus's ship.

Fossil Bone (Not Bone Bone)

There are several kinds of fossils, but the ones we most closely associate with dinosaurs are fossil bones. Fossil bones are the remains of skulls, hips, teeth, or claws from the original animal. They turn into fossils through a process called *permineralization. Per* means "through," that is, the minerals flow through the bone.

This process takes several steps, but it starts with the dinosaur dying in a nice cushy substance, such as mud or sand, preferably at the bottom of a river. The bones need to be sheltered from wind and predators, to keep them from eroding or being ripped apart. A river bottom allows materials to flow through the remains in an orderly manner. The bones need to decay carefully. No disorganized decaying allowed!

Muscles and flesh rot fairly quickly. Occasionally, soft matter like skin or feathers can be preserved, if the mud dries just so. But most of the dinosaur fossils that have been discovered so far consist of bone residue. Although bones are hard, they are themselves filled with blood vessels and organic tissue. At the cellular level—even for bones—there are gas bubbles, which leave openings.

These openings in bones, cells, and blood vessels leave places for minerals to be deposited as they wash through those bones, held fast in that river bottom. Mineralized water seeps into the openings and fills the holes while the organic matter decays. Over a long time— thousands and millions of years—the mineral hardens and turns to rock. Now, we have a three-dimensional copy of the original dinosaur.

Fig 23. Example of a complete fossilized skeleton of *Camarasaurus* at Dinosaur National Monument, Utah.

Fossils, then, are like a photographic negative of a dinosaur. They are not bones; they are rock. "Fossil bones" are what scientists call them, but the rock is not the original bone. The rock filled the holes in the bone. Filled holes is the best that scientists will get. Like Theseus' ship, the fossil ship is a copy of the original dinosaur, not the original dinosaur.

So for the purists who only want to show original *Diplodocus* "bones" and not copies, the skeleton dug up with Andrew Carnegie's money was neither bone nor the original. The plaster casts of the fossils are a copy of a copy, not a copy of the original.

Uplift

Uplift is another important part of the equation. Fossils are buried, deep all around us, underneath layers and layers of rock. The only reason we know they exist is that some of those layers have surfaced. This happens because some mountains formed *after* the animals lived and died and turned to rock. Uplift is not involved in creating dinosaur fossils. But uplift is how we can find the dinosaurs. This happens because the earth surrounding the buried fossils does a little dance.

Here's how uplift works. The tectonic plates underneath the continents and the oceans are always moving. They bang into each other, changing the shape of the world, even more slowly than the flow of minerals into bone. If one tectonic plate meets another and is stubborn enough, it keeps pushing. The other side has nowhere to go but up.

That's how the Rockies formed in the western United States, in an event called the Laramie orogeny, and I would make a joke about orogenous zones, but I suppose the geologists have heard that one. Anyway, as that plate kept pushing, the land buckled, like a bath mat slipping on a tile floor. As an entire half of North America went upward, the older layers of earth became exposed, which is why American national parks in the west are full of striped hills that are spectacular in the sunset. Eventually, erosion from wind or water exposes parts of the rock, and, suddenly, there's a wall of bones going upward. Fossils end up sticking out, ready to be discovered by excited fossil collectors.

It's not an accident, therefore, that so much fossil hunting occurs in Colorado, Wyoming, Montana, and even up in Canada near Alberta. The uplift of the Rockies and the dry air are perfect for exposing and preserving fossils. It's likely that there also are many fossils on the other side of the Rockies to the east, in Minnesota and Nebraska. But the climate is not as conducive to preservation or erosion, and there's little uplift, so very few fossils have been found. The same rules explain why so many discoveries occur near the young mountains in Asia, as well as in South America.

Uplift helps scientists find the fossils. After all, we can't just start digging up the entire world to find the fossils beneath us. Doing the digging itself might plow right through the evidence. We have to be satisfied with looking in the right places that had the right kind of soil and climate and mountains millions of years ago. Thank you, stubborn tectonic plates!

Footprints & Coprolite

Although most fossil discussions involve bone, almost any organic matter can be fossilized. The more quickly the dinosaur was buried under the proper conditions, the more intact a fossil might be. Fossil claws, teeth, and even skin ("S") are the stuff of a paleontologist's dreams.

Other kinds of fossils don't reveal what the animal was, but what it was doing. These "trace fossils" are different ways of seeing an extinct animal. *Ichnology* is an entire branch of science (*ich*=trace) devoted to studying what organisms left behind.

One good example of such a trace is a footprint. For instance, giant sauropods once plodded along a highway near Morrison, Colorado. The footsteps of the giants sank deep into the mud. The soil underneath the mud eroded away, and changes in geology exposed the rest to air. Those who first looked at the bumps might not have recognized sauropod feet, but other footprints nearby told paleontologists that these were no ordinary bumps. The depth of the bumps demonstrate how heavy the creature was who trod along this highway.

Fig 24. Trace footprints of a sauropod. The muddy tracks hardened to rock, while
the soft soil below eroded away.

Dinosaur footprints seen from underneath are fairly rare. Prints
seen from the top are far more common. Feet, whether small and
large, three-toed like a bird or round like an elephant, sink into soft
mud that turns hard (see Figure 3).

It's a familiar story. Soft mud is the key to a lot of what we know
of ancient beasts. Footprints get covered with sand, pebbles, or
whatever soil is softer than the dried mud. Time passes, yadda yadda,
erosion, uplift, and Bob's your uncle, we can see the footprints.

Almost any part of an animal could, in theory, be fossilized.
Fossilized eggs have been found with never-born dinosaurs babies
inside ("X"). Any part, you may wonder? Yup. Even dinosaur poop.
The fancy scientific word for dinosaur poop, or fossilized dung, is
coprolite:

> *Copro* (dung) + *lith* (stone)

Copro, that Latin word for dung, is at the front of other words as
well—coprolite, coprozoic, coprophagy—don't ask about that last
one. Analyzing fossil dung is another specialized category of
paleobiology. How dung gets fossilized would take ten to twenty very
technical pages to explain, so, trust me, the main point is that organic
matter simply needs to be more solid than whatever preserves it.

Otherwise, the process is similar to bone. Mineralization replaces the air bubbles in the original until *voila!* Preserved dino dung!

The 19th-century farmers of Cambridgeshire, England, were keen to find coprolite. This was before people enacted rules about preserving ancient things. Local fossil hunters loved finding coprolite because its high phosphate content made it great fertilizer. They'd dig it up and sell it to farmers for their crops. The ultimate in recycling!

Fig 25. Coprolite sample, including a fossilized deer toe visible in the foreground.

In modern times, there is another thriving coprolite industry—on the internet. People sell fake dinosaur poop. (Of course they do, because anybody will buy anything, which means anybody will sell anything.) Merely searching for information about coprolite will take you to dozens of fake sales offers. Unless you can confirm the phosphate content or verify that the place of origin is a dinosaur fossil ground, then you probably can't distinguish coprolite from a weirdly shaped pile of rock. So don't be tempted to buy any. Remember, too, even authentic fossilized poop isn't actual poop. It's only a copy.

Which leads to an intriguing philosophical question. If you made a cast of authentic coprolite, would it still retain the essence of dung? Wonder what Thomas Hobbes would think of that.

G is for Godzilla

Godzilla was definitely a dinosaur. If you're wondering what he's doing in this book, that's the answer. The question is not whether he was, but how do we know? And what do we know about Godzilla, scientifically, that would conform to a paleontologist's view? We can examine the G-Man's body parts like a paleobiologist, looking at his skull, tail, and other anatomical features.

To answer those questions, though, we also have to address one important issue. There have been 38 films made about Godzilla, beginning with the Japanese *Gojira* in 1954 and continuing through to 2023's *Godzilla x Kong: The New Empire*. So, we need to decide which Godzilla we are talking about.

One thing is for certain about the Big Guy. It's not that he is a "he." To avoid pronoun confusion, I will refer to Godzilla as "he" and G-Man, but Godzilla could be asexual, nonbinary, or female. Movie evidence has not been presented to give him a conclusive gender. And having a Japanese scientist saying "Godzilla is a male" is not scientific evidence.

No, the bigger certainty is that Godzilla is a superstar. As evidence of his stardom, Godzilla is the only dinosaur to have both an Oscar, and his own theme song.

Fig 26. Is Godzilla a dinosaur? How do we know?

Which Godzilla Are We Talking About??

Fair warning. I am almost as big a Godzilla dork as I am a dinosaur geek. I could spend a few dozen pages on just the ins and outs of all the movies. That's for another book. But we need to know a little about the movies to analyze Godzilla's dinosaur traits. So, how many different kinds of Godzillas are there? And, which ones should we analyze?

While there were 38 film Godzillas, there are three that we can use for our dinosaur-themed discussion. The 1954 Godzilla, from the first film, is the most useful for this purpose. Paleontologists would call him a *holotype*, meaning the standard-bearer for the entire species.[17] We can call him OGH, or the Original Godzilla Holotype.

---

[17] For example, the fragmentary *Diplodocus* discovered by Marsh in Wyoming was the holotype. Carnegie's funded expeditions discovered better versions of *Diplodocus* but they are called "referred specimens."

The first Japanese film, *Gojira*, which introduced OGH, carried an anti-nuclear message. Godzilla was roughly 25-30 meters tall, bipedal, and aquatic, but also oxygen-breathing, sharp-toothed, long-tailed, and fire-breathing. OGH was exposed to nuclear radiation, but it's not clear how he was changed from that radiation—was he originally a lizard? A fish? A Loch Ness-type serpent? We don't know, other than that he was awakened from the deep and subsequently spawned a whole series of sequels. In some of the 1960-1970 sequels, he fought other monsters from Earth (also radiated?) and banded with them against extraterrestrial monsters. Several of the sequels featured him with his son, for whom he seemed to be the only parent.

The second Godzilla has been called GINO—Godzilla In Name Only. This 1998 American film version of Godzilla (also unhelpfully titled *Godzilla*) designed him to look distinctly different. This was because the filmmakers wanted to create their own look. Plus, they didn't get cooperation or the licensing rights from the Japanese owners of OGH. However, by 1998, views of dinosaurs had changed, and GINO was more dinosaur-like and more animalistic. He looked less like guy in a rubber suit and more like an animal.

GINO held his tail out stiffly behind his body, which made him better at running. In the 1998 movie, GINO also turned out to be pregnant and laid eggs, though the movie claimed it was via asexual reproduction. Despite GINO's more "accurate" depiction, the movie itself was heavily criticized for its lack of plot and character development. Yet, complaints from film critics notwithstanding, GINO looked more like a dinosaur.

The third main Godzilla type, which has emerged in the most recent franchise reboot, is a return to the bipedal tail-dragger. No longer resembling an iguana like GINO, the GReboot is far larger than OGH, standing between 100-120 m on two massive legs. GReboot breathes blue fire and—so far—has not appeared with any offspring. He has both battled and allied with King Kong.

Overall, the OGH and GReboot Godzillas are the best known and have generated the most film sequels, as well as the most cinematic and scientific analysis. Even though GINO was, according to some, more dinosaur-like, the bipedal versions are the ones most worth considering.

A Matter of Skulls

Several scientists have put forth legitimate assessments of OGH, through peer-reviewed articles in scientific journals, not just knowledgeable fans chatting on Godzilla-wikis. The best-known study was written by Ken Carpenter, a veteran paleontologist from the Denver Museum of Natural History. Carpenter's 1998 article, "A Dinosaur Paleontologist's View of Godzilla," was both thorough and readable, based on solid research but taking the movies seriously.[18] Carpenter is a well-respected scientist who had been collecting and analyzing dinosaur fossils for decades. Hence, his fact-based approach helps highlight how science can draw conclusions based on data—even fictional data.

Fig 27. Proposed Godzilla skull configuration compared with
other meat-eating theropods.

Carpenter started, as I did in "A," with a comparison of skulls. His description of Godzilla's skull notes that the creature's eyes were forward-facing, which gave him stereoscopic vision. That vision is common to many predators, whether eagles or *T. rexes*. OGH also had large, pointed teeth and clawed feet, which marked him clearly as a meat-eater.

It's a logical classification, even though we don't see OGH eat on film. We see him pick up things with his teeth—subway trains, aircraft carriers, people—but he doesn't eat them so much as toss

---

[18] Kenneth Carpenter, "A Dinosaur Paleontologist's View of Godzilla," In Lees, J. D. & Cerasini, M. (eds), 102-106, *The Official Godzilla Compendium* (New York: Random House, 1998).

them aside like the puny things they are. Still, even if we don't see what he consumes, the physical traits, from three-toed claws to a mouth full of serrated blades, mark him as a carnivorous theropod, the clade name for the meat-eaters.

Some might argue that Godzilla is fed by nuclear radiation. He does absorb energy, which he spits back out in yellow or blue blasts, depending on the movie. But is he "eating" the radiation? And if he eats radiation, then what are the serrated teeth for? He certainly behaves like a predator, stalking, pouncing, and grabbing things with his jaws rather than with his arms. The more advanced theropods had tiny arms because they used their heads and jaws directly (see "T").

Therefore, says Carpenter, Godzilla's skull is best compared with that of other meat-eaters. OGH's head was more square than rectangular. So he is not like a *T. rex* or even an *Allosaurus*. Instead, he is similar to an earlier carnivore called *Carnotaurus*. *Carnotaurus* had a blunt nose, which made his head smaller. The carnotaurs had horns, where Godzilla clearly does not. But horns are a small adaptation, even if Godzilla has none. He could still be cousin to a *Carnotaurus*.

Carpenter also notes the distance behind OGH's eyes, which suggests that he had neck muscles strong enough to hold the large head with room behind the eyes for those diapsid holes where extra jaw muscles could attach. The better to chomp you with, my dear subway passengers!

Size (and Tail) Matters

Still, while the skull, teeth, and toes seem to suggest a theropod dinosaur, other anatomical features have problems. GINO is the Godzilla that holds his tail "correctly," but OGH and the GReboot do not. Theropods—dinosaurs—did not drag their tails. The 1998 incarnation that Godzilla-lovers hated walked in a manner closest to Carpenter's full-body skeleton in Figure 28. The tail was rigid and outstretched behind, which would have allowed a real *Gojirasaurus* to move quickly.

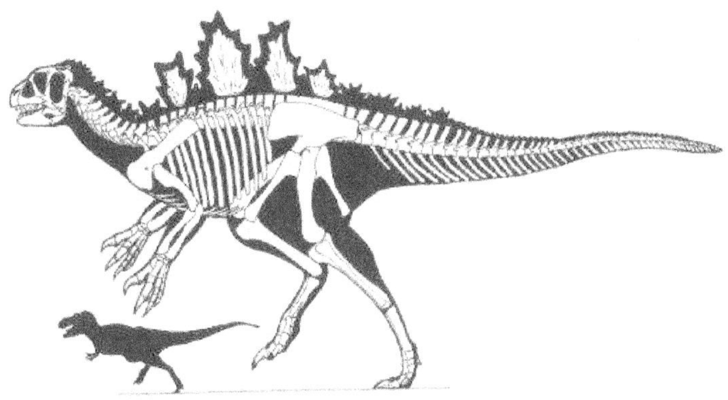

Fig 28. Carpenter's Godzilla skeleton compared with a smaller tyrannosaur.

In the first set of Japanese movies, OGH was portrayed by a man in a rubber suit, which probably made an outstretched tail impossible. The logistics of merely walking in a 220-pound rubber suit was difficult enough. Haruo Nakijima reportedly lost 20 pounds just wearing the suit because it lacked ventilation. A human being doesn't have strong enough legs or the right hip structure to hold a tail out in back, like in Figure 28. Those hip bones are adapted for a tail, not a human holding a tail.

Curiously, in the most recent Monster-verse reboot movies, when CGI was available, our GReboot still dragged his tail. The tail floats atop the ocean surface when Godzilla swims, but he walks upright on land. The GReboot version is more kangaroo-like than dinosaur-like. This might make sense if Godzilla is an aquatic creature, perhaps using his long tail to swim like an eel, rather than aiding him while walking. Yet advanced marine reptiles, like mosasaurs or plesiosaurs, developed fins. Neither OGH nor GReboot has fins.

Furthermore, OGH displayed some very odd tail behavior. In some of the mid-1970s movies, like 1973's *Godzilla v. Megalon*, OGH would slide forward on his tail. Even if he could use his tail like a kangaroo during a fight, bouncing backward to spring forward, that doesn't explain sliding around on a tail. This is physiologically impossible, and it brings up an important point on how science fiction does or does not work.

In science fiction, there is a scientific premise emerging from known laws: alien creatures, humans with superpowers, time travel. Either basic laws of science must be obeyed, or the movie must explain why they are broken. Godzilla is a fictional creature, but he was created by radiation. Science fiction must have rules, otherwise it should be labeled "magic" or "fantasy."

It could be argued that scientific analysis on any movie monster is a waste of time. But since paleontologists themselves have to draw conclusions based on small bits of bone, have to create entire ecosystems and biological arguments on things that happened millions of years ago, conjecture is the name of the game. The question is what we can conclude, given the laws that we know are in place. Godzilla can't appear suddenly to fly or scoot around on his tail. He must also obey the laws of gravity.

One more issue has been hotly debated in the Godzilla-analysis circles. GReboot's size may be a bigger problem than how he holds his tail. The size issue emerges because, over time, the CGI Godzillas have grown exponentially. While OGH stood about 50 m in 1954, the latest Godzilla is two to three times that size, depending on the movie and who you ask. But it's one thing to have different versions of Robin Hood or Moses, played by different people. All of those actors were human and only a few inches different from each other (5'10" to 6'4"). It's another to create a computerized version of Godzilla that defies physical boundaries of living creatures.

The Rebooted Godzilla has been described by the filmmakers as 350 ft/100 m, a size which could tower above the Statue of Liberty or 30-story buildings. Those with knowledge of paleobiology argue that a creature that size could not exist because his bones would be crushed under the volume of his body. The biggest *Titanosaurus* sauropods were only 20-30 m, and their bones were hollow. Moreover, they were quadrupeds, with hip structures that suggest they could not move quickly or move on two legs. Bipedal dinosaurs, even the biggest theropods, were much smaller at perhaps 5-6 m— even *T. rex*. The body has to make a trade-off if it is to be a realistic dinosaur.

Fig 29. Is the latest movie version of Godzilla too tall to be "realistic"?[19]

Could a 100-meter Godzilla have adapted in some other way to strengthen its bones? Perhaps, bombarded with nuclear radiation, GReboot's bones could have generated a unique cell structure similar to steel or titanium. The problem is that the movie does not address it, and good science fiction will justify the things that surpass the boundaries.

Meanwhile, it's hard to say what exactly nuclear radiation blasts would do to make your bones stronger. Usually, it's the other way around. Overall, the size of GReboot might just be his most unrealistic feature. Even more implausible than nuclear breath.

Serious Science? Or Silly Science?

While this may all seem too far-fetched for analysis, it's notable that multiple scientists have done serious work to assess Godzilla's

---

[19] The photo shows "Shin Godzilla," a Japanese 2016 variation similar, not identical, to the 2014 reboot version. If you care about the distinction, I agree that they are different.

biology. This shows how paleobiology works. For example, the ichnologist Anthony Martin, one of those people who studies fossil traces, waxes poetic about the trace evidence provided by movie scientists in the 2014 *Godzilla* film. When a monster moth hatches from an egg, crawls underground through an emergency burrow, and then leaves tracks, Martin is thrilled. Such tracks can be used to determine an animal's size and shape.[20] As Martin says, forget all the boring talking, let's get back to the trace evidence!

Another scientist, writing under the name *Tetrapodzoology*, provides a fully detailed literature review. A literature review is serious stuff. It's a type of research analysis that's provided in dissertations and academic journal articles. This blog summarizes all the scientific analysis done on Godzilla up through the 2020s.[21] The author cites both formally published and non-published papers, includes a properly formatted bibliography, and highlights several articles that were peer-reviewed. Peer review is a vital step because it means others could pick apart the scientific logic. If it was peer-reviewed, others took the topic seriously, too.

The key is to try and maintain that internal logic. A dinosaur with a long tail should hold the tail. If it has eggs, we need to know how it reproduced; there are reptiles that reproduce asexually, so that is based on existing science. There are animals that breathe oxygen but stay underwater for long periods of time. There are worms which, cut in two, can regrow both their tail or their head, as GReboot has sometimes done. There are a lot of weird things in the modern and animal kingdoms.

Ken Carpenter, for his part, bestowed a great honor on our Oscar-winning film icon. In 1997, after finding an 18-foot-long theropod, similar to *Coelophysis* from the middle Triassic, Carpenter gave it the name *Gojirasaurus quayi*. Since then, there's been a question about whether Carpenter had enough fossil material to distinguish those bones as a unique species. Those discussions are still ongoing. It may be that *Gojirasaurus* might not retain its status as a new species. But the name stands at the ready.

---

[20] Tmartin, "The Ichnology of Godzilla," *Life Traces of the Georgia Coast, May 23, 2014.* https://www.georgialifetraces.com/2014/05/23/the-ichnology-of-godzilla/. Accessed November 26, 2024.

[21] Tetrapodzoology, "The Science of Godzilla," *Scienceblogs.com*, November 1, 2010. https://scienceblogs.com/tetrapodzoology/2010/11/01/science-of-godzilla-2010. Accessed November 26, 2024.

Still, while there have been critiques of *Gojirasaurus*, Carpenter's specimen UCM 47221 as of 2024 still has its original name. Thus, not only does Godzilla have an Oscar and a theme song, he now also has a real-life namesake.

H is for Hip Bone

It's time to get into the hips. Hips are what the dinosaurs are all about, which is why I just spent the last half hour trying to find you a picture of a dinosaur doing the Time Warp. *It's just a step to the left*.…Did you know there's a whole wiki showing you how to do the Time Warp? You can learn anything on the internet!

Anyway, some of you already know your Ornithischians from your Saurischians. For those who don't, get ready to focus in on the pelvic bones. Dinosaurs are dinosaurs because of their hip design (and skulls and ankles, "A"). It's the hips that let them walk, stalk, and run away from the crocodiles. Although don't tangle with a croc in the water, and their hip design will explain why. The distinction among dinosaur hip bones was an early way to organize the dinosaur clades, although that's becoming controversial, too.

Hip Bone's Connected to the …

We need to uncover the *ischia* of it all, *ischion* being the Greek root word for "hip." Understanding dinosaur hips starts with anatomy. Let's start with the more familiar human hips before we delve into what makes lizard hips different.

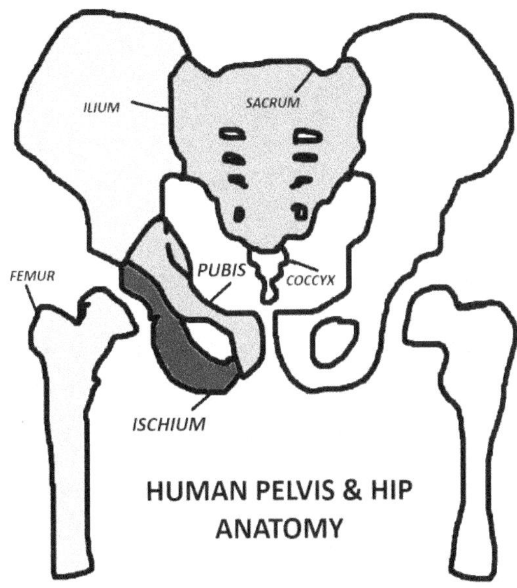

Fig 30. Humans have a ball-and-socket-joint for their hips. Note how the pubis and ischium bones (bottom right) create a convenient "hole" to anchor the femur.

Humans, like other land animals, have a pelvis with a top, bottom, and symmetrical sides. The human hip is triangular, wider at the top and smaller at the bottom. The torso and vertebrae attach to the top, at the *sacrum*, while the legs and tail—for humans that's our *coccyx*—attach to the bottom. The femurs, those important weight-bearing upper leg bones, attach to the hip with a ball-and-socket joint that snugs into a hole. In humans, the femur juts out of that hole at close to a 90-degree angle and quickly descends, allowing us to stand upright. The ball-and-socket configuration gives humans flexibility of movement and improved weight-bearing, which is a highly successful adaptation. The angle of the human pelvis allows us to stand straight.

That joint hole is created by two other bones, the *pubis* in front and the *ischium* in back. In humans, those two bones are fused. You sit on your ischia, your hip bones, but they are closely connected to the pubis in the front. In Figure 30, those bones are different shades for identification purposes, but in humans they are a single structure, as shown on the right. In other animals, they are two separate bones.

Why Crocodiles Can't Run

Reptiles, both back in the day and now, have similar bits and pieces: pelvis (ilium), ischium, pubis, and femurs. In non-dinosaur reptiles like crocodiles, the pubis juts out in front, while the ischium is tilted backward. The division of those into two unjoined bones distinguishes them from mammals, among other things. Crocodiles differ from dinosaurs in another hipster way. In crocodiles, the femur fits into a depression, not a hole. The femur—the absolutely vital, weight-bearing leg—extends outward at almost a 90-degree angle to the pelvis. But unlike humans, where that angle drops downward, in crocodiles, the angle is to the side. This is why crocodiles squat and crawl, rather than stand up and run.

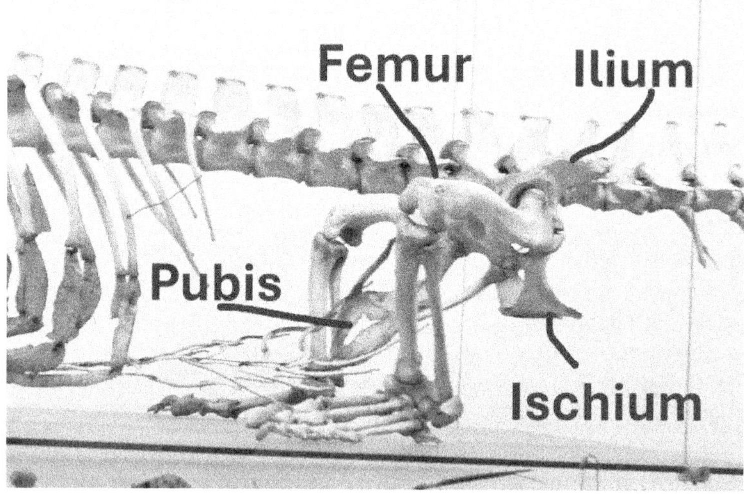

Fig 31. Crocodile femurs are situated differently from humans. They can't run, but they can swim more effectively.

The angle of a crocodile femur makes its move relatively slowly on land, though swinging its tail helps a little, However, crocodiles are lightning fast in the water, reaching speeds of 18 mph, as many dogs and ducks have found to their peril. In the water, long femurs sticking downward would encounter water resistance and slow them down. Better to have those foldable femurs.

The downward angle of legs became a competitive advantage for the earliest dinosaurs, who thrived on land after developing that hole to hold the ball-and-socket joint for their femur. Roughly 200 my ago, dinosaur femurs "broke through" the hip sockets. But even after the hole in the hip socket developed, dinosaur hip structures continued trying to adapt, and reptile hips split into two different types. These two variation of hip designs played around with the *ischium* and the *pubis*, creating extra work for people who draw clade diagrams.

Ornithischians Were Named Backward

Back in the mid-19th century, when only a few dozen dinosaur species had been discovered, the pioneer paleontologists were eager to create naming systems. One enterprising naturalist, Richard Owen, came up with the term *Dinosauria*: *dino*=terrible or fearsome + lizard. "Terrible lizard" became an instant hit. Forever after, everyone called them dinosaurs, even though they didn't agree whether they were lizards, terrible, or belonged in a single category.

Cambridge naturalist Harry Seeley took a step further. The rest is spelling misery for the rest of us. Seeley created the main two dinosaur branches on the tree. Hip bones were often one of the easiest parts of the fossil skeletons to identify, especially with large dinosaurs. Seeley thought it was easy to identify the hip bones, and dinosaurs did seem to have prominent pubis and ischium bones. In some, the ischium pointed backward, and, in others, the ischium pointed forward. Easy peasy, two handy groups!

The group with backward-pointing hipbones was designated as Ornithischian. The term "bird-hipped" was assigned because modern birds have both their ischium and pubis pointing backward. Find a skeleton of a chicken and check it out![22]

Ornith (bird) + *ischion* (hip)

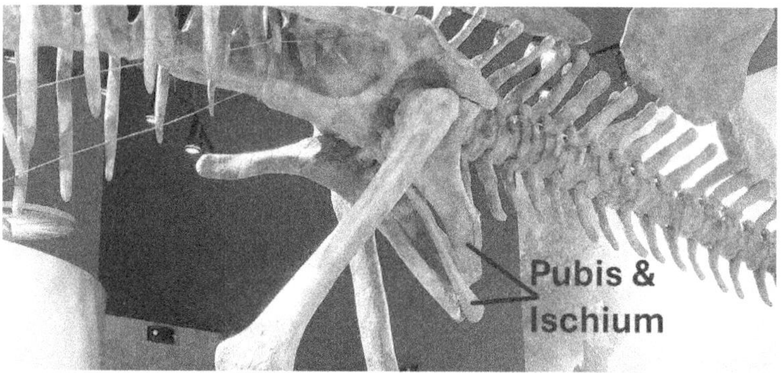

Fig 32. Close-up of the "bird-hipped" *Stegosaurus*, with its backward-pointing pubis.

The ornithischians were all plant-eaters. Like birds, they also had beaks, that is, curved bones right above their mouth, presumably to nip leaves with. The variation within the group was large. It included armored, squat ankylosaurs, bony-horned ceratopsians, and the curvy-backed stegosaurs. Each of these had different skeletal body features except for their similar hips and beaks. Along with the beaks, they sported teeth designed for grinding plant matter. Digesting a lot of leaves—and they had to eat a lot—is time-consuming, so it's thought that the backward hip bones made room for a larger stomach or even multiple stomachs.

Saurischians and Other Hipster Dinosaurs

The other category of dinosaurs identified by Seeley was named Saurischian.

---

[22] A labeled chicken skeleton, for example,
at:https://tbnranch.com/2012/01/15/chicken-anatomy/

Saur (lizard) + *ischion* (hip)

Seeley noted that this second group of dinosaurs, like crocodiles and other lizards, had a pubis which jutted forward (Figure 33). These skeletons had a ball-and-socket joint for the leg bone but also a forward-facing pubis.

Fig 33. Close-up of the "lizard-hipped" pelvic bones of a *Diplodocus*.

Unfortunately, Seeley's simple forking branch and naming convention created a big problem for paleontologists. The problem is, as we've already noted, modern birds are evolved from dinosaurs. In fact, they are still on the dinosaur family tree.

However, birds belong in the Saurischian arm of the diagram. Birds, who have bird hips, are grouped with the lizard-hipped. Oy vey!

How did Seeley go astray? The Saurischian dinosaurs, with a pubic bone that faces forward, most likely evolved first from crocodiles and other lizards. Their adaptation was the hole in the ball-and-socket hip joint that let them stand upward. This allowed them to move faster, eventually developing some bipedal variations.

The saurischian hips included both the giant sauropods and meat-eating theropods. The sauropods like *Titanosaurus* or *Diplodocus* might grow to be 40 m long, either from head to toe or tip to tail, however you wish to measure. Even though they stayed mostly on all four legs, they could theoretically rear up to reach the tastiest leaves on the top of a tree. So their back legs had to be really strong, with a balanced set of hips and a strongly anchored femur bone.

The theropod dinosaurs, like *Tyrannosaurus* or *Velociraptor*, needed to run easily in order to catch prey. These animals also had grasping hands and powerful feet. The sturdy pelvis not only stabilized their upward stance but helped them speed up significantly. Other adaptations in saurischians, from size to claws to teeth, came afterward to help either the gentle giants or speedy carnivores.

The adaptation of the backward-facing pubis for the ornithischians also likely happened later. Thus, some of the dinosaurs on the ornithischian line initially started out with forward-facing pubic bones. Yup. Bird-hipped dinosaurs, at some point, started with lizard hips. This is why simplistic classification systems become problematic when they're based on a dozen examples. Fast-forward several decades of fossil collecting, and the much bigger set of examples no longer fits on the tree as neatly.

On the theropod side of the saurischians, where they kept their lizard hips, some feathered theropods were eventually discovered in well-preserved, late-Cretaceous soil. These animals had all the main features of the predators: hole in the head, ankle joints, pointed teeth, sharp claws, and three-toed feet. They looked like small versions of their carnivore cousins. But *Maniraptor* and *Archaeopteryx* had feathers, a subject that will resurface in other chapters ("S," "W"). In these small dinosaurs, the pubic bones had again shifted backward. These became the ancestors of modern birds. That's how the lizard-hipped dinosaurs evolved into bird-hipped birds.

Seeley's system may someday be upended. The problem is knowing whether there is any single feature that embraces all the distinguishing characteristics. Paleontologists have long argued that the lizard-hipped/bird-hipped structure was too simplistic. The question is: what to replace it with?

Some now separate ankylosaurs and stegosaurs from other ornithischians. Others put the ornithischians at a different level from the saurischians. Still more even give the theropods their own branch, equal to the ornithischians and saurischians. This might seem a bit trivial to us, but the history books remember Linnaeus and Seeley for their classification system. Some professor who could come up with a brand-new branch that fits all the data perfectly would become famous. At the very least, tenured!

The more fossils that are recovered, the more data scientists will have to move the diagram around. Rearranging the hierarchy of dinosaurs will probably continue long into the future, which will cause perpetual evolution in the paleontology textbooks, too.

I is for Iguanodon

In 1820, Dr. Gideon Mantell was thrilled to discover a palm-sized rock, unnaturally pointed and curved. He knew it came from an animal, probably an ancient animal. It seemed logical that it might be a tooth, and since it was leaf-shaped, he thought it might be from a large plant-eater, like a hippo or rhinoceros. That would be unusual in Sussex, so he knew discovering an ancient English rhinoceros would make him famous.

Oh, what a howling error! Mantell would be known forevermore for his mistake, for linking his discovery so closely to a rhino. Was it his fault, given that the foremost naturalist of his day insisted the animal was a rhinoceros? Mantell was also ignored by other prominent scientists, only to have them gain fame from his ideas. Maybe history should be kinder to Gideon.

Previous chapters have dropped a few names of early paleontologists. This history-themed discussion will spotlight several, particularly those in Britain who first stumbled across large bones and wanted to know more. The *Iguanodon* plays a unique role in this story because of how naturalists of the day discussed its properties as they struggled to incorporate ancient reptiles into their belief systems. Gideon Mantell, his dogged analysis, and his obsession with classification, are at the heart of this discussion.

On the other hand, his obsession ruined his marriages, and his wife's support is often ignored in the history books. It was Mary who likely found the first famous tooth, Mary who let Gideon fill their dining room with samples, who organized his papers, who drew illustrations for his book, who raised his children … and who then was forced to move out when the house was turned into a museum.

On second thought, let's not cut Gideon Mantell too much slack other than crediting him with launching the *Iguanodon* hunt.

Who Found the Tooth?

Iguanodon (*don*=tooth, "iguana-toothed") was only the second dinosaur to be discovered and named formally by the scientific community in charge of such things, which in the early 19th century was the Royal Society in England.[23] The idea of dinosaurs, the understanding of their domination of the Earth in the Mesozoic, and the knowledge of their huge variation in function and design was decades away from becoming the science of paleontology in 1822. When Mantell found fossils in the quarry near his medical practice, he did not know their source.

There is also confusion about who actually found the tooth first. Encyclopedias credit Gideon. But author Deborah Cadbury, whose book *Terrible Lizard* is a meticulous and fascinating account of the dinosaur discoveries of the English Regency Period, claims Mary found it. According to Cadbury's reconstruction, Mary went with her husband on walks and brought the tooth to Gideon. Gideon told people at the time that she did so and wrote it in his diaries, which detailed all his activities, things like: *Murdered two evenings at cards.*[24] It was only later on, when the Mantells separated, that he changed his story. After the tooth became famous, he claimed its discovery.

---

[23] In the mini "bone wars" of the 1820s, Mantell and others vied to be the first. William Buckland is credited with publishing information about a creature he named *Megalosaurus* in 1824, though Gideon Mantell had written to him earlier with queries about the *Iguanodon* teeth.

[24] Deborah Cadbury, *Terrible Lizard: The First Dinosaur Hunters and the Birth of a New Science,* (New York: Henry Holt, 2000), 84.

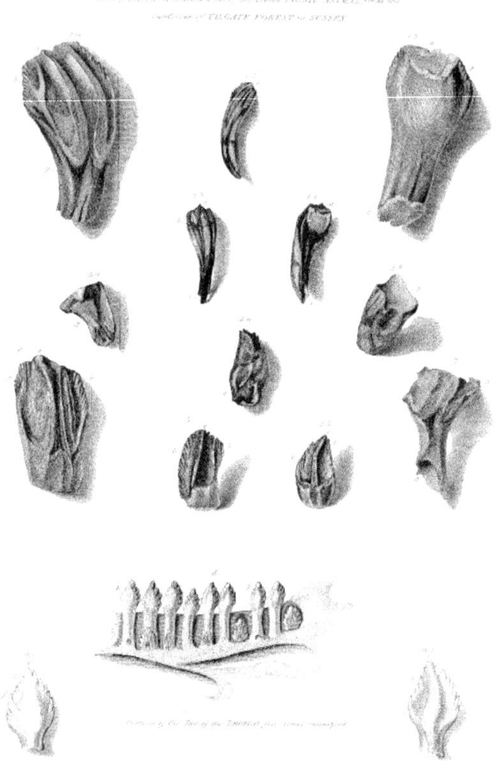

Fig 34. Illustration of *Iguanodon* teeth for Gideon Mantell's 1825 published book on fossils. Mary Mantell drew the pictures and probably found the first tooth.

To be fair, Gideon was the Mantell most passionate about fossil hunting. He had been picking through bones since attending medical school. Later, when he moved his medical practice near Whiteman's Quarry, he started finding dozens of bits of bones and leaf fossils. The bones were scattered, fragmentary, and terribly eroded. Were they from a giant fish? A giant mammal? There was very little information to go on.

But this tooth was different. It had vertical grooves (Figure 34, top left) as well as bumps along the top. Gideon thought it looked like an iguana's tooth, although naturally it was much bigger. An animal with such a tooth might be 10 to 15 meters long. Mary had found it on a walk, but together they went back to nearby Whiteman's Quarry, and Gideon found many more teeth.

Mary, as it turned out, was also an excellent illustrator. She made drawings of the finds, most of which were Gideon's, but her illustrations helped fill out the book he was writing on *Fossils of the South Downs*. She also was kept quite busy raising two of his children and keeping the large house organized, especially once Gideon started displaying his finds all over the parlor and dining room.

Only a Rhino, Scoffs the Frenchman

Gideon began circulating his finds among the naturalist minds of his era, eager for feedback on his ideas about ancient reptiles. Initially, his reptile comparisons were rebuffed. Georges Cuvier, a well-respected French scientist who had written the definitive work on Ice Age mammals, told Mantell the tooth resembled a modern rhinoceros. William Buckland, a creationist who wanted ideas of ancient animals to fit a Christian biblical timeline, told Gideon that he was mistaken about the geology of the quarry. Buckland insisted that Mantell must have found the bones in a different level of the soil than he claimed.

Mantell was told he was wrong six ways from Sunday, but he persisted. He spent more time at the quarry, dug up more fossils, scattered them all around the house, and talked to anyone who would listen for five minutes. Buckland continued to ignore him and published a book on his own finding, *Megalosaurus*. Some of his published illustrations, though, would be strikingly similar to Mary's illustrations.

Cuvier eventually agreed that the bones might be an ancient, rhinoceros-like reptile. As the powers-that-be debated, a young assistant to a natural history museum, Richard Owen, came out to see the teeth. Owen, who would eventually coin the name *Dinosauria*, spent a lot of time with Mantell. Owen had connections.

Eventually, the Mantell Museum (formerly his house) became so elaborate that Mary and the family were forced to move out. At first, she came back to visit, to help with the museum, and to give Gideon money. Over time, however, the separation became permanent. Mantell's dinosaur obsession left no space for his family.

The museum attracted plenty of visitors but made very little money. Despite trying to get royal patronage (and money), Mantell was ultimately unable to afford maintaining the museum. He had to sell most of his collection. By the 1850s, however, he had at last achieved the notoriety he sought. He was able to claim credit for discovering what he called *Iguanodon* and was acclaimed as a dinosaur expert. Sadly, he also developed a terrible case of sciatica and ended up overdosing on narcotics.

Gideon Mantell's discovery of the *Iguanodon* led to two other unfortunate incidents. One involved another fossil found near the treasure trove of teeth. This was a large, curved spike, bigger than a human hand. Cuvier and Buckland had both told Mantell that the creature might be a rhinoceros. Plenty of dinosaurs, as we now know, did have horns. The iguana that Mantell had compared with the original tooth was horned. It was not a giant leap for Gideon Mantell to suggest that the curved bone for his *Iguanodon* should go on the forehead.

Fig 35. Where to put the spike? Mantell thought the head, so sculptor Benjamin Waterhouse Hawkins created a rhino-iguanodon. Later, the spike was identified from other fossils as belonging to the hand.

However, *Iguanodon* bones began to be found in many other places all over northwestern Europe. Eventually, skeletons unearthed in Belgium and France were discovered where the pointed bone was attached to the creature's front hand. The pointed object was confirmed to be a thumb spike, not a horn. The error was firmly attached to Gideon Mantell's reputation.[25]

The illustrations of *Iguanodons* created in the 1830-1840 time frame showed the dinosaur as bipedal, sitting up on its longer hind legs like a kangaroo, ready to spike attackers. It was recognized that its hind legs were longer than its front legs, a skeletal structure common to many large plant-eaters. Later, turn-of-the-century designers noted that these were built more like quadrupeds. Eventually, the quadruped notion would win out, and modern depictions show *Iguanodon* on all fours. Mantell had argued that the key was the animal's tail. If it was bipedal, the tail could have been used for balance. At least, Mantell had gotten something right. After all, the rhinoceros had not been his first thought.

The Infamous Dinner in a Dinosaur

The other postscript to Mantell's discoveries involved his friend Richard Owen, the *Dinosauria* man. Owen turned out to owe more to P. T. Barnum than Charles Darwin. Owen had aristocratic patrons and confidence to spare, in contrast to Mantell's constant doubts. Mantell was a painstaking scientist; Owen liked to grandstand. They argued over the design and structure of the reptile discoveries. Owen ridiculed Mantell's size estimates, claiming that reptiles could not be that big. However, given a chance, Owen took the lead in publicizing to the Royal Society the dinosaur fossils and ideas that Mantell had struggled to explain.

The two naturalists were then asked to help showcase their discoveries for London's 1850 Great Exhibition, the World Expo built around a glass and iron marvel called the Crystal Palace. Mantell

---

[25] One of the drawings of the Iguanodon bone has been created as a lithograph, offered by the Fine Art online library and Litz collection as a "Nasal Horn." https://fineartamerica.com/shop/prints/iguanodon+nasal+horn

began collaborating with artist Benjamin Waterhouse Hawkins on a series of large sculptures for the exhibit. But Mantell died before they were completed, and he ultimately did not supervise the work.

Owen took charge, and his vision of the ancient animals was as clumsy, lumbering creatures like elephants. This ponderous dinosaur version was the one that took hold and endured for decades. It was Owen's portrayal of the *Iguanodon* that the world saw, despite Mantell's work in making the discoveries in the first place.

Perhaps the worst example of Owen's grandstanding came as the large structures were being assembled for display. Owen invited a group of wealthy donors to dinner and arranged the meal to be held inside the partially completed *Iguanodon* sculpture. The newspaper report and accompanying drawings were both intriguing and bizarre. The publicity did lead to an increasing public fascination with "Owen's" dinosaurs.

Fig 36. The "dinner in a dinosaur," as portrayed in the Illustrated London News in 1854. Mantell's name is hidden on the side (right).

However, the humiliation for Gideon Mantell was not yet over. While his discovery of teeth and spikes had earned the name *Iguanodon* prominence, his given name of *Iguanodon anglicus* was not to last. After decades of debate and review, the original parts discovered by Mantell were termed a *nomen dubium*, meaning that he had not found enough of a definitive skeleton to be considered a holotype, a unique species. Mantell's bones were recategorized under the species of *Iguanodon bernissartensis*, the name bestowed on the bones discovered in the quarries of Belgium. The *Iguanodon* legacy would not even be British!

The original *Iguanodon* tooth was bequeathed to Gideon's son, Walter, and Walter moved as far away from home as possible. The tooth that started it all, the one that created the interest in *Iguanodon* and sparked the British hunt for *Dinosauria*, now belongs to the Te Papa Tongarew museum in Wellington, New Zealand.

It's not even on display.

J is for Jurassic

Scientists are actually preoccupied with accomplishment…
focused on whether they can do something. They never
stop to ask if they should do something.

Ian Malcolm, *Jurassic Park*

Chances are that you have seen *Jurassic Park* or one of its sequels,
especially if you are rifling through a random book about dinosaurs.
Chances are that you found some part of it exciting. You might also
have found parts that were hard to believe. That's okay. The Jurassic
Park franchise is not entirely accurate. At first, I thought it was too
pandering, too dumbed-down to create realistic dinosaurs. But I was
wrong—at least about the relative realism of the dinosaurs.

No, they weren't exactly Jurassic. Some of the dinosaurs did not
act like their namesakes. In particular, the *Velociraptor* and
Dilophosaurus in the first movie were not right, if you know something
about velociraptors and dilophosaurs. But Spielberg got a lot of
things right. Plus, he made dinosaurs really popular, which probably
led to more people studying dinosaurs and more funding for dinosaur
studies. Well played, Mr. Spielberg. Well played.

Not Especially Jurassic

Jurassic is the term for the middle geological time period of the
dinosaur era. The Triassic began after one of the Big Five extinctions
("E") at the end of the Permian. Another wave of extinctions

happened after the Triassic, which led to the Jurassic and the Cretaceous. (See Appendix Two for a list of geological time divisions). This overall division of geological time includes periods, eras, epochs and other categories, chiefly to provide names for future geologists and paleontologists to memorize. Also, it's shorter to write *Jurassic* than it is to write *200 to 145 million years ago*.

The entire era of the dinosaurs is called the Mesozoic (*meso*=middle), sandwiched as it is between Paleozoic (*paleo*=old) and Cenozoic (*ceno*=new). It's an organized system, though those names are pretty boring. *Zoic* refers to the animal fossils, meaning these are eras which had animal forms in them. The era prior to the Cambrian Age of the Fishes is called the Pre-Cambrian era, which is no fun at all. But at least those names make sense.

On the other hand, the three divisions of the Mesozoic have more idiosyncratic names, kind of like unmatched socks. Many of the Jurassic fossils were found in the Jura region, a span between France and Switzerland. The name was suggested by a French naturalist, though the Latin name *Jura* comes from a Celtic word. At any rate, a French guy got the nod. Not to be outdone, the Germans suggested that the middle period should be called Trias after the three different divisions. Kind of like the basic rule of magic: if you say a thing three times, then it becomes real.

Naturally, then Cretaceous could not be named after a region or a number. Instead, Cretaceous refers to "chalk" (*creta*=chalk). Many fossils found in this geological strata were discovered in the chalk layer—picture the White Cliffs of Dover. Overall, these names suggest that European naturalists didn't have as systematic a way of coming up with names for the periods as they did for the eras Paleo-, Meso-, and Cenozoic.

I hate to break it to movie lovers, but there were no tyrannosaurs, no triceratops, and no velociraptors during the Jurassic period. The vast majority of the dinosaurs in Michael Crichton's book, and Steven Spielberg's movies, emerged during the Cretaceous period. There is a simple explanation for this mismatch. *Cretaceous Park* simply doesn't have the same ring to it. At some point, author Crichton was sitting in his office, flipping pencils at the ceiling, and staring out the window—y'know, writing—and he just started mumbling "Triassic park" … "Mesozoic park" … "Cretaceous park" …. "Jurassic Park—that's it!!!!"

The Message

Jurassic Park was not a documentary, not a scientific study, and not historical fiction. It was a fictional story, one which both author Crichton and director Spielberg wanted to wrap in a morality tale with a message about scientific meddling. The dinosaurs were a little bit of window dressing. Interesting, expensive, super-cool CGI window dressing, but window dressing, nonetheless. They could have been crocodiles or mastodons. I'm glad they weren't. (*Ice Age* was also a movie series, but not as scary.)

The underlying movie plot involves regenerating dinosaurs using speculative science that mixed and matched DNA. At least, it was speculative in 1996. Now? Not so much. A small part of the story's purpose was to show the general public how the dinosaurs lived. The main purpose was to send a warning message about playing with scientific ideas. Well, that and making a zillion dollars. In either case, *Jurassic Park* has more in common with *Frankenstein* than with Jacques Cousteau.

In the story, for the three of you who need reminding, a bio-engineer invents techniques that allows dinosaurs to be revived so that he can put them in a theme park. He uses some ancient DNA from their blood, somehow still preserved in 200-million-year-old mosquitoes—which is the least of the scientific problems with the story, trust me. The scientists who restore these dinosaurs then play around with the genes in order to prevent the animals from reproducing or displaying unwanted behaviors. It doesn't go so well. The real message is not that dinosaurs are dangerous or even scary, but that we have no business attempting to play with dinosaur DNA.

The history of animal adaptation, if the movie guys only knew their Darwin, isn't survival of the fittest but that life escapes all barriers. Life breaks free, as Crichton says. Life expands and adapts to new situations. Painfully, perhaps even dangerously. But life finds a way.

What Was Wrong with the Movie Dinosaurs?

Still, to satisfy the purists out there, I'll point out a few of the pluses and minuses in the movie's Jurassic dinosaurs. Spielberg should get credit for hiring a number of well-respected dinosaur consultants to guide his movie critters' design. For many people, seeing dinosaurs run with their tails for balance, the way that paleontologists had been describing for years, was exhilarating. Paleontologists of the time said that *Jurassic Park* was the first movie with dinosaurs in them that looked like what dinosaurs ought to look like. We can give the art direction credit for trying to get that part of the science right.

What was wrong? For one thing, dinosaurs don't roar. They don't have the vocal chords for it. Please delete all the roaring *T. rexes*. They did hoot, snort, and cry, but no roaring. *T. rex* also didn't have bad eyesight. He did have a spectacular sense of smell, though, which Jurassic rex has. And he had the jaw power to crunch a car, as he does in the film. But he could not run as fast as a car. He usually didn't have to.

Fig 37. The less impressive but more accurate *Velociraptor*, duck-sized and feathered.

The second big problem was with the velociraptors. Or small problem, maybe. Velociraptors were not human-sized, intelligent beings that hunted in packs like wolves. Instead, they looked a lot more like ducks. They were small, with long tails. It's quite possible they had feathers and plumage. But as feral as they might have been or as sharp their teeth, they probably wouldn't have been that terrifying. Unless there were fifty of them or something. Personally, I find some waterfowl—like geese—quite scary, but then I'll squeak when opening a canister of pop-n-fresh biscuits, so maybe I'm not the measurement standard.

Spielberg apparently knew very well that his velociraptors were inaccurate. The movie dinosaurs look more like *Deinonychus*, a carnivore with a raised claw, which was believed to live in groups. Spielberg wanted them to look like *Deinonychus* but thought Crichton's decision to name them *Velociraptor* sounded better. The misnomer stuck.

The last significant error in the original movie was with *Dilophosaurus*. That was the little dinosaur who meets the bespectacled, chubby fellow that was smuggling DNA off the island. A bunch of little dilophosaurs come out of nowhere, flip out these weird-looking frills, and spit paralyzing venom on the smuggler dude. Then, they eat him. That's a hard Nope. *Dilophosaurus* didn't have the crests or the venom.

Fig 38. The *Dilophosaurus* in the film had a frill, spit venom, and was quite small. Actual dilophosaurs were bony-crested and bigger than humans. Scary enough, even if you're Mrs. Peel.

The real *Dilophosaurus* had a bony head crest and was bigger than a human. Plus, it was a meat-eater. By no means did they look harmless. Still, even inaccurate, the movie ones looked awesome, didn't they? When one spits on the Bad Smuggler Dude, everybody cheers. Just like when the *T. rex* chomps the lawyer, everybody cheers. Maybe in this case poetic justice was more important than scientific accuracy.

The most recent movie sequel before this book was published was *Jurassic World Dominion*, which was long, meandering, and dopey. It was a strong argument for ending the franchise. Still, *J.W.D.* seemed to get the hadrosaurs correct, and I do like a good *Parasaurolophus* (see "P").

One of my all-time favorite scenes is when a massive sauropod—*Apatosaurus*, me-thinks—wanders into a logging mill. All the workers in the mill just get out of the way because even an herbivore is in charge when it's 30 meters long. As it should be.

K is for the K-Pg Boundary

You know about the asteroid. Big BOOM. You can't really look at a generic picture of dinosaurs on the internet without seeing them fleeing from hellfire and brimstone. But the story of the discovery of the asteroid involves two parts. The second part is what happened after the BOOM. I'll tell that story toward the end of the alphabet. You'll have to guess what letter.

But the first part of the scientific discovery is: how did they know? How could scientists tell that there was a giant asteroid that fell on Earth at the end of the Cretaceous? Maybe they could figure out from the fossil record that the dinosaurs disappeared. But how did they know it was influenced by an extraterrestrial event? Particularly when the impact crater was nowhere to be found.

They didn't know at first. And they're still not a hundred percent sure now. But they've only been debating the asteroid theory for forty years. Compared with 200 million years, that's not a long time.

Constipation, Eternal Damnation, and T. S. Eliot

Before 1980, paleontologists did know that dinosaurs disappeared—roughly around 65 million years ago, in fact. The end of the Cretaceous period was set at 65 my ago, and not 100 or 150, precisely because it was the time when dinosaur fossils disappeared. It was somewhat handy that it happened during a chalky geological period since that made the line easy to spot on the sides of cliffs.

But how? I happened to have taken Paleo in 1980, before the asteroid stuff gained media attention, so I remember the debate. For decades before 1980, scientists were perfectly well aware that dinosaurs, along with most marine life and a lot of plant life, died off in the Cretaceous (about 76%, according to the table in Figure 21).

In 1979, what were the causes given for the end? Tectonic changes were a likely culprit, since they had created large-scale climate change in other eras. Given that varieties of mammals expanded broadly in the age that followed the dinosaurs, many thought mammals out-competed the reptiles for food sources. The adoption of the progressive view of natural selection, survival of the fittest, suggested that mammals, i.e., the group that humans belonged to, were thought to have "won."

There were also a myriad of ways to explain how dinosaurs became weak. Theories included senility—I'm not making this up—parasites, viruses, and constipation. It's true! Professor E. Baldwin argued in 1964 that there was a mass die-off of a species of ferns near the end of the Cretaceous. These ferns contained a natural oil that acted as a laxative. When the plant-eaters lost their Metamucil, well… and then the meat-eaters went, without the plant-eaters as prey. The problem with this hypothesis is less its bizarre nature, which may or not have been intended for humor, but the lack of completeness. After all, what caused the ferns to die?

The difficulty of any hypothesis for extinction is that it has to account for what happened. It has to explain the dinosaurs, marine life, and plants, but not all life on Earth. For instance, Bible thumpers back in the day suggested that it was sin and immorality that caused the dinosaurs to disappear, and modern creationists echo some of the same ideas.

> Eventually, about 4,300 years ago, God judged man's wickedness with a worldwide Flood… Dinosaurs disappear above the K-T boundary…because the Flood and its aftermath dumped additional sediment on top of those dinosaur-bearing layers …[26]

---

[26] "How Did Dinosaurs Die?" *Answers in Genesis*, 2024. https://answersingenesis.org/dinosaurs/extinction/dinosaur-extinction/how-did-dinosaurs-die/. Accessed November 27, 2024.

Even contemporary creationists say that the dinosaurs were among the original beasts in the Garden of Eden but were too big to include on Noah's ark. Again, though, why the plants? Were the plants sinful?

If someone is going to argue climate change, then (a) there has to be a cause for the change; and (b) the change has to extinguish some types of life and not others. What's always been hard has been for the cause to cover the consequences in the right way. What kind of thing could kill off 76% but not 100% of life? The extinctions at the end of the Permian and Triassic had a broader impact than at the Cretaceous. None of these explanations seemed completely satisfactory, even as late as 1980. But the paleontologist population really balked at the asteroid suggestion. Why is it that an asteroid created so much more controversy?

This happened, in part, because once the word "extraterrestrial" was put into the scientific community, and by a legitimate, award-winning scientist, all hell broke loose. And not just in the Cretaceous.

The Boundary and the Bombshell

It is an unusual story. Science usually does not advance because a smart guy looks at his kid's science project and says, "That must have been extraterrestrial." Or, if he does, no one takes him seriously. Not even if he's a Nobel Prize-winning astrophysicist and his son is a geologist.

Luis Alvarez won the 1968 Nobel Prize in Physics for building a hydrogen bubble chamber that discovered resonance states. I don't know exactly what that means in physics, but it certainly means he understood testing and the scientific method. He has a tiny part in the movie *Oppenheimer* because he was at Berkeley when they were building the you-know-what.

Alvarez's son, Walter, was a geologist studying magnetism in ancient rocks in Italy. He was interested in dating geomagnetic reversals, which is what happens when the magnetic positions of the north and south pole change. We'll have to save that for the future volume, *The A to Z of Physics*. The point is, Walter A. wasn't looking for asteroids or reasons for dinosaur extinctions. Instead, he was focused on the Cretaceous-Tertiary, or K-T boundary.

Fig 39. (Left) Luis Alvarez in 1969 with his fancy science machine; (Right) Luis and son Walter in 1983 pointing out the chalk-colored K-Pg boundary in Gubbio, Italy.

By the way, why was it called K-T then and is now K-Pg? Don't scientists know their alphabet? Remember that scientists have all sorts of funky ways of naming things ("J"). Sometimes, it's systematic—Paleozoic, Mesozoic, etc.—but sometimes it's based on where a guy was standing. For a long time, the boundary between the two eras was called Cretaceous-Tertiary, or K-T. The Germans used a "K," so scientists thought they would sound smarter if they talked like German scientists.

Meanwhile, an Italian guy back in 1759 decided to divide all of time—every bit of it—into three periods. Didn't lack for confidence, that's for sure. Remember the wizard's rule of three from the Jurassic chapter? Giovanni Arduino divided all of time—back to the very beginning, which in 1759 meant "let there be light" and all that—into three sections. He helpfully called them One, Two, and Three, or Primary, Secondary, and Tertiary. Quickly, other scientists realized that One and Two weren't very descriptive, but for a long time, they didn't know that Tertiary means "three," so they kept using it. Tertiary and Quaternary are the periods that make up the Cenozoic

Era, our own era. Humans emerged in the Quaternary. Yes, that meant a fourth section. Arduino had a comprehensive system but couldn't count as high as four.

Besides, now that we have computers and are better at math, scientists have re-decided that Tertiary isn't descriptive or German enough, so they've reverted to calling the "third period" the Paleogene. Therefore, the boundary isn't the C-T or the K-T, but now it's the K-Pg. Why isn't it the K-P? Don't ask.

Anyway, Professor Alvarez was looking at the composition of the layers across the time periods, specifically examining the stratigraphy—i.e., layers—for his north–south pole switching scheme. He happened to notice that this boundary had a lot of an element called iridium in it. *Dad? You're an astrophysicist…do you know anything about where iridium comes from?*

Why, yes, son. Iridium is extremely rare on Earth. But guess where it's not rare?

Yep, outer space. To be clear, then: The Alvarezes were not sitting around eating their mashed potatoes and suddenly decided BOOM went the dinosaurs. Walter just noticed something weird in the rocks. And his dad knew something about rare earth elements. Yet a lot of science moves forward because someone notices something weird and someone else has a bright idea from another field.

The Alvarezes published their findings in *Science* magazine in early 1980. This was a legitimate research article using footnotes and everything: "Impact Theory of Mass Extinctions and the Invertebrate Fossil Record."[27] The core of the argument was simply that there was a statistically significant amount of iridium at the K-Pg boundary time period and NOT elsewhere. The implication led to the suggestion that something very big came from space and hit the earth, which might have affected the creatures of the Cretaceous.

---

[27] Luis Alvarez and Walter Alvarez, "Extraterrestrial Cause for the Cretaceous-Tertiary Extinction," *Science* 208, no. 4448 (1980): 1095–1108. http://www.jstor.org/stable/1683699.

Or Could Be Volcanoes

Gerta Keller wasn't satisfied. Keller is a geologist and paleontologist from Princeton whose research has long focused on the geology of mass extinction events. In other words, she was in expert in the subject, probably more so than either of the Alvarezes. She had done groundbreaking work focusing on the Eocene-Oligocene extinction event that led to the Ice Age at the dawn of early humans. She knew the Ice Age event was influenced by volcanic and tectonic changes from the Indian subcontinent, whose plates were still moving toward Asia 30 million years ago. Keller gained significant knowledge in the region and its western coastline of volcanic land. The volcanic strip along western India is called the "Deccan Traps." Keller became convinced that they also played a role in the demise of the Cretaceous.[28]

It's worth noting that Keller was not the only scientist in the early 1980s dissatisfied with the asteroid theory. Many felt that an extraterrestrial event was not only melodramatic but over-rated, and it didn't explain the data. For example, three paleontologists published a 1981 article, "Out with a Bang," arguing that the die-off of certain species at the end of the Cretaceous was way too gradual to have been caused by a huge, single impact. They ended their paper, a la T. S. Eliot:[29]

> *This is the way the Cretaceous ended*
> *Not abruptly but extended.*

Keller herself had noticed an early die-off in some of the better-known flora and fauna ("biotic" material), prior to 65 my—that is, a few hundred thousand years before the end of the Cretaceous. She

---

[28] Gerta Keller, Paula Mateo, Johannes Monkenbusch, Nicolas Thibault, Jahnavi Punekar, Jorge E. Spangenberg, Sigal Abramovich, Sarit Ashckenazi-Polivoda, Blair Schoene, Michael P. Eddy, Kyle M. Samperton, Syed F.R. Khadri, Thierry Adatte, "Mercury Linked to Deccan Traps Volcanism, Climate Change and the End-Cretaceous Mass Extinction, *Global and Planetary Change*, Volume 194, (2020): 2-17. https://doi.org/10.1016/j.gloplacha.2020.103312.

[29] W. A. Clemens, J. David Archibald, and Leo J. Hickey. "Out with a Whimper Not a Bang," *Paleobiology* 7, no. 3 (1981): 298. http://www.jstor.org/stable/2400675.

thought the Deccan Traps, whose lava ducts were emptying during that period, were either the initial cause or a major contributor. Of course, long is relative; initially, it was thought that the Deccan eruptions lasted for several million years. That broad spread would not account for some of the precision around the K-PG boundary, so Keller's idea was not originally accepted.

Decades of data collection suggests now that the Deccan Trap eruptions started around 66.25 my ago and lasted for less than a million years. That time period would span the K-PG boundary, coming right before, lasting through, and continuing for a short time after the end of the Cretaceous. Don't forget that the end of the Cretaceous itself is somewhat approximate and coincides with whatever the heck killed off everything. It could have been volcanoes in India, pumping out lava for 800,000 years. That certainly would have impacted the climate.

Keller's work repeatedly concentrated on the timeline to show that the Deccan volcanic traps occurred first. Her results strongly suggest that, at a minimum, volcanoes were spewing out toxic material for a long time before any old asteroid started its countdown toward Armageddon. The fossil record now has plenty of evidence to show that there was the beginning of a die-off *before* the end of the Cretaceous. There wasn't a specific day that the dinosaurs died, no matter how loudly the kettle drums beat in YouTube videos of flaming objects from outer space.

Still, Keller's Deccan Traps argument was a harder sell, at least to the amateur scientists of the world. Volcanoes *had* been identified as causing other extinctions. But, somehow, massive erupting volcanoes across a chunk of the Indian subcontinent didn't seem to have the same ring to it for national media as an asteroid. It took until the 2020s for that same media to start switching to new headlines, from "An Asteroid Killed the Dinosaurs" to "What Really Happened to End the Cretaceous."[30]

---

[30] Now, even AI has to get into the act. Matt Simon, "An Epic Fight Over What Really Killed the Dinosaurs?" *Wired,* September 20, 2023. "
https://www.wired.com/story/what-killed-the-dinosaurs/

Fig 40. A little less research-oriented, a little more shock value. Artist's rendering for "What Really Killed the Dinosaurs?"

One Big Thing Missing

Scientific information advances through public debate. Whether you're Walter Alvarez or Gerta Keller or Gideon Mantell or Charles Darwin, the way you prove a theory is to put it out there and get feedback. Other scientists poke holes, and you respond and/or gather more data. Alvarez's original article proposed a theory about the asteroid as a likely explanation, although it left open the possibility that there could be other explanations. That's how the scientific method works. Alvarez found something odd—lots of iridium at one time period—and collected enough information to create a hypothesis.

The earliest response to the Alvarez theory was a little unique. Before it was scientifically validated, it got some media airplay. Because Luis Alvarez was not a geologist but an astrophysicist, some scientists ridiculed the theory from the get-go. Basically, *Mind your own business. Stick to astrophysics. Nobel Schmobel, you don't know anything about paleontology, butt out.* Some scientists, like those in the 1981 "Not With a Bang Paper," were more polite about it, but still *blunt. Your theory doesn't cover all the data and doesn't account for other facts.* Other feedback was more derisive, implying that lack of knowledge undercut the argument.

Aside from whether the asteroid theory would explain enough, it did have two big gaps. First, in early 1980, most of the data on iridium had been found in only a few places: Gubbio, Italy, and count-on-one-hand elsewhere. There wasn't enough data to support the argument on behalf of a giant megaton asteroid wiping out all life on Earth. However, after several years of data collection, geologists around the world had collected enough data, and the iridium spike was noticeable and international.

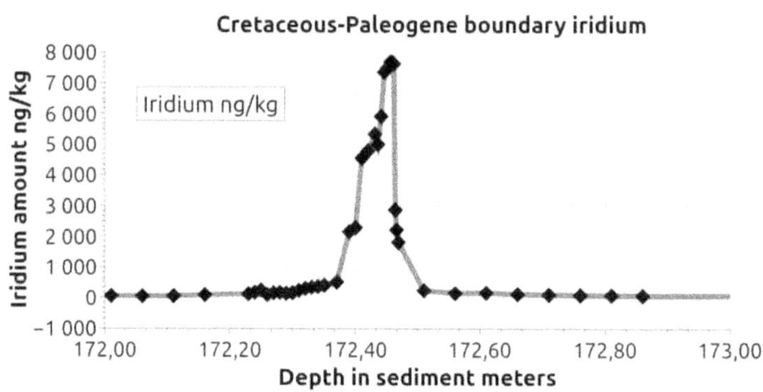

Fig 41. By the 1990s, data on the iridium spike clearly indicated something unusual happened right at the K-Pg boundary.

Still, the biggest problem of all was one that Luis himself mentioned at the end of his original paper:

> …we would like to find the crater produced by the impacting object[31].

---

[31] Alvarez and Alvarez, "Extraterrestrial," 1107.

A giant asteroid, big enough to throw iridium all around the world, would leave a darned big hole. No such hole at the end of the geological end of the Cretaceous had ever been found.

The antidote for not having enough data was easy: Go get more data. The antidote for the crater was to find it. The antidote for being told to butt out was a lot more problematic.

Chapter "Y" will finish the story.

L is for Living Relatives

Dinosaurs could see in color. The EPB-living relative theory says so.

EPB: those letters can tell us a lot about how dinosaurs lived. They represent difficult words—*extant phylogenetic bracket*. But don't worry. They'll be defined shortly, and you can use the idea of "living relatives" as a proxy. It's just that Extant Phylogenetic Bracket are like magic words for researchers because they allow scientists to look at fossils and make suggestions about extinct animal behavior.[32] Looking at 100-million-year-old fossils, a paleobiologist can be fairly certain about the animal's blood vessels, its muscles, and even its eyesight. Scientists do this by comparing extinct creatures to the closest Living Relative.

EPB: Big Words, Brilliant Idea

Let's break this acronym down.

Extant means living. It's the opposite of extinct. Instead of being related to something long gone, extant means something related to a living thing.

---

[32] The EPB model was first proposed by Lawrence Witmer in L. M. Witmer, "The Extant Phylogenetic Bracket and the Importance of Reconstructing Soft Tissues in Fossils," in Thomason, J.J. (ed). *Functional Morphology in Vertebrate Paleontology, 19-33.* (New York. Cambridge University Press, 1995).

Phylo=race or tribe while *genetic*=origin. *Genetics* relates to the smallest unit of life, DNA. So, phylogenetic means the origin of a tribe or group, a fancy way to refer to the family tree.

> *extant* (living) + *phylogenetic* (family tree) + *bracket* (group) =
> EPB

Extant phylogenetic bracket is a complicated but efficient term that means you can decipher unknown things about a creature on a branch of the biological tree by looking at similar things on the tree, things that are either on the same branch or on a very nearby branch. A simple example of the EPB might address giant swimming reptiles. Some of the earlier ancient reptile skeletons found in England had flippers. Knowing how whales, snakes, or lizards swim can tell paleontologists how giant reptiles, twenty times the size, might have patrolled the deep waters.

EPB helps with some debates but not others. For instance, they could measure the size of blood vessels running through fossil bones. This might tell a sauropod expert that the giant dinosaurs might have had hearts that weighed 600 pounds.[33] That could lead to a lively debate about whether they could hold their head up high. Surely, the blood pressure for a *Diplodocus* to raise and lower its head up would make their brain explode!

EPB to the rescue—a logical response is that a long-necked sauropod might have had special soft-tissue structures like a giraffe. Even though a giraffe, being a mammal, is not on the same part of the evolutionary tree as the reptiles, it is a living animal that can suggest aspects of circulatory design.

On the other hand, drawing conclusions about metabolism based on living relatives is harder to do. If we return to the cold- and warm-blooded debate mentioned earlier, scientists thought about using EPB to settle the argument. Could they infer something about metabolism and blood circulation in extinct dinosaurs from the extant descendants, i.e., from the living relatives? The structure of dinosaur blood vessel openings in the bone suggests that dinosaurs had a four-chambered heart. As it happens, both mammals and birds have four-chambered hearts, so using EPB could lead you to conclude that

---

[33] Nature on PBS, "The 500-Pound Dinosaur Heart." February 12, 2016, YouTube, 1:22. https://www.youtube.com/watch?v=8YBDqFWRbPI

dinosaurs are warm-blooded like mammals and birds. Crocodiles, however, also have four-chambered hearts, even though many reptiles don't. Therefore, the heart construction alone can't tell you whether the dinosaurs were warm or cold-blooded, since two different kinds of living relatives—birds and crocodiles—had different metabolic systems. EPB, in this case, does not resolve the unknown.

Chubby Cheeks

A clever use of the EPB was applied to something very different: the cheeks of *Triceratops.* Those who specialize in how the herbivores ate have long argued over how they chewed. Seriously! A 100-year-old debate! Paleontologists knew, certainly, that the jaw muscles of a *Triceratops* were huge because they could see the multiple holes in their head. Those holes, the temporal and antorbital fenestrae (Figures 4 and 5) might simply make a massive *Triceratops* head lighter, but they also were where muscles would be attached. *Triceratops,* then, must have had many strong jaw muscles.

Teeth can also be very revealing about an animal's overall behavior. *Triceratops* teeth were made for plant-eating. Pointy teeth are for ripping meat, whereas flat or bumpy-edged teeth were for pulling off and grinding up foliage. Extinct animals might also have multiple kinds of teeth, just as humans do. Paleontologists even knew that some dinosaurs didn't chew the leaves because their teeth couldn't grind. The three-story-building *Brachiosaurus* just pulled and swallowed, probably letting multiple stomachs do the rest of the work.

So teeth can tell you *what* an animal might eat, but not *how* they ate it. Flat teeth means the leaves were ground up, but were they ground side to side or up and down? *Triceratops,* as it turns out, had five different layers in their teeth, one of the most sophisticated dental structures ever found. Plus, huge heads made chewing a complicated endeavor.

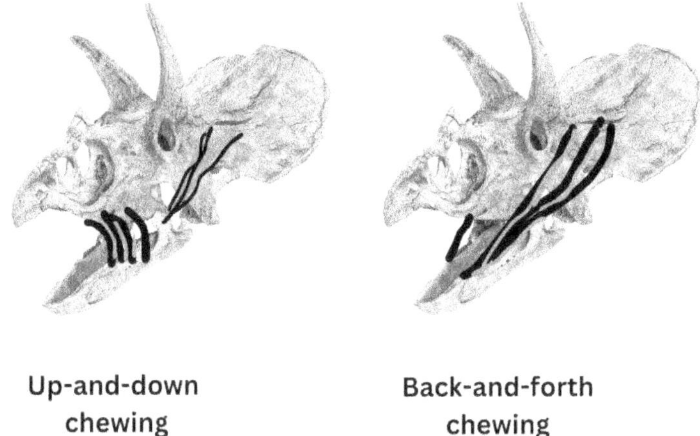

Fig 42. Researcher Ali Nabavizadeh argues convincingly that *Triceratops* chewed back and forth, with jaw muscles attached horizontally, rather than up and down. (Graphic created by author after Nabavizadeh.)

The first paleontologists to study *Triceratops* believed that it chewed up and down, which suggested it had vertical cheek muscles (Figure 42, left). Cheeks play several roles. First, cheeks keep food from falling out, regardless of whether their muscles are vertical or horizontal. Second, cheek muscles dictate the direction of chewing. Most mammals, whether humans, mice, or cows, chew up and down. The up-and-down chewing of mammals was used as the living relative comparison, just as giraffes were used for sauropods.

But in this case, mammals weren't necessarily the closest living relative. Ali Nabavizadeh noted that looking at reptilian cousins would be a more useful comparison, since reptiles are direct ancestors of dinosaurs.[34] He found reptilian relatives whose cheek muscles extend from the back to the front, horizontally (Figure 42, right). In this way, *Triceratops* would chew back and forth, grinding food like a wood planer rather than like a hammer.

---

[34] Ali Nabavizadeh, "Did Plant-Eating Dinosaurs Have Cheeks?" *Science Connected Magazine*, February 14, 2019. https://magazine.scienceconnected.org/2019/02/did-plant-eating-dinosaurs-have-cheeks/

Color Vision

Applying the living relative model to vision demonstrates both the limits and the advantages of the model. The forward-focusing eyes of eagles suggested to paleontologists that carnivorous dinosaurs had great depth perception, since theropod eyes were situated in a similar place on their skulls. Scientists went a step further and wondered whether they could see in color.

Many animals on the animal family tree have color vision. Both birds and crocodiles, for instance, see in color. That leads to a pretty strong conclusion that dinosaurs could see in color. However, crocodiles can't distinguish ultraviolet color (UV), while birds can. Because of that difference, we don't know whether UV was a trait that dinosaurs developed or one that birds developed later in their evolutionary journey. You can't simply look at one descendant of a dinosaur, pick a trait, and decide all the dinosaurs had that trait. You have to look at multiple animals and pick a trait that came from a common ancestor.

On the other hand, scientists did isolate a gene (CYP2J19) that lets animals see a range of colors in red. They knew that birds had the gene, then found the same gene in turtles. Ah-ha! They concluded that this gene very likely existed before turtles and birds split very early on the evolutionary tree. Therefore, they think dinosaurs had the gene.

Fig 43. The brightly-colored *Velociraptor* hops toward its mate, waggling its red tail feathers—oh, bother! This is in black and white. You will have to imagine the red in order to see it as a dinosaur would.

What this "red gene" allows birds and turtles to do is distinguish among many variations of red. If they can see variations of red, then they can display variations of red. As one researcher put it, the CYP2J19 gene's purpose was to help the female birds and turtles pick the brightest red males[35]. That means that instead of reptiles all having green skin for camouflage, dinosaurs probably displayed tremendous variation in color. Add feathers, and your average *Velociraptor* could easily be imagined doing that little dance of allure that birds do, when it's springtime in the Cretaceous and the angiosperms start to bloom…

---

[35] Hanlu Twyman, Nicole Valenzuela, Robert Literman, Staffan Andersson, and Nicholas I. Mundy, "Seeing Red to Being Red: Conserved Genetic Mechanism for Red Cone Oil Droplets and Co-option for Red Coloration in Birds and Turtles," *Proceedings of the Royal Society of Britain*, 283,20161208.
https://royalsocietypublishing.org/doi/full/10.1098/rspb.2016.1208

M is for Mary Anning

She sells seashells by the seashore,
The shells she sells are seashells, I'm sure.
So if she sells seashells on the seashore,
Then I'm sure she sells seashore shells.

Mary did sell seashells. And fossils. She was well-known for doing so, although she was not credited at the time by the Royal Society, full of naturalists who took her collected evidence and used it to improve their own intellectual standing. Many say the poem is about her, though at least one expert on folklore argues that it was not.

She did, indeed, sell seashells—if we must be purists, they were the bones of sea creatures found in the rock. Sea bones found in the cliffs. Sea bones painstakingly removed and cleaned, drawn by a woman with no artistic training, theorized about by a woman with no formal education. Mary Anning found sea bones and drew plesiosaurs by the Lyme Regis seashore.

She also practically invented paleontology.

Mary, Mary

No, that's another rhyme…. although in the other nursery rhyme Mary's garden grows with cockle shells, so maybe… And truthfully, Mary Anning did not invent paleontology. However, paleontology didn't exist as a scientific discipline until she collected hundreds of fossils and started drawing, mounting, and discussing them with a parade of naturalists who trailed out to Lyme Regis to examine her findings. And after that, it did.[36]

Fig 44. An 1847 portrait of Mary Anning, not credited to the painter, but given to the Anning family. Mary is pointing to an ammonite shell next to her beloved dog, Tray.

The coastal area of southwest England, where Mary Anning resided, is full of tall chalk-based cliffs. A smart fossil hunter might be able to extract samples—carefully—from multiple geological time

---

[36] The word "paleontology" was coined in 1820 by French naturalist Henri Marie Ducrotay de Blainville after he had looked at fossil fish, the ichthyosaurs. Which Mary Anning had discovered.

periods, multiple layers up the hill. Close to the Atlantic, the tide of Lyme Regis brings in plenty of sea life in from the deep. There were always lots of fossils to sell. If the collector also made copious notes about what was found, she could help support the idea of time periods and provide evidence that not all types of animals lived at the same time. Or, the more radical idea in 1823 that some animals might have lived long ago but were no longer around.

There were ten Anning children, born in this poor family. Only Mary and her old brother Joseph survived to become teenagers. Their father was a cabinetmaker, although he also liked fossils. He showed the children how to find bones in the mud and to extract them without breaking. But he was not himself careful enough. He died falling off one of the cliffs, leaving his family to fend for itself. Mary and her brother Joseph were good enough collectors to find fossils to sell in their tiny shell shop. Occasionally, a windfall might let them buy a few sticks of furniture. When the pickings got slim again, away would go the table and chairs to cover rent and enough food to prevent starvation.

The Monster

Mary Anning was best known locally for finding fossils called ammonites, spiral-shelled creatures common during the Age of Fishes before the Permian extinction. She had been taught to dig them out without cracking the shells, to brush away the dried mud, and to clean the fossil carefully to leave it whole. She knew that you could find shells in the cliff at different levels, although naturally you should not dig out the cliff from the bottom, which would create landslides.

One day, shortly after her father passed away, her older brother found the tip of a large snout. Mary took over excavating the 15-foot-long beast. Was it a kind of crocodile? A small whale? A giant fish? She knew it wasn't something modern. She mounted it with painstaking care, as a naturalist might.

The monster skeleton sold for 23 pounds—six months' worth of food—then was quickly resold by someone else to the British Museum for 45 pounds. By the time the museum put it on display, they had named it fish (*ichthy*) lizard: *Ichthyosaurus*.

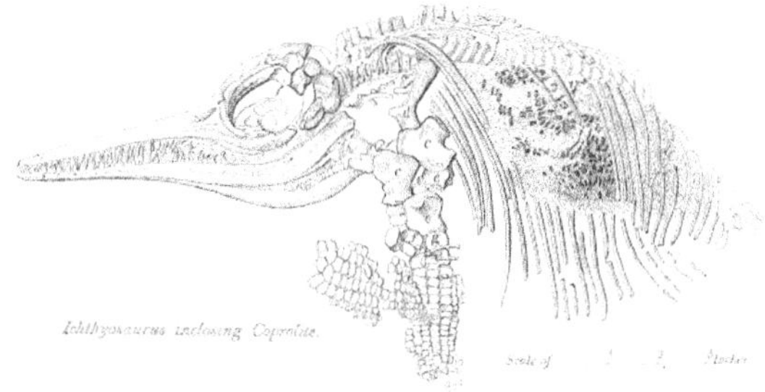

Fig 45. Drawing of Anning's *Ichthyosaurus*, used by naturalist William Buckland's for his 1836 book on geology.

The *Ichthyosaurus* was neither dinosaur nor crocodile. It wasn't even a land creature, so technically not a lizard. It could be identified as an air-breather, so it was not a fish. It was the unimaginable—a giant marine reptile that had patrolled the waters. Based on where the Annings found it in the cliffs, *Ichthyosaurus* (so hard to type!) must have been thousands of years old. That means there was a time when giant marine reptiles had ruled the sea.

People Came from All Around

The *Ichthyosaurus's* size and completeness caused quite a stir in London. All the usual suspects from Chapter "I"—Gideon Mantell, William Buckland, Richard Owen—weighed in on the finding. Georges Cuvier, of rhinoceros fame, called it a hoax and insisted that she was lying or mistaken about where she claimed to have discovered the bones. All the well-known naturalists, including Charles Darwin, beat a path out to Lyme Regis to talk to Anning. A lot of their eventual "research" emerged from those discussions. For decades, the men presented findings without mentioning Mary Anning, their source of information.

The discovery of the giant reptile did push forward one prominent idea: extinction. Many Anglo-European scientists believed that the world was as it had been described in the Bible, with contemporary animals being the only species invented by Adam and saved by Noah. The idea of a giant animal that had swum through the deep waters was interesting, but the stuff of dragons and mermaids. Finding the bones suggested that things might not always have been as they were in 1821. Hence, the interest from Charles Darwin.

Anning, meanwhile, found another giant set of bones in the rocks. This time the head was smaller and the body bigger. People had found similar bits and pieces before, but Anning's skeleton was nearly complete. The *Plesiosaurus*, or "near lizard," as it was dubbed (*ples*=near), was similar to its cousin the *Ichthyosaurus*—a giant, prehistoric marine reptile.

Anning cleaned it up and sold it to buy food for a few months. Lather, rinse, repeat. By 1823, then, she had gained at least enough of a reputation that Cuvier had stopped saying hoax. Those who repeatedly came to visit saw the poverty of the rooms. Some tried to help. A well-known geologist painted a scene (Figure 46) that included many of the animals that Anning had found and gave her the proceeds when the picture sold.

Fig 46. Mary Anning's friend, Henry da Beche, painted *Duria Antiquor* as a representation of a prehistoric scene with animals she had discovered. He gave the money from the painting's sale to her.

Anning and Buckland talked, many times, about the giant reptiles. Anning told the celebrated naturalist that she found additional fossil rocks inside the skeletons. These fossil rocks contained bits of smaller skeletons within them. Though not formally educated, she understood natural processes. She told Buckland that they must be fossilized feces—dinosaur poop—which was still inside the body when the animal died. She and Buckland together named them coprolites (dung stone), and an entire wing of fossil study was born ("F").

For most of her life, the male scientists came to visit and ply her with questions. Anning eventually complained about all the naturalists who would show up with some flimsy excuse, "suck her brain," then go off to present papers to the Royal Society. The ichthyosaurs and plesiosaurs displayed in museum had lost all trace of Anning's original work. Finally, when Buckland presented a paper on coprolites, he did at last mention Mary Anning's name, crediting her scientific help in the discovery, analysis, and hypothesis of coprolites.

At last in 1840, while Mary was still alive, a Swiss-American naturalist named two species of fish after her. A century later, in 2015, another species found in nearby Dorset was named *Ichthyosaurus anningae* in recognition of Mary Anning's contributions.

Ammonite, Seashells, and Mary's Rediscovery

While Anning was not credited by scientists and museums much during her lifetime, many since have been trying to redress the balance. She has been getting her due most recently, a rock star (couldn't resist, sorry) of the 21st-century history books. She seems to be particularly well-integrated into children's history books. You can access dozens of elementary school lessons online, for example, to have students write diary entries as if they were Mary finding a fossil on her daily walks. For some reason, much of the recognition is aimed at younger people. Multiple photos show museum docents dressed like Anning's portrait, presenting at the classic fourth grade field trip for children to the British Museum.

Many lessons and articles start just as this chapter did, by citing the poem which links her name to a nursery rhyme: the plucky girl who found the giant seashell. But some categorically deny that the poem is about her. For example, folklorist Stephen Winick delves deep into historical evidence and argues that the poem was not about her at all.[37] Winick traces the origin of the phrase "she sells seashells" to an 1858 handbook designed to improve pronunciation of English.

Winick notes that the examples include "he sells seashells," which could not be Mary. He also stresses that this phrase appeared much earlier than is usually credited. Winick further points out that the Annings lived in town, not by the seashore, and that, as everybody knows, they sold fossils and not seashells. The historical detective work here is sound and getting the facts straight is important.

Still, the evidence could suggest that the 1858 writer was aware of the Annings. After all, Joseph found shells as well; he did sell seashells. Moreover, whether the shop was literally on the shore or not, Lyme Regis is a seashore town and the fossils were found there. Plus, ammonite, the most common type of fossil which Mary found, looks an awful lot like a nautilus shell. Do we know for certain that the British writer of the 1858 book was not thinking of Mary Anning, the famous discoverer of sea bones, who had died only a decade earlier? Even if the words were not a direct tribute to Anning, might they not be about her? The struggle to define Anning's legacy, with so little to go on, continues.

A few years ago, the 2020 movie *Ammonite* told part of Anning's story, showing how she searched daily for fossils in the cliffs and mud, revealing the danger of the work and the poverty of her life. In the movie, Anning also has an intimate relationship with the wife of one of the aristocrats who repeatedly visited the shop to view the fossils. Anning's biographers griped that no such relationship ever occurred, and one of her relatives claimed to be upset at the thought. Every movie review takes great pains to point out that it was absolute fiction. Anning did not mention any such relationship in her notes, though they were scientific. Family members were not aware of it, nor were they aware of any other relationship she had. Still, no one mentioned it; therefore, it didn't exist. Would they have complained so hard if it had been a fictional relationship with one of the male scientists? And, what exactly was documented? What exactly is known?

Anning did not keep a daily diary, although she took scientific notes, drew pictures of her finds, and corresponded with many

---

[37] Stephen Winick, "She Sells Seashells and Mary Anning: Metafolklore with a Twist," *Folklife Today: American Folkslife and Veterans History Project* (blog), *Library of Congress,* July 26, 2017. https://blogs.loc.gov/folklife/2017/07/she-sells-seashells-and-mary-anning-metafolklore-with-a-twist/.

women and men about her scientific finds. She never mentioned any relationships. Her family was often near starvation, selling the furniture at times for food. Women in that day and age married for survival. It was highly unusual for a woman to live unmarried as Mary Anning did, even taking care of a parent.

She had so many valuable things around her, yet apparently none of the men who visited ever suggested an arrangement, romantic or otherwise since she did not marry. There is no documented relationship with a man. For a woman who needed money in that day and age not to marry was highly unusual.

There is another, newly developed way for historians do historical research called reading "against the grain," which is particularly useful for marginalized historical figures. Knowing that someone was already ignored, a historian reading against the grain might look at other pieces of evidence beyond what was written or preserved. Could historians reasonably infer that an unmarried woman might have relationships with women? It's a matter of supposition, but not unlike the Living Relative EPB theory.

If we can draw inferences about a dinosaur's color vision or metabolism based on only a skeleton, then when it comes to the gaps in a historical figure, we ought to be allowed to draw some inferences based on her unmarried status. However, Mary Anning's newfound recognition as a heroine for children may have created a new problem, a desire not to explore certain questions.

During Mary Anning's lifetime, men came to finger her seashells, ask her detailed questions, and learn all they could about fossils to present their "findings" to the Royal Society. She was not thanked properly then, nor was much written about her personal history. Now, as others rush in to compensate for that lack, they may wish to control how the gaps are filled in.

What we know about Mary Anning is simply far too little.

N is for North Pole

Yes, you read that correctly. Dinosaurs in the snow.

There were dinosaurs in the Arctic and in the Antarctic. Fossils have been found in the extreme north, across Siberia and in Alaska, and south, in Argentina and Antarctica. These new bones have upended the conventional notions of where dinosaurs might have thrived.

We should not be surprised. All those National Geographic and David Attenborough documentaries about life on Earth stress that life exists in the deepest oceans, the highest mountains, and the darkest and coldest places on land. The ruling reptiles were spread all across the continents when their rule ended 65 million years ago. Why wouldn't they also have adapted to the deepest, darkest, coldest?

Where in the World is the World?

A brief diversion into Mesozoic—a.k.a. the Age of the Reptiles—geology is helpful here. Once upon a time, there was a single mega-continent called Pangaea (Appendix One has maps of the land masses and their changes across the Mesozoic). When the dinosaurs first emerged during the Triassic, the band of continents was still singing a single tune. Roughly 210 my ago, the Arctic and Antarctic were not at the poles, where they are today, though they were at the farthest points north and south of Pangaea. The Antarctic was roughly at a latitude where South Africa is now: a chilly zone, but not frozen.

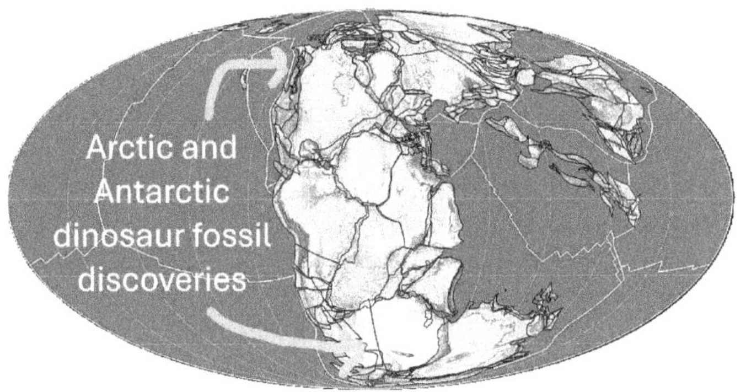

Fig 47. The super-continent, Pangaea, roughly 210 million years ago. Dinosaur fossils found in Alaska and Antarctica were from regions not, at the time, at the poles. See Appendix One for continental maps of the Dinosaur Age.

Multiple creatures once crawled, walked, and stalked the Antarctic. Fossils found in the Antarctic suggest that small proto-dinosaurs lived alongside small proto-mammals, even where it was a bit cooler. However, around 200-210 my ago, the continents began to change.

Under Pangaea, volcanoes called the Central Atlantic Magmatic Province (CAMP) went into action and started a big CAMP-y dance. Pangaea split up. North America said farewell to Africa, and the North Atlantic Ocean formed. All this movement led to the Triassic-Jurassic die-off ("E"), since massive volcanic eruptions aren't especially fun whether you have one, two, or three holes in your head.

Once the smoke cleared, what was bad for the early quadrupeds was much better for the saurischians and the ornithischians. Dinosaurs proliferated across all the continents even as the tectonic plates drifted apart. While much of the world after the band broke up was swampy, especially toward the equator, the northern and southern climates were more forest than swamp. Still, even those extremes at the time were quite warm because of the volcanic CAMP. Not to mention the water: the middle of North America looked much different from today. Kansas and Nebraska were under water. Eventually, the water receded and continental uplift occurred to create the Rockies.

There are key takeaways from this mini-paleogeology lesson. First, dinosaurs started one place, but those places drifted. It's not like dinosaurs had boats to leave. (Or did they? Is there where The Ark comes in?) Continental drift explains how places now far and away from each other, like Argentina and Mongolia, were once closer land masses.

Second, what is Arctic and impossible to live in *now* was relatively warmer *then*. There was land at the North Pole, and it was not a frozen mass. Dinosaurs could live among trees. Still, there was less light nearer the poles, because the earth was still round (technically ovate) and still tilted on its axis, meaning less sunlight reached the poles.

When modern scientists think about dinosaur survival conditions at the extremes, they still think about basic biology: food sources, predator-prey strategies, body adaptations, and reproduction. Some of these are things that a few bones might not convey.

The air temperature of these cool climates is estimated to be roughly 36-55 F in the north and 28-40 F in the south. Cool, and not swampy. How can they know? Leaves of plants have different shapes in cold versus hot weather. By looking at the fossils of leaves, they can determine the temperatures 150 million years ago. At those temperatures, paleontologists think it likely these dinosaurs could survive with either a thick skin or a covering, like feathers.

Frozen in Another Language is Still Darned Cold

Discoveries of these cool-climate creatures date back decades. Canadian expeditions have unearthed fossil dinosaurs since the early part of the 20th century. Several cold-weather species, such as *Edmontosaurus* and *Albertosaurus*, have been found in large fossil beds in the Canadian Rockies, courtesy of the same uplift that aided the fossil beds in Wyoming and Montana.

During the ill-fated 1912 Antarctic expedition of British explorer Robert Scott, Scott and his team collected dozens of specimens of fossils found in the snow on his journey to the South Pole. Unfortunately, his group made several fatal errors and died near the South Pole. Searchers later found bags and bags of rocks with fossil ferns in the tents. Scott had collected multiple examples of other forms of life, proof that plants at least had once existed in the frozen soil. Since then, paleontology expeditions—much better equipped— have traveled routinely to the Antarctic as well as to Northern Alaska to unearth dinosaur fossils to add to the ferns.

They've also come up with better names than "Place-osaurus." *Cryolophosaurus*, for instance, means *cryo* (frozen) + *lopho* (crested) + *saurus* (lizard), "frozen-crested lizard."

In the discoveries nearer the Arctic, like the Prince Creek region of Alaska, scientists have begun coordinating their finds and works with the local indigenous people. Names are taking on a new flavor. *Nanuqusaurus*, a type of tyrannosaur, was granted the name "polar bear lizard," since *nanuqu* is "polar bear" in the Inupiaq tongue. It sure sounds a lot more interesting than *princecreekasaurus*.

Fig 48: *Nanuqusaurus*, or polar-bear lizard, was found in Northern Alaska and partly named with Inupiaq words. Researchers believe dinosaurs sported feathers for warmth Note: this original graphic was light green and orange, not polar-bear white.

Antarctopedia ("frozen shield") was a squat, armored ankylosaur. *Issi saaneq*, found in Greenland, was given the indigenous name for "cold bone." There's also *Imperobator antarcticus* (powerful warrior from the Antarctic) as well as *Glacialasaurus*. That last one lacks a little imagination. Much more interesting is the name and story behind *Ugrunaaluk kuukpikensis*.

Ugrunaaluk kuukpikensis—which is a mouthful!—means "ancient grazer" to native Alaskans. It was a duck-billed hadrosaur, a type of plant-eating dinosaur that lived in herds. Hadrosaurs generally walked on all four limbs but could rear up and bolt quickly on two legs if a predator was spotted ("P"). Hadrosaurs are also known for having rows and rows of teeth, which they would need for chewing the tough vegetation that survives the cold.

The researcher who found *Ugrunaaluk*, Patrick Druckenmiller, thought they were very similar to *Edmontosaurus*, one of the early Canadian fossils found a century earlier. Druckenmiller lobbied to have *Ugrunaaluk* recognized as a unique species with its own unique name. The final scientific decision has not yet been confirmed. Depending on whether the information is in Polish, Spanish, or English, *Ugrunaaluk* is either recognized on its own or still lumped in with the edmontosaurs.

Druckenmiller and others argue that *Ugrunaaluk* should be unique, but others think his evidence reflected a juvenile version of another existing species.[38] Some of the scientists who have entered the fray are in Japan because there are similar hadrosaur fossils in Japan. That's a long way to run away from predators! More proof that even in the Cretaceous, some land that is separated today was once attached. I don't know how this scientific donnybrook will be resolved, but my vote is that *Ugrunaaluk* ought to win the naming contest.

Fig 49. *Ugrunaaluk kuukpikensis* may have cousins in Alberta. Do you suppose they were the origin of the Calgary Stampede?

---

[38] Mike, "Is this the Demise of a Duck-billed Dinosaur?," *Everything dinosaur* (blog), June 25, 2020. https://blog.everythingdinosaur.com/blog/_archives/2020/06/25/is-this-the-demise-of-a-duck-billed-dinosaur.html

The indigenous northern people have a lot more words that might need to be used before paleontologists are done. They have, reportedly, dozens of words for snow.[39] We may yet need them all to define the snow dinosaurs.

Migrating? Or Living?

Part of the difficulty scientists have for understanding how dinosaurs could live among the ice was that metabolism argument. If dinosaurs were cold-blooded, how could they survive in a place with little light and weak sun? When fossil hunters first started finding fossils under the tundra, they believed that the dinosaurs may have migrated. Canadian geese migrate; whales migrate. Why not dinosaurs? Perhaps the giant reptiles could travel north in the summer to find new vegetation, lay eggs, raise the children, then return south with the bambinos.

Druckenmiller, the fellow fighting to have *Ugrunaaluk* recognized as its own species, has been intensely focused on this question of migration. Many of the fossils he pulled out of the northern mud were quite small. Dozens of fossils, many smaller than a penny, were found in the soil near the Colville River, which dumps into the Arctic.[40] Today, this is at the tippy top of Alaska.

Small dinosaur bones mean small dinosaurs. This was partly why others thought *Ugrunaaluk* might be a juvenile version of something else. There were a lot of juveniles there. For Druckenmiller, if these tiny bones meant that baby dinosaurs hatched up north to their big hadrosaur mommies, he wondered if they migrated south.

Because of the distance to warmer food sources, Druckenmiller believes that they didn't. Based on the size and number of specimens

---

[39] I tried to verify whether the Inuit have a dozen—or fifty or whatever the number is—for snow. The research results were "it depends on which culture" and "it depends on how you define a word." Let's skip the esoterica and just agree that the northern people probably had at least as many words for their local climate as there are flavors of Doritos.

[40] Zaria Gorvett, "The Polar Dinosaurs Revealing Ancient Secrets," *BBC.com*, November 30, 2022. https://www.bbc.com/future/article/20221130-the-polar-dinosaurs-revealing-ancient-secrets

found, he believes they lived up north. In an inference to living animals, he draws a parallel with caribou. Caribou migrate, but only after the babies reach a size big enough to survive the journey. Druckenmiller argues that the size of the fossilized teeth and other fossil remains mean that the babies wouldn't be big enough to make a long, arduous trek. The migration itself would be more harmful than adapting to the cold.

The Bitter Cold for Dinosaurs...and Paleontologists

No doubt about it, though. The dinosaurs had to get real busy when there was a spring thaw. They had the same range of temperatures from spring to fall that humans do today, even if their extremes of light were far more dramatic. Those hadrosaurs and cryolophosaurs had to put on the Barry White records pretty quickly as soon as the weather warmed up a tad in February.

Those eggs had to be laid and incubated, so that the babies could hatch and grow big enough before the weather changed again in late September. Even if the juveniles couldn't migrate, they still needed to get big fast. While Druckenmiller determined that the animals could survive nearer the poles, he also demonstrated that their reproductive cycle was very accelerated.[41]

Finding out this information wasn't that easy, either. In Alaska, doing anything means working with the extremes. The paleontologists themselves have only a few months each year to complete their field-work. In that brief summer, the mosquitoes and other bugs are giant, even while the ground is still partly frozen. Just excavating fossils takes perhaps three times as long as it might in Wyoming due to the climate. Wyoming isn't exactly tropical, but its dirt isn't permafrost.

But as with other new ideas, the very notion of polar dinosaurs changes what we can imagine about them. Scientists will keep at it. They want to know how some adapted to the dim light. Thicker

---

[41] Patrick S. Druckenmiller, Gregory M. Erickson, Donald Brinkman, Caleb M. Brown, Jaelyn J. Eberle, "Nesting at extreme polar latitudes by non-avian dinosaurs," *Current Biology*, Volume 31, Issue 16 (2021): 3469-3478

skins, layers of feathers, and different types of claws may have helped adapt to the weather and the soil. Plenty to study!

Paleontologists like Druckenmiller are on the cutting edge of new science. Perhaps global warming will eventually affect this work. If permafrost starts to melt in areas never before used as fossil grounds, there may be many more discoveries. It brings up another question that might be resolvable in fifty years: did the North Pole dinosaurs meet Santa?

O is for Origin

I hope this doesn't burst anyone's bubble, but Charles Darwin did not single-handedly invent the theory of evolution. Several naturalists between the 17th and 19th centuries observed that animal species changed over time. Darwin added his own special sauce, by doing experiments in the isolated Galapagos to strengthen his ideas. His work, *On the Origin of Species,* was part of a chain of scientific proposals on the topic. Some of these proposals preceded or ignored the fossil findings. Others tried to fit them within grander narratives, biblical or otherwise, despite evidence that said differently.

This chapter will look at "origins" from several points of view. One involves the history of those who found fossils and drew conclusions, a topic we've brushed against before. Another is about the first dinosaur discovered, a topic at the mercy, naturally, of whoever was lucky enough to find it first. Last, there is a question of what came after, what animals originated once the ruling dinosaurs were forced to bow before E.T. and his Merry Asteroid. There are different kinds of origin stories.

The Origin of Evolution

The theory of evolution, and the resistance to the theory of evolution, was not just about monkeys and humans. The radical idea that Earth was not the way it had always been strayed from traditional Christian beliefs. For those who read the Bible literally, God had created everything in seven days, and that was it. Even an ordained priest like paleontologist William Buckland might compromise only by interpreting Genesis slightly differently.

Buckland and many others of his day accepted the religious interpretation called Gap Theory, which suggested there was unaccounted-for time somewhere between the end of the sixth and the seventh days. Kind of like the missing seven minutes in the Watergate tape. As naturalists started finding old bones, however, the idea that millions of years had passed in the Gap didn't square the religious narrative.

Darwin was certainly not the first person, or even the biggest name in the early 19th century, to cause dyspepsia to the ministers. Georges Cuvier—who keeps popping up in my story despite his lack of dinosaur expertise, what a show-off!— was respected precisely because he had used fossils to argue for a deviation from the Bible while still adhering strongly to church values. Cuvier had come across some mastodon teeth and noticed their similarity to contemporary Indian elephant teeth. His groundbreaking reference guide on mammals proposed that animals might be related and how they might have changed over time, i.e. gone extinct. It's one of the reasons he kept suggesting rhinos to Gideon Mantell; he was a mammal-loving guy.

Mary Anning and her myriad of fossils added to the story of origins in two ways. First, she dug up giant forms of fish-reptiles. Like Cuvier's giant mastodon teeth, the bones suggested that animals of the sea were huge once, even if no longer. Second, she found fossils that came from different parts of the cliff. That caused her, and the many scientists who came to see her fossils, to confirm theories of how geology worked. It's not that hard to understand that ammonites near the bottom of the cliff must have been older than those near the top of the cliff.

William Buckland initially disputed what Anning thought about the age of the bones because they didn't fit the Gap Theory. But others, like Charles Lyell, found a different way to keep God in charge. Lyell was once of the major proponents of *orthogenesis*, the progressive view of evolution that said that change was always about better because God was in charge. God started out with amoebas then fiddled with them to make them better. Continuous improvement eventually led to Adam and humanity, the crowning achievement. The family tree of animals moved upward, ever upward, toward the heavens.

Darwin's Big Idea

Darwin was not married to the idea of evolution as progress. The "survival of the fittest" were not his original words, and he only adopted them later to augment his idea of "natural selection." Natural selection is not synonymous with fittest. The strongest and fittest is not always the best adapted. Nature might select the smallest, such as a skinny little nocturnal mammal that eats insects when the big plants and dinosaurs die off.

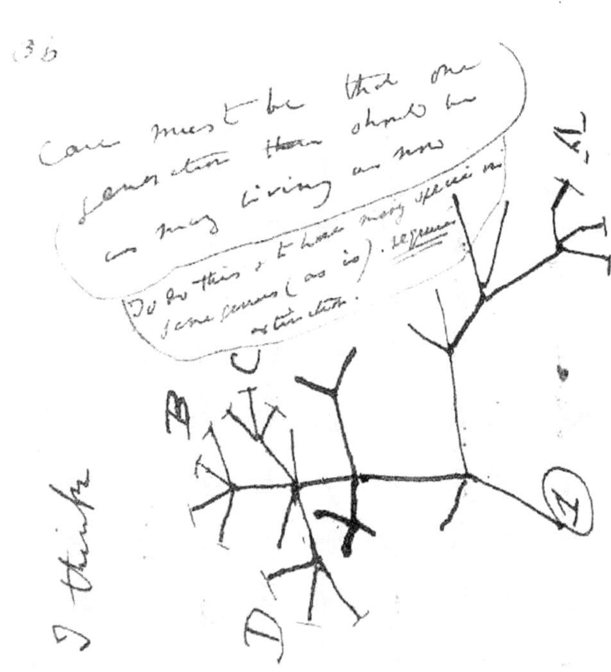

Fig 50. A drawing from Darwin's notebook, doodles of the evolutionary tree. A & B, he thought, would differ starkly while B & C would be more like each other, despite them all springing from a single ancestor.

Darwin's notebook doodles suggest he was working out how animals adapted, how the tree branches suggested relationships. Change might improve a species in a single time and place, but there was no sense of absolute improvement. As Darwin looked at the birds, mammals, and even barnacles of the Galapagos, he saw constant change. Natural selection was about "exploitation" of ecological niches—continuous exploitation. Living creatures changed to adapt better to the environment around them. Some species would adapt well to the environment, and others less so. There would be origins of new species, and deaths of less adaptable species.

It would be much later, in the 20th century, when survival of the fittest was applied to biology, then politics, economics, and elsewhere. Dinosaurs were branded as losers, humans as the ultimate winners, and mad scientists began playing around with eugenics and race purification. Darwin was left in the dust, even though his idea was that organisms shifted to meet the environment, not rule the universe, *bwhahaha*.

Geologists and the biologists both noted that habitats change and change again. Volcanoes and earthquakes crop up. Plants adjust as they compete for nutrients with other plants. If plants change, then the animals need to change, too. Change is continuous, and it produces opportunity. A beak might get longer to get a new type of food, but if the food source changes, the beak can evolve to become shorter again.

Darwin's big idea of natural selection explains the variation in size, behavior, and function of the dinosaurs. Since they had millions of years and lots of land to spread across, there was a lot of opportunity for dinosaurs to diversify across the Mesozoic.

The First Dinosaur Found

As the evolutionists were dreaming up their theories of selection and survival, other types of origins were happening. Credit for the discovery of the first dinosaur is given to Edward Lhuyd. In 1699, Lhuyd found a giant tooth. Note that this means the first tooth found by someone who had enough scientific knowledge to draw it, categorize it, and share with other scientists, whose writings became the official history accessible in English today.

Of course, this means European men. History has not recorded when the first dinosaur tooth was found in China, India, Asia, Africa, or South America. There were undoubtedly Chinese scientists in

1699. English reference works do not tell us what their dinosaur discoveries entailed. Just sayin'.

Anyway, we can give Lhuyd credit for finding what came to be called *Megalosaurus*, officially the first discovered dinosaur. *Megalosaurus* stood for "big-assed lizard," *mega* meaning "humongous." Other bits of *Megalosaurus* had been found—a thighbone (femur) in 1677. They just were not sure what the bulbous shape was.

When the fossil bone of *Megalosaurus* thigh was first passed around, scientists believed it might have come from an "elephant" or other big quadruped. When biologist Richard Brookes and chemist Robert Plot put a booklet together on the *Natural History of Oxfordshire*, they intended the illustration to be described as a thighbone.

Someone forgot to tell the person applying the captions, however, because it was labeled: *scrotum humanum*. Plot's illustration was carefully drawn in pen and ink, but the typesetter didn't get the memo.

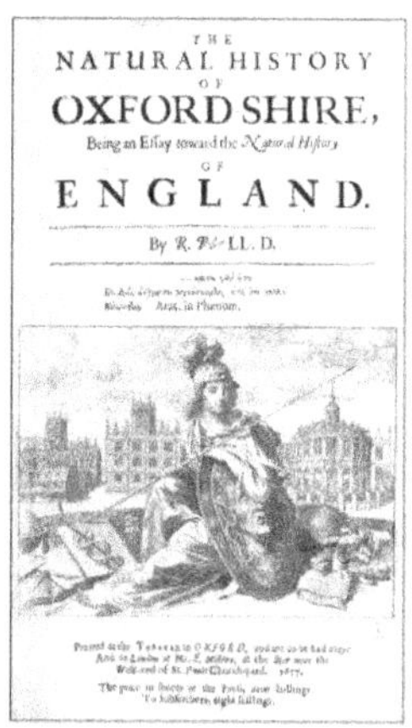

Fig 51. Was it the illustrator or the person writing the captions? Someone made an error in this 1677 *Natural History of Oxfordshire*, which labeled the *Megalosaurus* femur as *Scrotum humanum*.

You can fill in your own jokes involving stones and bones at this point. I'll just wonder whether this was when giants walked the earth.

Origin of the Species

A discussion of origins should probably end with another beginning. It's long been known that the Age of the Dinosaurs ended with the Cretaceous extinction. It's also long been known that this was when mammals diversified, during the Cenozoic, which is nicknamed the Age of Mammals. For most of that time, it was thought that all the mammals during that later period evolved out of a small quadruped, a distant cousin to the modern tree shrew.

It turns out that's almost right. Actually, there were lots of mammals in the early Mesozoic with the early, adapting dinosaurs. Almost 30% of those early Triassic animals were smallish quadruped mammals, duking it out with the smallish quadruped dinosaurs. Both had ball-and-socket hip joints, and both had holes behind their eyes to hold jaw muscles. They shared a common ancestor with their crocodile cousins.

Fig 52. One of the earliest mammals was *Morganucodon*, a monotreme, or egg-laying mammal (top); a descendant, the duck-billed platypus, still lives in Australia (bottom).

One of the little guys hanging out before the volcanoes split the Atlantic was *Morganucodon*—named for a place in Wales called Glamorgan (so why wasn't it *Glamorgandon*? The German fellow who named it didn't speak Welsh.) Looking a bit like a mole, our Welsh friend Morgan walked on all fours, had claws, and probably ate insects. Unlike his dino third cousins, however, he had fur, mammary glands, and permanent teeth. However, like dinos, he laid eggs.

This valiant little mammal was nocturnal, which accounts for the large eyes. It hung out in the dark, while the dinosaurs wandered around, trying to figure out how to take over the earth. As the sauropods were sprouting for the tops of trees, the morganucodons were still scuttling around. Luckily for their mammal descendants, they stayed hidden for thousands of years, biding their time and waiting for the Big BOOM.

The mammalian descendants of *Morganucodon* still exists. They're called the monotremes (*treme*=hole, so "one hole") because they lay eggs. Birds only have one hole, too, but only mammals can be monotremes.

Today, the only remaining monotreme species is the duck-billed platypus, native only to Australia. A lot of folks make fun of the platypus, that duck-billed, egg-laying mammal that seems like an animal built by a committee. If only they knew that his great-great-great-granny was around before Pangaea split up! Maybe the platypus would be granted a little more respect.

P is for Parasaurolophus

Parasaurolophus is my favorite dinosaur. Partly because I just love how that word rolls off the tongue. You'll get it…

para—like "parachute"

saur—like "sore"

olo—like "ah-lla" (The big accent is on the "ah" part)

phus—"fuss"[42]

para + *saur* + *olophus*

"beyond or near" + "lizard" + "crest"

As in, that dinosaur dude has one heavy-duty crest. It's beyond, man!

---

[42] I prefer Par-a-sore-OLL-o-fus, which is what most Internet pronunciations suggest. Some point out that Para-and-so-on was intended to be similar to a species already discovered, the *Saurolophus*, pronounced Sore-O-LOAF-us. Which means our buddy should be Par-a-sor-a-LOAF-us. Nope! That just doesn't roll off the tongue the right way.

Walks on Four Feet But Runs Like an Ostrich

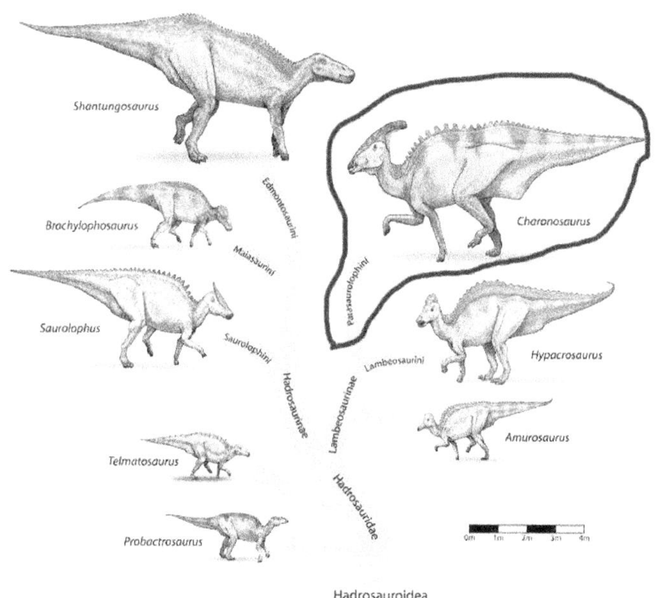

Fig 53. The parasaurolophini occupied a branch of the hadrosaur tree. Hadrosaurs were a prolific family of plant-eating quadrupeds in the late Jurassic/early Cretaceous. Imagine horses that could run on two legs, who had with fanciful headgear.

Like the duck-billed dinosaurs found up near the North Pole, Mr. P was a hadrosaur (hadr=thick, bulky). The hadrosaur body design started with sturdy back legs, anchored by those ball-and-socket joint hips. Add a thick midsection, short front legs, a strong tail, and a long face with headgear. Despite the shorter "arms," they did walk mostly on all four legs.

Hadrosaur feet have prompted much research and speculation.[43] In at least one species, *Edmontosaurus* (or was it *Urug*…never mind, "N"), a hoof-like nail was present. The bones had keratin covering

---

[43] For example, see Nick Schofield, "The 'Hoof-Like' Nail of Dakota the Dinomummy," *RexMachinablog* (blog), March 18, 2020. https://rexmachinablog.com/2020/03/18/dakota-dinomummy-hoof-nail/

their digits, a substance thicker and harder than skin but not as hard as bone, like human fingernails or animal hooves. Did the nail mean that this was a hoof and that hadrosaurs ran like horses?

Other studies have proposed hadrosaurs had separable toes but walked on those toes, more like camels. Some suggest they may have had a fleshy pad that worked as a shock absorber, while others think they might have had webbing between the toes, even under the keratin. Their back legs were built for long-distance running, not sprinting. Like camels, they may have been able to walk across multiple types of soil.

In addition, because their back legs were so strong, hadrosaurs could rear up on their back legs when they needed to become speedsters. Two-legged camels! In fact, it's thought that the youngsters ran around before their forelimbs grew long enough to support their weight. Adults mostly walked on four legs, unless they needed to run, as they did in *Jurassic World Dominion*. Again, not a great movie. But I sure loved the majestic herds of parasaurolophini sweeping across the plains.

Dig that Crazy Crest!

Of course, most of the conversation about the *Parasaurolophus* has not been about its feet, but its head. Ever since that first skeleton was discovered up in Alberta in 1921, paleontologists have tried to give this unique animal its due to set it apart from the other duck bills. Their flat and wide mouth reached vegetation that other animals could not. That broad jaw housed rows and rows of teeth—between a hundred and a thousand—packed together like arrow bundles to shear off the toughest material. By the time a row of teeth reached the chewing surface, it could be ground down to nothing without pain, even though the row was attached to those below. One researcher calls it "the most complex dental system ever made."[44]

Still, the most prominent feature of our friend the Big P was that head crest, a four- to five-foot-long tube, which curved past its neck. What was that thing for?

---

[44] Elaine Smith, "With 300 Teeth, Duck-Billed Dinosaurs would Have Been a Dentist's Dream," *Phys.org*, August 16, 2016. https://phys.org/news/2016-08-teeth-duck-billed-dinosaurs-dentist.html

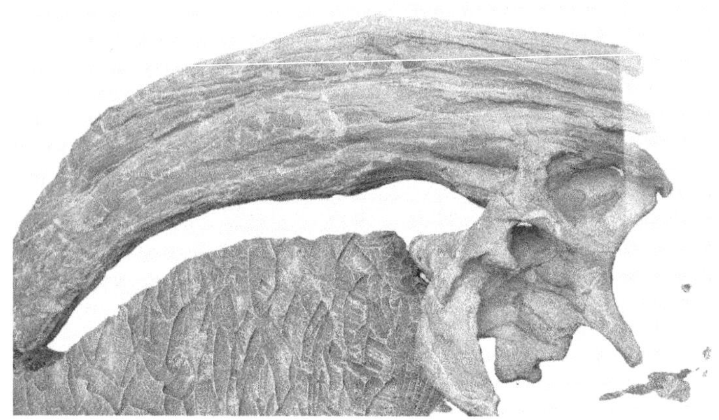

Fig 54. The crests of the parasaurolophus have been discovered all over western North America. Often just the tube was found without the remaining skeleton. Why such a long stretch of bone?

Was it for mating rituals, such as males fighting each other? Scientists wondered if they used them for mating rituals as well as protection. Other dinosaurs had horns, possibly for similar rituals. Ceratopsians (*kerat*=bone, i.e., "bone face") might have two, three, or even five horns, sprinkled around the head.

Another type called *Pachycephalosaurus* had a bony dome nearly a foot thick. The pachys—*pachy*=thick, *ceph*=head, so "thick head"— were thought to perform headbutting rituals, similar to modern rams. Recent research suggests that the pachys may have had vertebrae designed to absorb the shock of such crashes. However, *Parasaurolophus* didn't have a neck alignment to support headbutting. Plus, the crests would have gotten tangled in a way that domes could not. So maybe not fighting rituals.

More unusual uses for the crest were suggested, too, though not necessarily supported by evidence. Some thought maybe it was a breathing tube, like a snorkel. Perhaps our parasaurolophini friends waded into the copious waters of the mid-Jurassic to hide from predators. On the other hand, there were plenty of giant marine reptile predators, and *Parasaurolophus* was built for running, not swimming.

Perhaps the crest contained salt glands? That made no sense, because those are usually for seawater animals, not land-dwelling quadrupeds. Maybe it was a "foliage deflector," i.e., a way to avoid branches while searching for tasty leaves. Perhaps a place for extra muscles to attach to hold up the neck? Lots of crazy ideas.

Remember that for a long time, all the paleontologists had were bits of skeletons. If the fossilized rock didn't have an air hole, it was guesswork to know whether the original crest had a hole in it or not. When fossils form, it's partly because silty water is replacing bone. It was hard to tell how the crest was actually formed.

The World's Oldest Musician

Spoiler alert! The crest was a trombone. Ta-da! However, it took decades and a lucky find to confirm it.

In early 2017, while digging with others in New Mexico, paleontologist Terry Gates spotted a bit of bone sticking out of a rock. That's nothing new—that's how most fossil discoveries start. Usually, it's only a bit of bone, and let the conjecturing begin! In this case, the bit of bone was followed by a lot more. By the time he and his colleagues pulled it out, they were shaking with delight, which is how paleontologists respond to fully intact bony crests.

Part of the mystery with crests is that they had only found bits and pieces, or the crest but not the rest of the body. In particular, the skeletons known from the species *Parasaurolophus cyrtocristatus* had eroded (*curtis*=shortened, *cristatus*=crest). You may well wonder how "crest" can be both *olophu* and *crista*, and the answer is that scientists switch from Greek to Latin on a whim.

Even as late as the 1960s, paleontologists had to do a lot of guesswork at the internal design. Paleontologist John Ostrom, who will feature heavily in "R," prepared a detailed anatomical discussion for *P. cyrtocristatus*, where he argued that it was a separate species. The problem was that the skeleton he was working with had a much smaller crest than its better-known cousins, *P. walkeri* (named after a 19th-century guy named Walker) and *P. tubicen* (named after—oh, not yet!) species. Many believed that Ostrom's *cyrtocristatus* was just a smaller version of the other, more famous, parasaurolophisticates.

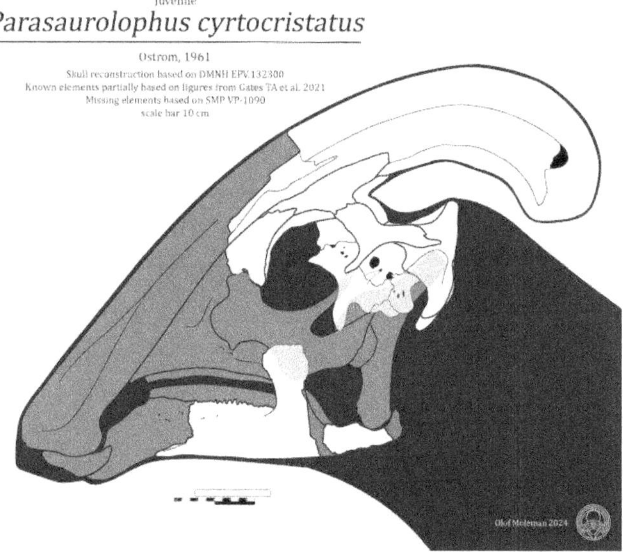

Fig 55. An updated view of the inside of the nasal cavities of *P. Cyrtocristatus*, described by Ostrom, but now known to be hollow and likely capable of producing incredible sounds.

What they all believed but didn't know, was that the crest bones were hollow. Ostrom drew them that way in a Field Guide he wrote in 1963. However, he had to fantasize—um, theorize—about the nasal passages. He was also looking at skeletons that had been discovered decades earlier, which were not as well preserved as more modern specimens.

Still, in 1963, paleontologists guessed as best they could about the air holes. Between the bones' exposure to the original air and handling later, researchers couldn't see what the crests were inside. In order to see, they would have to break them apart, which just would not do.

Technology triumphs once more! In 1998, Sandia Labs in New Mexico applied "brand-new" CT scanning technology to look inside a skull. What they discovered was, indeed, branching inside the nasal cavities, something like a trombone. The fossil of *P. Tubicen*, found in

Sweden in 1931, had originally been named "trombone" (that's what *tubicen* means in Latin). It turned out to be a pretty accurate guess.

This was why the 2017 finding was also so important. Gates's newly found skeletal crest was fully intact, "exquisitely preserved" according to the paper that detailed all its beautiful, impossible to pronounce, Latin parts.[45] Previously, the partial crests had eroded quite a bit. These new ones were fully intact, and they confirmed what the scans had shown and what Ostrom had drawn. The crest was full of cavities. The nasal passages even seemed to wind around in the crest, which would have amplified the sounds.

Not only did Gates prove that *P. cyrtocristatus* was a unique, third species of *Parasaurolophus*, but they had enough information to show how the crests worked. So, number one, they got to rewrite the clade—and in pen!

Number two, they knew what it might sound like. Some enterprising sound technicians ended up working with the design, both from the Sandia Labs version and the more recent findings. If you can wander off to YouTube, you can hear its call.[46] Those sounds could have had many purposes: mating (for sure), warning of an approaching predator, or maybe calling the young in for dinner.

Whatever its purpose, the music of the *Parasaurolophus* must have been glorious.

---

[45] T. A. Gates, D.C. Evans, and J. J. Sertich, "Description and rediagnosis of the crested hadrosaurid (Ornithopoda) dinosaur *Parasaurolophus cyrtocristatus* on the basis of new cranial remains." *PeerJ, 9,* (2021).
https://pmc.ncbi.nlm.nih.gov/articles/PMC7842145/

[46] According to my brother, the musician, the scientists at Sandia Labs created the parasaurolophus sounds using musical fifths.
https://www.sandia.gov/media/audio/dinosaur.mp3

Q is for Quetzalcoatlus

Dragon dinosaur. Winged serpent. If you've ever seen 1960s cartoons, perhaps like Turu the Terrible on *Jonny Quest*—another Q![47]

Quetzalcoatlus is the largest flying animal that has ever been discovered. She had a fifty-foot wingspan, as big as a small aircraft. In fact, the first paleontologist named it *Q. northropi* after—what else?—a Northrop light aircraft. Massive jaws. As a tall as a giraffe. Weighed five hundred pounds. However, not, technically, a dinosaur.

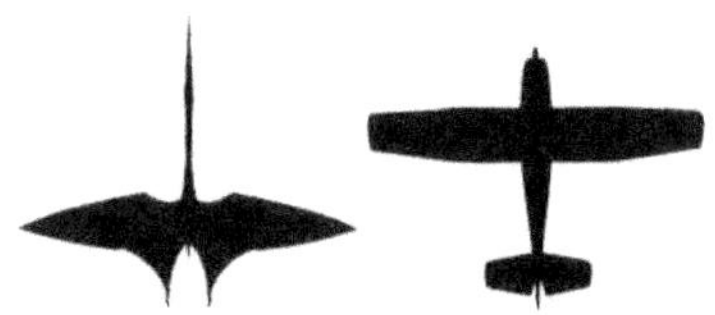

Fig 56. Comparison of *Quetzalcoatlus* to a Cessna 172.

Q. Northropi belonged to the group called pterosaurs (*pter*= winged, i.e., "winged lizards"). Like the giant marine reptiles that Mary Anning found in the cliffs of Lyme Regis, the giant fliers also lived during the age of the huge land lizards. But they had no

---

[47] "Matalos Turu!" from *Jonny Quest (1968)*. Uploaded by ForemanDomai. January 31, 2011, YouTube, :05.
https://www.youtube.com/watch?v=0XwEIjSSgzM

antorbital fenestra and the wrong kind of hips. Their ancestors had separated from the *-ischian* families long before. They were close cousins, closer than, say, turtles or bats. They were, without a doubt, reptiles. Like the other ancient reptiles, the pterosaurs disappeared after the K-Pg boundary.

In all other respects, the pterosaurs were giant reptiles that crossed the Cretaceous sky. Like their land third-cousins twice-removed, they were present across a long stretch of the Mesozoic and proliferated all around the world. Arguably, *Quetzalcoatlus* seems a reasonable compromise for the letter "Q." Even though, let's all say it together, not dinosaurs.

Giants in the Sky

The discovery of the first *Quetz*—I'm going to just type *Qu* from now on and you'll know what I mean—the finding of a colossal arm bone and part of a wing occurred in 1971. Doug Lawson was a PhD geology student in Texas, digging near the Mexican border, and was thrilled at the size of his discovered bones.

Lawson estimated the flying reptile's size, based on its parts, to have a wingspan of perhaps 52 ft (16 m). The size of a glider, a crop duster, a Piper Cherokee: the best comparisons are small planes. His article in *Science* magazine showed *Qu* side by side to an airplane.

What was unique about *Qu* was the length of its neck in proportion to the long wings. This pterosaur had a short, stubby tail. Some of the Northrop plane's designs were like that, like a modern Stealth bomber, with wide wings and an almost nonexistent tail.

After Lawson earned his PhD, he went on to design computer models based on animal behavior for corporations, specifically airlines. For example, using ant behavior theory, he showed Southwest Airlines why it is quickest for passengers to board without assigned seats.[48] As the ants were putting their luggage in the overhead bins, Lawson's original *Science* article caught fire and, suddenly, everyone wanted a *Qu*. Today, *Qu* flies across museums

---

[48] Lawson showed it's quicker to board a plane without assigned seats because the middle seats will be chosen last, which means only the aisle-seated person will have to get up to allow the last person in the row.

from North Carolina to Oregon, although she does pose a challenge. Whose museum foyer is big enough to hang a 50-foot skeleton?

Fig 57. *Qu* gracing the giant hall of the Royal Ontario Museum.

No Teeth, Though They Did Fly

Despite its lovely wingspan, *Qu's* skeletal structure confused paleontologists in more than a few ways. First, it had no teeth. Other flying reptiles, like pterodactyls (*dactyl*=finger, "winged finger") had pointy, sharp teeth, though not all the flying reptiles did. Most modern birds don't have teeth, except for the occasional egg tooth that helps them get out of their shell. As giant and scary-looking as *Qu* must have seemed, it had no dental structure. What did it feed on?

Coming up with the right model for food-gathering habits of a giant, toothless flier is more complicated than you might think. Suppose you think it may have skimmed the water for fish, like a modern pelican. Fifty-foot wings create so much drag that skimming would not work—too energy-inefficient. Could they scavenge dead carcasses? Probably not. You need a special beak hook to do that to pull meat from a carcass, and *Qu* had none.

The best theory that researchers have put forth is that *Qu* would land and !*gulp*! swallow a few small prosauropods as a snack. Modern storks do feed on small animals that way. Without teeth, a *Qu* would have to down the food intact. Like birds, they could have had a multi-part stomach with gizzards, grinding stones, or special stomach acids that quickly digest food. Gotta keep it light to get back in the air!

Fig 58. Toothless *Quetzalcoatlus* likely swallowed small prey whole, but on the ground, not as a skimmer or scavenger.

A Non-Flying Pterosaur?

Plenty of paleontologists have proposed designs to explain how pterosaurs walked, as in Figure 58. But paleontologist Donald Henderson went wild and crazy. He speculated that *Qu* couldn't even fly. He claimed that its body size and weight had been underestimated. Using computer 3-D models of ducks and ostriches, he claimed that the animal would have been too big to get off the ground. It was a fascinating poke in the eye to the pterosaurs, no doubt.

Still, even an amateur dino enthusiast might suggest that a hollow-boned, fifty-foot-wingspan skeleton makes no sense. Darwin would have said that a creature would not adapt to have specialized wings for no purpose. It might have been able to feed by landing near small prey, but it really could not walk all that far. Why would a creature have such wings and then not use them? Contrast wings with feathers, which could have been an adaptation originally for warmth. Wings would have little purpose held folded up next to a walking body. Meanwhile, the big carnivores could easily catch something clomping around half on its knuckles. Ostriches manage because they run 40 miles an hour. They also don't have long wings. And they're mean-tempered and kick.

Being a little provocative in scientific circles is not a bad idea. Multiple scientists leaped to the challenge to prove Henderson's calculations were wrong. Sometimes a reason to propose something is so that other people can come up with a way to refute it.

In this case, other paleobiologists used math to extrapolate from the size of breastbone of *Qu* to suggest that large muscles would have kept it aloft. Michael Habib also suggested that Henderson was using outdated models of pterosaurs and overestimated the mass of *Qu*. Habib and Mark Witton calculated that not only could *Qu* fly, but it could reach speeds of 80 miles an hour. Those long wings were ideal for soaring. *Qu* might, in fact, sustain long distances as a glider, efficiently using its food to stay aloft.

Habib estimated that *Qu* might go as far as 8000 miles—the length of Asia! Such estimates have stirred the pot even more, and recent studies have disagreed, claiming that *Qu* was more of a short-distance gal.[49] It depends on whether or not *Qu* was good at thermal soaring, a hotly debated topic. Long-distance or not, most do agree now that *Qu* was a powerful flier, even if for only short distances.

Ancient Views on Flying Reptiles

> There are extinct organisms that defy the imagination and push the boundaries of what we knew life was capable of. We name them accordingly, with etymologies taken from mythology and history.
>
> *Morphology and taxonomy of Quetzalcoatlus*[50]

---

[49] "Quetzalcoatlus and Other Giant Pterosaurs were Short-Range Flyers, Study Suggests," *SciNews, May 20,2022.*
https://www.sci.news/paleontology/quetzalcoatlus-flight-10828.html
[50] Brian Andres, and Wann Langston. "Morphology and Taxonomy of *Quetzalcoatlus* Lawson 1975 (Pterodactyloidea: Azhdarchoidea)." *Journal of Vertebrate*

Many cultures have legends that mention dragons and serpents. Chinese dragons, for example, are thought to symbolize fortune and fertility, positive qualities. The Chinese Year of the Dragon is supposed to bring good luck to everyone, especially to those born under its sign. Chinese apothecaries have long included "ground dragon bone" in their tinctures.

Such ideas might often be treated as silly or primitive, yet it's long been known that the Gobi desert and rural China have heaps of dinosaur fossils, for many of the same reasons as the North American Rockies (uplift, climate). Medicine "collectors" likely found or paid others to find dinosaur bones for their mixtures. It's not that different from farmers in Cambridgeshire digging up coprolite and spreading it on their crops because it's great fertilizer.

People who came before us recognized that there were ancient creatures, whether they were called dinosaurs or something else. Chinese science far predates Western science, so it seems logical that knowledge might be built around discovered fossils. Some of the bones might have been recognized as belonging to a flying animal, and others from creatures that swim or slither.

Chinese dragons are often compared to crocodiles, but perhaps they were simply based on dinosaur or pterosaur fossils. Asian culture built a mystique around them that emphasized good fortune. Even if *Quetzalcoatlus* was never found in Asia, plenty of pterosaur fossils have been found. Dragons have been described in cultures around the world, drawn with lion's heads (carnivores), serpentine bodies (crocodiles or plesiosaurs), or wings (pterosaurs). Dragons are dinosaurs, people! Let's be real.

The Mesoamerican cultures had access to flying reptile fossils, too. While the Aztecs were centered near Mexico City, they surely found fossils across the deserts to the west, near to the Rio Grande, where Doug Lawson first found *Qu's* long wings. The Aztec culture had an important god, named in the Nahuatl language "plumed serpent." The feathered snake. Dragon. Also known as Quetzalcoatl.

Paleontology 41, sup.1 (2021): 46–202.
https://www.tandfonline.com/doi/full/10.1080/02724634.2021.1907587#abstract

Fig 59. Quetzalcoatl graced multiple temples and images created by the Aztecs, like this temple at Xochicalco. The white outline around the Aztec serpent god made by the author for emphasis.

The Aztec god Quetzalcoatl symbolized both wind and the planet Venus—fertility! He wore a conch shell around his neck with the spiral of nature that meant wind, chaos, and rebirth. Surely, the Mesoamericans found those bones, had their own paleontologists reconstruct the skeletons, and concluded that such ancients had ruled the sky. It might make perfect sense for them to name their god Quetzalcoatl, so that Doug Lawson and his friends could come along centuries later and dig up fossils and apply a name that already fit like a glove.

A perfect name for a sky god that could sail across an entire continent. Just not a dinosaur.

R is for (Dinosaur) Renaissance

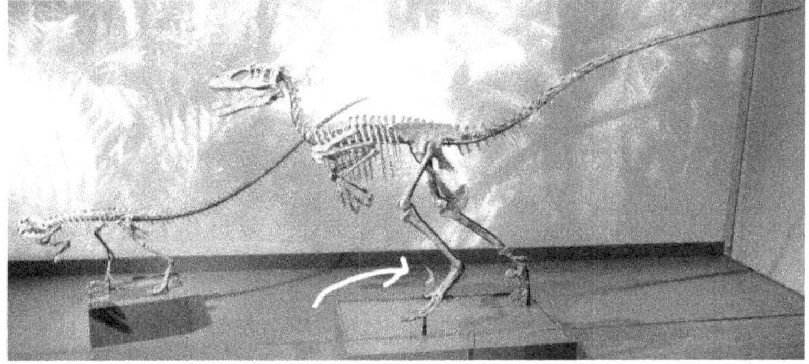

Fig 60. *Deinonychus* was the dinosaur that got the renaissance party going. Note the upturned foot claw and the correctly positioned tail, outstretched to balance for speed.

If you think the renaissance was all about art—you're right. That is, the dinosaur renaissance was, in part, about how dinosaurs were drawn and how their bodies were positioned. Would Da Vinci have painted them so their eyes followed you around the room? I'll leave that for another book. One of the hottest debates about these giant creatures from the 19th century forward was over how they moved around. Could they run? Could they bolt from a predator or chase prey? Did they have to live in water to offset the weight of those massive bones?

The position of a dinosaur's tail become the center of the debate. So did feathers and toes. The key dinosaur that unlocked the renaissance was *Deinonychus* (*deinos*= fearsome + *onukhos*=claw). *Deinonychus*, who had feathers, a long tail, and a famous, upturned claw.

The dinosaur renaissance is now looked at as a historical phenomenon, one which spawned books and video series and is, in fact, "aging." It's captured the popular imagination so much that there are games and apps which advertise "Dinosaur Shakespeare!" complete with anthropomorphic dinosaur versions of Romeo, Juliet, and Friar Lawrence. Now that's just silly. We don't need to put a triceratops head on a biped wearing a dress to understand what the dinosaur renaissance was about. We just need to know about the relatively recent history of paleontology.

Cue the Go-Go music, because this story starts in the 1960s.

The Missing Link: John Ostrom

When the first few giant reptile skeletons were discovered, the 19th-century public was pretty intimidated. They visualized monsters dominating everything in their path: scary, menacing, and fast. It was only toward the beginning of the 20th century that the idea of dinosaurs changed. The more the early naturalists dug, the more they discovered something definite. They realized that the disappearance of the dinosaurs was sudden—in geologic terms.

Sure, there were a lot of reptiles those millions of years ago, some quite big and others quite fierce, but *poof* they lost out. In the Darwinian interpretation, i.e., "survival of the fittest" stuff, the dinosaurs weren't fit enough. Mammals took over. Birds, too. There were a few reptiles still around, but they didn't evolve into humans— mammals did.

If the reptiles lost, then they must be different from mammals. In particular, the dinosaurs must have been slow and clumsy. Their bones were big, so it seemed to make sense. The dinosaur tree led to a dead branch. All the rest of the living lines which were fast, agile, and successful came from other branches.

This refrain probably echoes earlier discussions about Darwin ("O") and dinosaur metabolism ("B"). We know now—we the world *and* we who are leafing through this book—that dinosaurs were not slow, and that one of their family branches evolved into birds. But whose idea was that?

Fig 61. John Ostrom's ideas linking *Deinonychus* and the feathered *Archaeopteryx* changed everything.

When Yale paleontologist John Ostrom was digging up fossils in 1964, he came across bones of a mid-sized predator called *Deinonychus*. Pieces of *Deinonychus* had been found earlier, but not quite as much as Ostrom discovered. He was able to build the skeleton in a way that hadn't been done before. He could see that *Deinonychus* was clearly a reptilian predator, with the lizard hips of the Saurischians and an upraised claw. However, the other toes on its feet, aside from The Claw, looked very similar to the feet of birds.

It's one thing to build out a dinosaur skeleton. It's another to re-connect the pieces in such a way that you can redraw the entire tree branch. But that's what Ostrom did. First, he established a theory, then he gathered enough evidence to solidify the claim. *Deinonychus* helped create a link between the earlier meat-eating predators and the line that led to birds.

Archaeopteryx, the feathered fossil that had been discovered in Germany in the 1860s, will be spotlighted later ("W"). The 19th-century scientists believed that it was the oldest known bird. But Ostrom noticed the resemblance of its claws to *Deinonychus's* claws. He concluded that *Archaeopteryx* was a reptile, and a feathered reptile at that. It sparked a revolution.

Ostrom's theory was built around the following: *Deinonychus* and *Archaeopteryx* had similar feet. *Archaeopteryx* had feathers. Birds have feathers. Therefore:

(1) Birds evolved from dinosaurs, probably from theropods like *Deinonychus*; and

(2) Dinosaurs might have had feathers and other characters similar to birds.

It seems simple, but the beauty of this idea is that it is like a palindrome—it goes both ways. It explains where birds came from and how they fit on to the family tree of existing animals. It also explains how dinosaurs may have functioned if they were like birds. For instance, they might have been warm-blooded, with a high metabolism. Ba-da-bing!

If dinosaurs were like birds, then they would have to behave very differently from the clumsy giants that had dominated the discussion prior to 1960. We may notice in paintings that, at some point, dinosaur tails were no longer dragging on the ground. But that didn't happen because paleontologists discovered soft-tissue fossils that had dinosaur muscles. Rather, it happened because Ostrom made a connection between 150-million-year-old bones and the bones of birds today. If birds are, in fact, the descendants of dinosaurs, then that changed the view of what birds' ancestors might have been like. Suddenly, diorama designers at museums had to start building out structures to hold those tails up.

Red in Tooth and Claw: Robert Bakker

> Who trusted God was love indeed
> And love Creation's final law —
> Tho' Nature, red in tooth and claw
> With ravine, shriek'd against his creed ...

> No more? A monster then, a dream,
> A discord. Dragons of the prime,
> That tare each other in their slime,
> Were mellow music match'd with him.
>
> Tennyson, *In Memoriam A. H. H.*[51]

Ostrom's student, Robert Bakker, extended the renaissance in dinosaur ideas one step further. Bakker started building a strong case to support all dinosaurs as active, warm-blooded creatures. Metabolism was at the core of defining dinosaur diversity. If they were not tied to warmth and sunlight, then they could live at the North Pole, they could come in all sizes, and they could adapt in innovative ways.

Bakker was a talented artist, which was a useful skill for a paleontologist. As he argued that *Deinonychus* could be speedy like a road runner, he drew it with its tail held backward. His illustration made it into Ostrom's article, and museums forever afterward had to get very clever on how to pose their fossil bones. Speedy predators, in particular, made more sense but would need a reboot.

When dinosaurs were new in the early 19th century, the English poet Alfred Lord Tennyson had heard of them and incorporated extinct beasts into a poem, calling them "Nature, red in tooth and claw…" In other words, in 1833, they were considered fearsome, royal beasts. After a century passed, opinions had shifted by the early 1900s, with King Kong destroying the slow and plodding dinosaurs on movie screens. What Robert Bakker and the renaissance paleontologists did was return the dinosaur status to "red in tooth and claw."

---

[51] Alfred Lord Tennyson, "Canto LVI and LVIII," *In Memoriam A. H. H.*, 1850 at *Allpoetry.com* /allpoetry.com/In-Memoriam-A.-H.-H.:-56. Accessed November 27, 2024.

Fig 62. Robert Bakker, holding an *Allosaurus* hand. A student of Ostrom, Bakker sealed the deal, both providing evidence that dinosaurs were warm-blooded and resetting views about dinosaur movement as a whole.

Bakker became the standard-bearer for the young revolutionary paleontologists. He looked the part, sporting a ten-gallon hat and full "hippie beard," as opposed to the crew cut and button-down shirts worn by his mentor. But he had the same scientific chops that Ostrom had, and he had published well-argued works in *Scientific American* and other peer-reviewed journals. In the mid-1980s, he pulled together many of his radical ideas into a single volume: *The Dinosaur Heresies: New Theories Unlocking the Mystery of the Dinosaurs and Their Extinction.*

Heresies is now considered one of the most important books ever written about dinosaurs. In non-scientific language, Bakker lays out the case for warm-blooded reptiles and the resulting implications. Warm-blooded animals could grow big or small, could live in swamps or forests, and could be agile as well as strong.

Some of Bakker's ideas in the book have not proven to be ironclad. He claims that dinosaurs invented flowers because the evolution of ground feeders in the late Cretaceous coincided with a time when angiosperms (flowering plants) came to dominate the plant world. Biologists today respond: *meh*.[52] He also did not support the extinction-asteroid theory, at least not at first. He claimed that dinosaurs more likely succumbed to interspecies disease when animals from different continents crossed the Bering land bridge.

Much more data has come to light on those and other ideas since Bakker's book was published. The high metabolism of dinosaurs has held up as a scientific theory. The land-bridge extinction theory, not so much. Still, more than anything, what Bakker and Ostrom built was cases that fit evidence which had accumulated over decades. Dinosaur science did not advance much in the early 20th century, and the dinosaur renaissance upended conventional notions so much that it rebooted paleontology as a profession.

The increased opportunity for paleontologists was then augmented by political events as well. The end of the Cold War in the early 1990s led to the reopening of fossil sites that had been dormant across Asia. Particularly around the Gobi desert, fossils were newly identified that supported various theories, and this helped a flowering of new research. While the North American Rockies were—and are—a place that yields up plenty of fossil evidence, the expansion of evidence from places around the world helped even more. Once scientists had a lot more bones to work with, theories would change even more. It's how science works.

The Glee of Walter Cronkite

There's one more "missing link," if you will. Dinosaurs have been popular with the public for decades, but this fascination was on the rise even before *Jurassic Park* burst into the summer blockbuster season of 1993. One reason was because of Walter Cronkite, the venerable news anchor of the 1960s and 1970s, who, it turns out, was also a big dinosaur geek.

Cronkite, with his round face and deep, slow voice, was Everybody's Grampa. He marveled at the Moon Landing and calmed

---

[52] Paul M. Barrett and Kathy J Willis, "Did Dinosaurs Invent Flowers? Dinosaur—angiosperm Co-evolution Revisited," *Biological Reviews* 76 (2001). https://www.semanticscholar.org/paper/Did-dinosaurs-invent-flowers-Dinosaur%E2%80%94angiosperm-Barrett-Willis/f1d6f6fd9410cc889d8f0aa36b44c5b9009c4347

the public throughout the turmoil of the Vietnam War, the Nixon administration, and rough economic times. He also played a key role in a series on dinosaurs that would follow on the heels of the dinosaur renaissance.

The nightly news anchor had been a lifelong dinosaur fan since 1960, when he had helped with a project called *Digging for Dinosaurs*. The "family-friendly" package curated by the American Museum of Natural History included a book, a record album narrated by Cronkite, a series of slides, and a handheld slide viewer. In other words, the 1960 version of a video! Cronkite describes dinosaurs on the recording with excess zeal even as discordant modern music thumps in the background.[53]

In 1991, when A&E asked him to narrate their new series on *Dinosaurs*, he must have jumped at the chance. That show now seems dated by 21st-century standards, but it centered around the brand-new ideas of the renaissance scientists: dinosaurs as birds and running dinosaurs with their warm-blooded metabolisms. A&E's show was the gold standard until, two years later, Steven Spielberg came along with a much bigger budget and multiple dinosaur experts as consultants. In the A&E series, the animation by Ray Harryhausen was laudable, although no match for the *Jurassic* CGI.

Yet what's fascinating about the A&E series—now housed at the Internet Archive—is Cronkite's glee as he hosts the show. He marvels at new museum exhibits, talks to paleontologists starry-eyed, and explains everything to school children with an eagerness that matches their own. Both Robert Bakker and John Ostrom make an appearance. Still, the hands-down highlight must be when he does a dinosaur dance.

At the time, people might have thought that 75-year-old Walter Cronkite was kind of a dinosaur. Most likely, he would have been mighty pleased to be viewed as agile, warm-blooded, and ready to fly.

---

[53] Walter Cronkite, "Digging with Dinosaurs (1968)," uploaded by Mark Ryan, February 10, 2021, YouTube, https://www.youtube.com/watch?v=AOP0xUYNDX4

S is for Skin

Dinosaurs had a lot of skin in the game. Of course, fossilized skin can be hard to find, buried in the ground for 200 million years. Many dinosaurs were giant reptiles, so they had giant skins. Paleontologists long believed that if they were patient enough, they might find some skin that made it through the mud.

Fossilization of bone, of course, replaces the bone bits with minerals. That's no help with skin, however. Skin has to be preserved through mummification: the Egyptians were onto something! In order for a dead animal's skin to be preserved in the earth, it has to be geologically captured under a precise set of circumstances. Its cells can't be replaced with anything but must be held intact, neither eroded nor dissolved. That makes skin extremely tricky to find.

However, a few examples have been found. They tell us plenty about what the reptile rulers were like. Skin was needed to hold in the body parts, certainly, otherwise it would be inconvenient to trail intestines and so forth everywhere. But skin has other purposes, whether to blend in and avoid predators or to stand out and attract mates. Skin can even offer clues to the great dinosaur mysteries, since skin might be covered with scales or features.

Dino-Mummies

The year 2017 was an exciting one for paleontology, when miners in Canada found a beautifully preserved—it can hardly be called anything else—nearly full skin of a nodosaur. The dinosaur was dubbed with the genus *Borealopelta* (*boreal*=northern; *pelta*=shield). The skin was complete with horned edges and the face of a dino that did not want to be interrupted while eating, thank you very much.

The nodosaurs were a sister group to the ankylosaurs. Nodosaurs had short, flexible tails, in contrast with the ankylosaurs, whose tails had a spiked clubs. Like the ankylosaurs, *Borealopelta* had a spiky face and was covered with bony plates. And, like ankylosaurs, it was armor-plated, and the "armor"—the keratin covering—was what survived nearly intact.

Fig 63. *Borealopelta* skin found in a Canadian mine. It took a paleontologist more than five years to extract the skin from the rock originally surrounding the scaly skin.

The circumstances of preservation were unusual. This *Borealopelta* fell into water when it died, then flipped upside down. That wasn't particularly odd, as corpses do float after death, often filling with gases. Perhaps because its thick top layer was so much heavier than the dead, soft underside, the animal turned belly-side up, then sank into the mud. It was held fast so that the skin did not decay. In this case, the sands inside the water acted as a mummifying agent rather than as a conduit to replace living tissue with rock.

Borealopelta was discovered in the Canadian Rockies after a mining machine went *clonk*. The miners had the presence of mind to recognize it as something useful for other scientists and called the Royal Tyrell Museum hotline. Well, maybe there was no red phone in a mining trailer up in Alberta, but somebody guessed it involved dinosaur fossils, and they stopped the work to let the paleontologists come and get it.

Can you imagine those Canadian paleontologists, carefully scraping this thing away, accustomed for decades to getting excited over tiny bits of bone? Then, they find an entire intact skin? A full set of claws, clearly defined horns, and the whole enchilada of armor and spikes! One of the scientists involved was our friend from the *Quetzalcoatlus* controversy, Donald Henderson, the guy who suggested *Qu* couldn't fly. This time, Henderson jumped at the chance to oversee the extraction of the specimen since he is, actually, an expert paleontologist.

After two weeks of carefully extracting the entire block of stone that contained the upside-down skin, *Borealopelta* was sent to Alberta and turned over to a senior preparation technician, Mark Mitchell. Mitchell had the tedious work of grinding away the rock without destroying any of the skin tissue attached. Basically, 7000 hours with a vibrating metal toothpick. Five and a half years' worth of work. It seems only fitting, then, that the species was ultimately christened *Borealopelta markmitchelli*.

Camouflage and Other Functions

B. markmitchelli wasn't just beautiful because it was a preserved full dinosaur skin, complete with scales and horns. Mitchell and the scientists who dug further found something else. The skin contained remnants of skin-marking melanosomes. Melanosomes create melanin, which colors skin; melanosomes sit within cells to dictate the pigments that make up those colors.

Humans, for the most part, have a single skin color, while animals might display several distinctly different colors. *B. markmitchelli's* melanosomes suggested that it had "counter-shaded camouflage." That means the animal would have dark colors on its back, to blend in with leaves, and lighter colors on its belly. Without counter-shading, when light falls from above, things appear light on the top, making them easier to see. Counter-shading, where the top is shaded darker than the bottom of an animal, counteracts that effect, making an object harder to see. For instance, with fish, the lighter bottom also makes them harder to see from underneath, since usually the light source is above the water. This works for predators, too. Sharks are dark on the top and light on the bottom, which means they are harder for fish to see.

Still, *B. markmitchelli* was probably happy to be camouflaged. In addition to its thick skin *and* spikes *and* being low to the ground… *Borealopelta* blended into the foliage. Just a bush, folks, just a bush. The Canadian one who courteously left most of its outer bits in the northern rock was fairly old when it died, likely because it could hide well from the things with big heads and teeth.

Skin provides camouflage. But skin has a lot of other purposes, which is why the bits of other skin that paleontologists found previously came in dozens of patterns, shapes, and sizes. Dinosaur skin has both unique texture and elasticity. Some is smooth and stretchy while others is bumpy or pitted. Reptiles, don't forget, were known for scales—thin, flat, sometimes overlapping or patterned structures. Even if they were specialized reptiles, dinosaurs could still have scales.

Thick skin was protective. Thick skin might help with thermoregulation, to let the animal stay cool in the heat and provide a little warmth when it's cooler. Additionally, some skin can be more waterproof than others. A lot of skin might have been sensitive to the touch, allowing nocturnal dinosaurs to succeed in darker environments.

All in all, a lot of different kinds of dinosaurs meant that there would be a lot of different kinds of skin. Some skin might have been specially designed to hold curious attachments.

A Burst of Bristle

Skin attachments were at the center of a controversy involved *Psittacosaurus*. *Psittacosaurus*—(*posit*=parrot, "parrot-head") is a well-known species in Asian paleontology circles. It might be the one non-avian genus that has the most different species. Not counting birds, the genus group *Psittacosaurus* has twelve different species. So many specimens have been found in Asia that an area in Chinese geology has been nicknamed after them.

Aside from their parrot-shaped faces, all twelve species (*P. sinensis, P. albigensian,* and so on) were unique for a special reason: bristles. Embedded in the fossils were keratin-covered nodules, tubes, reeds—they go by many descriptors. Keratin is that material that makes up claws, nails, or nodosaur armor, not as thick as bone but certainly hard to the touch.

Enough of the *Psittacosaurus* samples have been found with tube-like bristles that it prompted the question about whether these were like feathers. We already know, birds=dinosaurs... except that *Psittacosaurus* was not a theropod. It emerged from the ornithischian branch of the tree. If the parrot-heads developed feathers, that would turn the paleo world upside down.

Several scientists have claimed that the bristles were not like feathers. They did not branch, they were keratin-covered, and they did not emerge from follicles as feathers do. They were more like quills. But unlike quills, the bristle remnants were too thin to ward off predators. What could they be for, if not display?

Psittacosaurus, with counter-shading & bristles

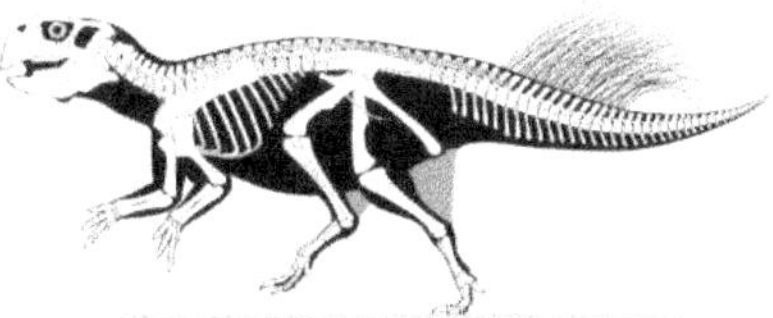

Psittacosaurus, skeleton containing bristles

Fig 64. *Psittacosaurus* (top) had counter-shading skin and bristles. The bristles attached to their vertebrae on the back (bottom) have created feverish debate about their purpose.

Earlier ("L") we noted that dinosaurs might have had color vision because birds and crocodiles have color vision. Seeing colors, such as red, means you might display red. Colored skin could help a dinosaur attract a mate. So, too, might bristles be waved to attract the lady parrot-heads. It's called plumage even if, instead of feathers, it was bristles on the tail of the parrot-faced, non-bird dinosaurs.

Scales to Feathers

We can leave the debate over whether bristles are proto-feathers to the nerdiest of paleontology circles. But a related question involves the way the bristles—or feathers—attach. The *Psittacosaurus* bristles were fused to the bone. Feathers emerge from individual cells, in the same way that hair does. The feathers have to attach. Unless skin is preserved, the places where the feathers attached isn't preserved. Ignore whether bristles or whether quills are feathers. Whatever they are, how did they get there? How did scaly reptile skin adapt places for bristles to attach?

Things that attach to skin, like feathers, are pretty sophisticated. Fish don't have them, and crocodiles don't have them, so they had to get on to reptile skin somehow. They emerge from *integument* structures, which is a complicated word for "covering." Skin is one kind of covering. So is hair. So are feathers. In order to have feathers, skin has to develop spots for fibers to grow. Skin has to create places for follicle cavities, which is where stuff attaches. Reptile skin was already not smooth and identical; it had scales, horns, plates. Adding a follicle cavity for something to emerge would just be another kind of adaptation.

Scales were a kind of early reptile filament. Did the earliest dinosaurs, or their proto-dinosaurs diapsid ancestors, have the filaments or not? Maybe other lines and branches of the dinosaur tree had feathers, aside from the birds, and they just were not well preserved enough to be discovered. Maybe even pterosaurs had filaments. Wouldn't that muck up the plans for those who have proved that pterosaurs are different from dinosaurs?

Naturally, some researchers had to dig into the question.[54] With a lot of statistics and cautionary warnings about data limitations, a 2015 study on dinosaur skin found that the dinosaurs along the bird-developing line, the theropods, might have had filaments. The dinosaurs along the other non-bird-developing line didn't. They don't know whether pterosaurs had them, but they think not.

Not finding evidence of something does not make it false. However, there is an important corollary when it comes to paleontology. If you don't have any evidence, then stop speculating about it. Filaments have not been found on reptiles other than those on the theropod evolutionary line. Period. As far as we know, the theropods and their bird descendants are the only ones who developed feathers.

No crocodiles with feathers. However, when it comes to the *T. rex*, that's a different story…

---

[54] Paul M. Barrett, David C. Evans, and Nicolas E. Campione, "Evolution of Dinosaur Epidermal Structures," *Biol. Lett.*, no 11 (Feb. 20, 2015). https://royalsocietypublishing.org/doi/10.1098/rsbl.2015.0229

T is for T. rex

Mr. T!

Tyrannosaurus was a formidable guy. He was the ultimate carnivore, with a skull bigger than most 12-year-old humans are tall. Then, he was 40-feet long from nose to tail. Longer than the average house is tall. His teeth could grow to be a foot long, which is why paleontologist Kevin Padian called them "lethal bananas."[55] Since the first set of bones was unearthed at the turn of the 20th century, dozens of *Tyrannosaurus* skeletons have been found. They're now worth a lot of money, and natural history museums bid big money to have them (see "U"). One exhibit in Japan put five skulls in a circle, like a carousel of chomp-mania.[56]

T. rex was a carnivore that belonged to the theropods, whose branch on the dinosaur family tree eventually ended in birds. It's been argued that other theropods, such as *Deinonychus*, had feathers, so it is possible that Mr. T had them, too. That debate remains live. He was an apex predator—maybe he could have whatever body features he wanted! Well, except for long arms.

---

[55] "The Tyrant Lizards: The Tyrannosauridae," *UCMP Berkeley*, https://ucmp.berkeley.edu/diapsids/saurischia/tyrannosauridae.html. Accessed November 27, 2024.
[56] https://commons.wikimedia.org/wiki/File:Tyrannosaurus_skulls_Japan.jpg

Fig 65. Could *Tyrannosaurus rex* have had feathers? His cousins and great-great-great-grandnieces did. Even Wikimedia slapped a warning label on this imaginative drawing, suggesting that its feathers are too extensive and its tongue too long. Everybody's a critic!

Even though almost a century of dinosaur bone collecting had passed between the coining of the word *Dinosauria* and the first *T. rex* banana-tooth being pulled from the ground, the king of meat-eaters was almost instantly popular. He was given the species name *rex* before many other dinosaurs had been discovered. He's never lost the fame and the flash. He's still the king, the apex dinosaur, as far as we puny humans are concerned.

The Very First T. rex Fossil

The first person to find *T. rex* fossils was himself named after P. T. Barnum, circus showman, which seems appropriate. The fossil collector was named was Barnum Brown, and he was the new naturalist running the brand-spanking-new American Museum of Natural History (AMNH) in New York. AMNH had great funding in 1900, so they sent Brown and a crew out west digging for bones, much as the same as Andrew Carnegie did. Brown found them.

What Brown found first was a six- to eight-inch tooth. Others, like paleontologist Edwin Cope ("U"), had found other pieces, like vertebrae, but couldn't identify the animal. When Brown pulled out giant teeth, even if he didn't know which brand-new animal it was, he knew it as a big predator. Brown was known to pay locals "good money" for fossils, but he also put in his own time collecting. The fossil hunters in Hell Creek, Montana would recognize him, supervising the digs in a full-length fur coat.

In 1902, Brown found pieces of what at the time was called a *carnosaur*, a meat-eating lizard. Those eight-inch spikes must have belonged to a massive jaw. The full jaw was also unearthed, along with more than thirty bones. It was undoubtedly a giant reptile skeleton, which New Yorkers would flock to see. As they kept digging, they ultimately excavated two complete skeletons. Barnum's boss, Henry Osborn, also working in the field, chose the name *Tyrannosaurus rex*. Even here the two skeletons found by Barnum Brown vied briefly for naming supremacy. Brown called one *Dynamosaurus imperator*—"emperor power lizard"—and the other got the name *Tyrannosaurus rex*. But *Tyrannosaurus* is the one listed first in his scientific publication. Later, when *D. imperator* was identified as the same species, *T. rex* "won" the battle for naming rights.

Tyrant-lizard (Tyrannosauridae) is now the family name; *Tyrannosaurus* is the genus. One of Brown's discovered skeletons went to London and the other to Carnegie in Pittsburgh. But Brown and Osborn found an even better full skeleton in 1908. The third one graces the New York AMNH. That 1908 skeleton is the one used to design *T. rexes* for many purposes, such as the cover of the original book *Jurassic Park*.

Fig 66. Although the tail of *T. rex* is incorrectly dragging on the ground in this 1905 illustration for *The New York Times*, you can clearly see the saurischian hips and antorbital fenestra.

The New York Times ran a feature in 1905 on the newly discovered predators: "The Prize Fighter of Antiquity Discovered and Restored."[57] The illustration shows the full skeleton, towering above a human set of bones. The five-column spread also depicts a man installing the display, looking up at the shin bone. Given how limited the scientific knowledge was at the time, it's not a bad depiction.

There Is Only One T

In the century since those first finds in Montana, paleontologists have uncovered another 42 different skeletons of *Tyrannosaurus*. Some of the bits and pieces stuck on other specimens have also been reclassified as part of *T. rex*, so some fossils today date back to the 1850s.

In the Tyrannosauridae family, between three and fifteen unique genus groups have been identified. The spread is wide because lots of animals, and their discoverers, want to jump on the bandwagon with the popular tyrannosaurs. Of course, it's terribly prestigious for a paleontologist to discover a unique dinosaur, which leads to an ebb and flow in the scientific literature. One person claims a "unique find!" Another argues that it's just one more of something already known.

All the species in the tyrannosaur family are predators: bipedal, long-tailed, strong-bodied, sporting a long rectangular jaw and rows of jagged, menacing teeth. The other species of Tyrannosauridae have names like *Gorgosaurus* and *Daspletosaurus*—"dreadful" and "frightful." All synonyms of scary.

The genus is *Tyrannosaurus*—a branch of a branch of a branch of Tyrannosauridae. For most if its history, *rex* was the king, the only species attached to the *T.* genus. You may have wondered, if there is a *T. rex*, why there wasn't a *T. regina* as well? Why no Queen of the dinosaurs?

---

[57] "The Prize Fighter of Antiquity Discovered and Restored," *The New York Times*, December 30, 1906, 21.
https://timesmachine.nytimes.com/timesmachine/1906/12/30/101814992.html?pageNumber=21

Some think that there was. In 2022, Greg Paul noted that everyone was constantly chucking anything that looked like a *T. rex* skull into the same pot. Paul suggested some might belong to a different species, like a *T. imperator* or a *T. regina*. King, Queen, and Emperor. Despite his organized plan, the work has not been accepted as yet. Detractors have claimed that differentiation based on number of teeth and size of the femurs is not enough to justify new species. Some of the other specimens could be juvenile, female, or a simple variation in size. There are high barriers to reach to become a new tyrannosaur.

Another new species analyzed in 2024 may finally break through as a new kind of *Tyrannosaurus*. While the fossil was discovered back in 1983, a second review of the specimen led to its being called *Tyrannosaurus mcraensis*, after the Mcraen rock formation. What is crazier about this discovery is that the rock was dated to 72 my ago, and that is older than most other *T. rexes*. The older dating both supports the idea that these fossils belong to a different species and raises new questions about its precise placement on the family tree.

How can a 1983 fossil get reclassified? Technology changes since the discovery allow scientists to re-examine old material. Such changes are ongoing. Since they can continuously re-examine other bits and pieces, who knows what they may eventually find? After all, birds used to belong to their own major branch of the animal tree.

Tastes Like Chicken

We should address the feathers thing, too. Birds, as modern dinosaurs, emerged from the line of theropods that also generated most of the meat-eaters. It's a surprising fact: In geological time, chickens are closer to *T. rex* than *T. rex* was to *Stegosaurus*.

It is fascinating to consider whether *T. rex* did have feathers. The idea is pure speculation, since none of the bones of those 42 *T.* specimens had feather-like impressions, follicles, or filaments ("S"). Some years ago, a few tyrannosaur fossils from China—the booming site for new species now—had bumpy somethings. The researchers suggested these might include proto-feather filaments and the infamous integumentary structures from which feathers emerge. These days, when the internet reads even so much as a proposed theory, it decides the question is concluded. Suddenly, there are dozens of painted variations of our feathered, banana-toothed friend floating around.

But the paleontologists who debate such things are still debating. Just as it's difficult to convince knowledgeable scientists that there are multiple *T.* species, it's difficult to simply slap feathers on the apex predator.

Plus, Darwin's ghost is clearing its throat. If the largest predator ever did have feathers, what were they for? Clearly, not flying. Clearly, not to frighten away other predators. Not likely for warmth, since *T. rex* lived in the places that were humid and swampy. The most likely possibility, if *T.* had them, was for display to potential Mrs. *T*s, and more likely to attract a mate than to scare off a rival.

On the other hand, the tyrannosaurs had other birdlike features. They were strongly bipedal and used their head and three-toed claws for hunting, rather than their arms—more on that in a moment. They had an excellent sense of smell and could dart quickly.

They also had outstanding vision. Like eagles, the *Tyrannosaurus* had a long jaw, with eyes set high above the jaw. Looked head-on, as seen in Figure 67, they had stereoscopic vision, whether there was skin on those jaws or not. Good thing we're looking at 65 my old bones, too. Can't imagine that very many things looked directly at a *T. rex* and survived to tell the tale.

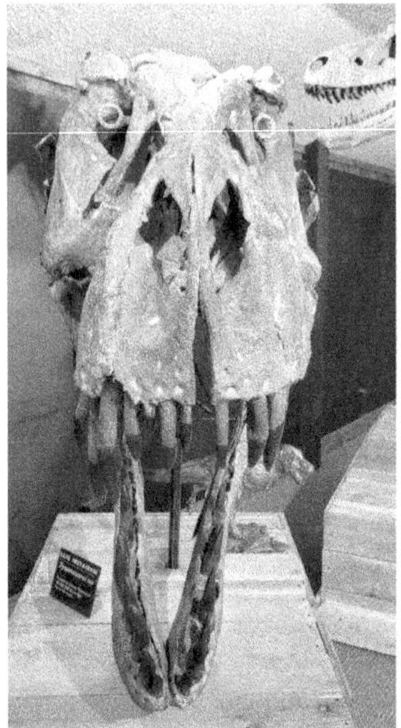

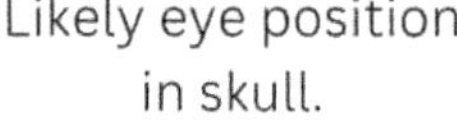

Likely eye position
in skull.

Stereoscopic vision
(eyes faced front).

Fig 67. A *T. rex* could see images in 3-D like modern eagles and other bird predators. The Morrison Museum in Colorado (left) makes this clear in the eye socket placement, while the Dinosaur Museum in Utah (right) also adds skin.

That means that although their eyes were set on the side of their head, they could see three-dimensional images. One more improvement for capturing prey. Of course, they could swing their head easily from side to side, too, but their eyes worked together, not independently.

All in all, *T. rex* was giant, lightning fast, with excellent vision and sense of smell. In those movies where the scientist says, "Just stay still…" Nuh-uh. That doesn't work. Mr. T can see, hear, and smell you, whether you move or not. The only chance you had, unless you had a handheld rocket at the ready, would be to dart sideways. The only thing *rex* couldn't do very well was change direction or back up.

Well, or pass the salt.

Tiny Arms: A Feature, Not A Bug

Yes, we've all heard the jokes. *T. rex* can't pass the salt. Can't be happy and know it. Can't reach the toilet paper. Because we are mammals with big brains and long arms, we've decided that the relatively short arms of the *Tyrannosaurus* must be proof of its failure. After all, they aren't around anymore, are they?

Fig 68. Barnum's original 1908 skeleton mounted at New York's natural history museum. Note the contrast between size of the square shoulder bones (scapula) compared with arm bones highlighted in white by author.

The paleobiologists will patiently explain, for multiple reasons, that the short arms of Mr. T were evidence of how adaptation works. Humans think the arms are ridiculous because, to humans, arms are vital. But, to *T. rex*, they were a bit unnecessary, and, in fact, a trade-off. As Kenneth Lacovara puts it in his book, *Why Dinosaurs Matter.*

> …the puny arms of *T. Rex* represent one of its greatest strengths…a key adaptation that allowed it to terrorize its landscape and dominate its ecosystem.[58]

---

[58] Kenneth Lacovara, *Why Dinosaurs Matter,* (New York: Simon & Schuster/TED Books, 2017), 58..

How could tiny arms be a successful adaptation? The tyrannosaur's arms got shorter because they just weren't needed. However, success is more than that. Natural selection occurs because the organism (or its genes, over time) chooses a better option. One better option, according to Lacovara, is that arms are a trade-off to other muscles. No body part is "free." The muscles that attach long arms to a shoulder actually compete with other muscles. In particular, the muscles that might attach to a jaw.

Humans (and mammals) don't have giant jaws because we have these long arms. But if you don't need long arms, then you can have a really, really big set of banana-sized, razor-sharp teeth on a jaw that could slice through concrete. Or a ceratopsian skull in one bite.

Besides, the two-fingered, clawed arms did have a function. Once that massive mouth grabbed you by the whatever—neck, leg, arm… oh, you have a loose arm waving about grabbed by a *T. rex*? Too bad you have all those extra unnecessary appendages! Anyway, once Da King had you up close and personal in its teeth, it could use those three-foot-long arms as seam rippers to open your belly up and expose all the good stuff.

But wait—there's more! Kevin Padian of UC Berkeley, further argues that tiny arms were not just small because they were unnecessary and because the jaws were using the muscles. He notes that when the predators fed, sometimes they fed in groups on the same carcass.[59] They also fought with each other because there's been some evidence that the tyrannosaurs might kill and eat each other. Cannibals, too! When they are group-chomping on a hadrosaur, if those big heads dive in for a big bite, anything that has long arms will get in the way. Predators that get their arm chomped off might bleed out. Thus, says Padian, it could be a competitive advantage to have arms too short for your cousin *T. Rexes* to bite off.

Overall, there might be several reasons that tiny arms make a lot of sense. They might have been the perfect complement to an 8,000-pound bite and 60 teeth. If the evolutionary path were reversed, and the tyrannosaurs hadn't been taken out by—volcanoes, asteroid, climate change, whatever—maybe they would have evolved into *Tyrannosaurus* scientists, looking at the absurdly long arms of mammal

---

[59] Robert Sanders, "Why *T. rex* has Tiny Arms," *UCBerkeley Paleontology*, April 7, 2022. https://www.universityofcalifornia.edu/news/why-t-rex-has-tiny-arms

fossils and wondering what Charles Darwinasaurus was thinking. They might have a hard time visualizing the purpose for us.

So we, in turn, can dream about what *T. rexes* were like.

Did they have lips? Probably not, though that generated yet another paleontology study, with too many graphs and new words to learn. Could they see red? Yep. Were the ladies bigger or smaller? They're not sure. They know there were lady *T. rexes* because there are bone cell markers related to egg storage. Could they run fast? Not as fast as a jeep. If you were agile enough, say the stories, you could get away.

I, for one, would not want to find out if I am agile enough.

U is for Unscrupulous

Who owns the bones?

The dinosaurs wandered across all the continents, including Antarctica and Australia. When they lived, they owned the earth. But who owns them now, as they lie buried? If I walk along my land and see a *T. rex* tooth sticking out, big as my hand, I would assume it belongs to me. But if someone pays me to dig fossils on my land, do they get to keep what they find? What if the land is unincorporated? What if it belongs to the government—to the United States, China, Mongolia? To a Native American tribe? A national park? An oil mine?

In addition, there is a complicated relationship between collectors and scientists, between those who find the fossils and those who study the results. Even when collector and scientist is the same person, the results may be tainted when controversy arises over the dig. Three stories from the history of fossil hunting shed light on this messy alliance. Dinosaur mania, then and now, has created incentives for collecting but also exacted a heavy toll on some who do so.

The Bone Wars

Scientists have always disagreed. The spirited debates among the Cuviers, Mantells, Annings, Owens, and Bucklands of 19th-century Britain, as told in Chapters "I" and "M," were comparatively genial. Although there were occasional hard feelings, paleontology moved forward through the buffing and battering. Robert Bakker calls it the "good rule": "Be kind to colleagues, ruthless with theories."[60]

But when money and prestige become involved, the environment changes. When the public's interest is piqued, the chance for notoriety and for a paying audience either to flock to a museum or buy a newspaper, then non-scientific entities change the mix. When men race to be the first, sometimes they don't follow the unspoken rules of scientific cordiality. That's what happened in the American Bone Wars of the 1870s.

The story of scientific rivalry between Edward Drinker Cope and Othniel Charles Marsh is told in wonderful detail elsewhere, such as in David Rains Wallace's excellent *The Bonehunters' Revenge*. Cope and Marsh were both brilliant paleontologists with access to wealth and influence. Hard-working and scientifically knowledgeable, they were also both quarrelsome, distrustful, and competitive. In their passion to be recognized, they left science in the dust.

Cope's family made its fortune in shipping. Well-educated, he was a wunderkind, a university professor at age 24, already churning out papers. He would publish over 1400 in his career, sometimes rushing to print before his work had been carefully checked. Marsh's background was less affluent, although he had a rich uncle. Marsh convinced Uncle George Peabody, to help fund a natural history museum at Yale, with Marsh as a director. Ten years older than Cope, Marsh was slower to advance in academia, more circumspect about publishing. Perhaps when they met in 1863 in Berlin, Marsh found the younger man's eager brilliance irritating. Later, when Cope showed Marsh his favorite fossil pit in New Jersey, Marsh secretly paid the pit owner to send all future discoveries to Yale.

A few years later, Cope wrote a paper that included a description of a plesiosaur skeleton. He incorrectly placed the head on the tail end, an error captured in the illustration. He showed the printed publication to Marsh, who gleefully noted the error. Cope then attempted to buy up all the available copies, but Marsh secured one, happily showing it to anyone who mentioned the other guy.

---

[60] Robert T. Bakker, *The Dinosaur Heresies: New Theories Unlocking the Mystery of the Dinosaurs and their Extinction* (New York: Zebra Books, 1986), 27.

Fig 69. Original Charles R. Knight illustration for Cope's 1869 article, with the head
of the plesiosaur (called *Elasmosaurus* by Cope) incorrectly placed on the tail.

Beginning in the 1870s, both paleontologists moved west in
search of new bones to fuel their publications and prestige. Their
tactics in searching for fossils, allegedly for the Philadelphia and Yale
museums, became increasingly underhanded. One would bribe the
other's workmen to smuggle out finds. The other would send spies
between camps. They used dynamite to get the fossils out as quickly
as possible, destroying other bones and fossils. After an excavation
was finished, they would fill in the pit, making it difficult for anyone
else to know what had been done. They would send telegrams after
partial finds, hoping to be credited far in advance of publication.

Meanwhile, a growing news media found the pictures of bones—
and the stories of sabotage—fascinating. Both men aired their
grievances in salacious accounts with tabloid papers such as the *New
York Herald*. The scientific community was appalled. Paleontology
was barely decades old, and now it was being trashed by the slash-
and-burn tactics out west.

Eventually, both men exhausted their financial resources and
ruined their personal reputations. Cope died in 1897 but first
managed to spearhead a large magazine spread: "Strange Creatures of
the Past" in *American Century*, which included the famous *Leaping*

Laelaps (Figure 10). Marsh was irked that the story highlighted Cope's years of success, as if he had single-handedly driven the knowledge of dinosaurs forward. In the end, Marsh discovered and named far more dinosaur species—80 to Cope's 56.

The Bone Wars helped initially fan the flames of dino-mania for the American public, who became eager to see more of the strange new creatures. From the 1905 *New York Times* announcement of the *T. rex* to Spielberg's velociraptors in 1993's *Jurassic Park* to the present day, the public has remained fascinated. But the vicious competition between the two rival paleontologists soured the funding for exhibitions, and the money, which dried up in the Depression and world wars, did not return for a long time. Many were relieved when the frenzied Fossil Find was over.

Fast-forward a century, and that frenzy would begin again.

Sue, Stan, and the FBI

The renewed public interest in dinosaurs sparked in the 1980s has now become a double-edged sword. The dinosaur renaissance generated new ways to imagine the past, as paleontologists upended musty old taxonomies. Museums repositioned those dragging tails to be balancing acts for lively, warm-blooded dinosaurs, and meat-eaters suddenly sprouted feathers. As film and television transformed dry academic diagrams into running, roaring reptiles, suddenly everyone wanted to see dinos. I'm not gonna lie—the current public enthusiasm for paleontology is part of why I wrote this book.

But if the last few decades have seen a renaissance for dinosaur hunting in general, it has also rekindled the debate over how science ought to be conducted. Increasing amounts paid for fossils have raised hard questions. Should science remain pure, above the interference of governments or the sordid marketplace of commercial collecting? Is that even possible? Who, then, funds the digging? And who gets to decide what a skeleton is worth and where it should be displayed? No case exhibits these issues more than the story of Sue the tyrannosaur.

Sue was named for fossil hunter Sue Hendrickson, part of a team of fossil experts from the Black Hills Institute of South Dakota. On a dig in 1990, Hendrickson spotted bones in an area outside their initial excavation area. The result yielded a *Tyrannosaurus* skeleton nearly 90% complete, one of the best specimens ever found. Peter Larson, leader of the Black Hills group, had paid a hefty $5,000 to the landowner, Maurice Williams, for permission to dig, hoping for a few good fossils to justify the investment. This exceeded his expectations.

There was only one problem. The Black Hills Institute was a private, for-profit corporation, which specialized in extricating, replicating, and selling dinosaur bones. They were scientists; Larson had dozens of scientific publications to his credit. They dug carefully, reconstructing skeletons meticulously. They got permits. They didn't use dynamite, steal fossils, commit sabotage, or make outrageous claims. But they did participate in the dinosaur fossil market.

Fig 70. Photo from inside the Black Hills Institute, 2011, showing their highly valuable inventory of fossil finds.

Scientists with degrees in chemistry, physics, or geology go to work for private industry without anyone batting an eyelash. With paleontology, however, there is a view that the fossils are somehow a resource that belongs to the public, and that those who dig for profit are plundering. Maybe if Sue the *T. rex* had also not been so perfect, what happened next would not have happened.

The Black Hills team spent 17 days pulling out the bones. It's tedious work, as each bone must be carefully encased in a plaster cast for transport. Then it must be re-extracted in the lab and submitted to a painstaking removal of plaster, dirt, and rock. Think of Mark Mitchell and the *Borealopelta* skin, spending five years removing it from the rock.

As landowner Maurice Williams watched Larson and his team extract the bones, he wondered if Sue might be worth more than $5,000. He asked Larson for more money, arguing that the money was for permission to dig, and anything found was extra. When Larson rebuffed him, Williams went to the authorities. Then, it got really messy.

Williams was a member of the Sioux tribe, which meant that the tribe believed it owned the dinosaur. Except that the US Bureau of Land Management controls what happens on Sioux land. Williams also owed a lot of back taxes to the IRS. The US Government suddenly had a stake in the outcome. On top of that, there had been previous complaints that the Black Hills collectors were taking some fossils from public land and had some illegal imports.

Roughly 18 months after Sue's extraordinary discovery, the FBI and the South Dakota National Guard raided the Black Hills Institute. Larson and team had no warning. One day, local kids were donating money to the museum from a bake sale and technicians were scraping off dirt with X-acto knives; the next, FBI agents were tossing every vertebrae, claw, and tooth into boxes.

Peter Larson was charged with 158 counts, although from other fossils seized, not because of the Sue skeleton. Sue sat in boxes for months as the trial proceeded. In the end, a jury convicted Larson on only four counts: two felonies for having brought back Japanese traveler's cheques ("overseas cash") without filing customs reports, and two misdemeanors related to taking a fossil worth less than $100 from public land in Montana. Despite the minimal nature of the offenses, however, the judge imposed a harsh penalty, sentencing Larson to two years in prison. Apparently, he thought it would send a message to deter private fossil collectors.

Five years later, Sue's skeleton was auctioned under the government's direction for a record price of $8.4 million. If the message was that collecting doesn't pay, that message was turned upside down. The proceeds went to Maurice Williams, with the Black Hills Institute receiving nothing, despite prepping Sue's skeleton for sale in the first place.

The winning bid went to the Field Museum of Chicago, in combination with a consortium of universities and corporate partners. The Chicago museum now advertises Sue as a marquee attraction, facing her away from the admission desk, where $45 must be paid before she can be seen (the admission covers the whole museum, not just Sue). I stopped by a few years ago but only had 20 minutes and could not bring myself to pony up that much money for so little time. I managed a shaky photo standing on a bench near the coat room.

Fig 71. Author's cheapskate blurry photo of Sue at the Field Museum in Chicago, 2017.

It's unclear what lessons might be learned from the case. Kevin Schieffer, the South Dakota prosecutor who pursued the case with relentless zeal, may have been angling for permanent appointment as the US Attorney for South Dakota. If so, the negative publicity and his heavy-handed tactics ultimately tanked his nomination. For Peter Larson, what started as a contract dispute with Williams ended up costing him dearly, although he returned to the Institute, which still operates in 2024 as it had before. Probably the Institute has become more careful with its paperwork. Maurice Williams got a $7.6 million windfall, though the IRS likely took its share. Ultimately, the Field Museum seemed to gain the most from the event, as its revenue is now more than $90 million annually.

If the goal was to reduce the likelihood of for-profit fossil hunting, the results probably did not achieve it. If anything, Sue's high auction price upped the ante. In order to resolve another contract dispute, the Black Hills Institute was later forced to sell another Tyrannosaurus skeleton, "Stan." Stan's 2020 auction fetched $31 million, and a museum in Abu Dhabi, expected to open in late 2025, claims Stan will be their featured attraction. As of now, the payoff for diggers is higher than ever, although so are the risks for shady behavior.

US vs. One Tyrannosaurus Bataar

The collectors noticed the financial payoff. Shady behavior remains shady. In another high-profile example from 2012, a fossil collector and importer from Florida named Eric Prokopi was arrested for attempting to auction an entire *Tarbosaurus bataar* skeleton that came from Mongolia. Suddenly, international political strategy became part of the deal. Because Mongolia does not allow unauthorized removal of its dinosaur bones, they asked for help from the United States in policing collectors. Mongolia, sitting strategically between Russia and China, is vital to America's Asian strategy. The United States was happy to help Mongolia enforce its laws against paleontology smuggling.

Eric Prokopi might have wanted to pay more attention to geopolitics. Instead, he built his career as a commercial fossil collector: digging, buying, and selling in the thriving market for old bones and rocks. Unlike Larson, Cope, and Marsh, Prokopi had no paleontology degree and had published no papers. He had simply spent his life digging up bones, and he supported a family from those excavations.

While the paleontology community may frown on those who dig up fossils for money, they have relied on amateurs since the days of Mary Anning. Entire conventions have cropped up, for example, in Tucson, which bills its Gem, Mineral and Fossil Showcase as the "New York Stock Exchange of the mineral world."[61] Scientists are also not the only ones in search of fossils. Prokopi had sold bones to celebrities like Leonardo DiCaprio and Nicolas Cage. The wealthy liked having dinosaur bones in their living room, displayed next to other antiques like Civil War pistols or African masks.

---

[61] Paige Williams, *The Dinosaur Artist: Obsession, Betrayal, and the Global Quest for Fossils* (New York: Hachette Books, 2018), 55.

The richest source of dinosaur fossils at the moment is from overseas, in particular, the Gobi desert in Mongolia. The Gobi has benefited from the tectonic drama of the Himalayas, combined with its dry climate, perfect for preserving old bones. Mongolia happens to be a poor country, recently democratized after the breakup of the Soviet Union.

Aside from its nomads, yurts, and fermented mare's milk, Mongolia is primarily known for mining. While they want to build a dinosaur tourism industry, they do not want to create a dinosaur mining industry. Whatever is found in the Mongolian soil, the Mongolian government would like it to stay in Mongolia.

Despite Mongolian laws, though, the Mongolian black market for dinosaur fossils is thriving. At least Prokopi thought so, because he saw Asian bones sold at the Tucson exchange and openly on the internet. Though he was aware of the strict laws against Mongolia exporting fossils, he thought dinosaur bones advertised online in catalogs suggested lax enforcement. He arranged with a Mongolian dealer to purchase several items and flew to the Gobi to observe the dig. He had a shopping list that included an openly advertised *Tarbosaurus bataar* skeleton. *Tarbosaurus* is in the tyrannosaur family, though a separate genus, but close enough for Prokopi to pay several thousands of dollars to the dealer. He flew to Mongolia multiple times to ensure the crates were shipped. The customs paperwork listed the source as Great Britain. He viewed that part as "red tape."

Prokopi then contracted with a New York auction house to sell the *T. bataar* skeleton, listing its start value as $1 million. Several people knowledgeable about Mongolian dinosaurs saw it. Tarbosaurs have only been found in one place: Mongolia. The suspicious scientists contacted the US District Attorney for New York, who launched a case, originally misidentifying the fossil: *US vs. One Tyrannosaurus Bataar Skeleton.*

Fig 72. US Immigration and Customs Enforcement (ICE) returning the *T. Bataar* skeleton to the government of Mongolia, 2013.

Prokopi was charged with multiple counts of smuggling fossils out of a foreign country, falsifying documents, and possessing stolen property. Though he was still confused about why activities that other people practiced so openly were wrong, he pled guilty. His sentence was relatively light—only six months. He served three months in a minimum-security prison and three months house arrest, ended his marriage, liquidated his assets to pay fines and legal fees, and was last seen heading away in a boat off the coast of southern Florida.

None of this may deter future fossil collectors. While risks have made it more costly for them to cut corners, the paleontology industry—universities and museums—still benefits from their finds. Andrew Carnegie bought himself and the city of Pittsburgh a beautiful *Diplodocus*. Sue the *T. rex* graces the immense hallway in Chicago, although you have to pay a high price to see her face. Museums for the wealthy, in places like Hong Kong or Dubai, will continue to pay; they may or may not inspect the paperwork for the place of origin.

It's an ongoing mess. Cope and Marsh vied with each other to be the first and collect the most, setting a tone that still hangs like a pall over the public perception of collectors. Peter Larson operated in plain sight, meticulously documenting and preparing his work, but was punished harshly, in part by a grandstanding prosecutor. Eric Prokopi also operated in plain sight but was just one among many in a crowded field of illicit smugglers. Perhaps the outcome reduced the open market of exporters offering bones from the Gobi. Mongolia, at least, did build a museum around their repatriated *Tarbosaurus bataar*.

Four months ago, in July of 2024, a fully mounted *Stegosaurus* skeleton was auctioned for $44.6 million. It had been found by a "commercial paleontologist" on his property in Colorado, after which he spent two years extracting and preparing it for sale. You can bet he had paperwork to show that he owned the land where he said he found it. The buyer was Ken Griffin, a multi-billionaire owner of a hedge fund. Griffin promises to lend it to a museum.

V is for Variety

Gone are the days when all the dinosaurs were drawn the same way: green, tail-draggin', oversized lizards. If there's one thing the dinosaurs are known for now—other than *not* being green, tail-dragging, or lizards—it's that there were so many different kinds of them, all shapes and sizes. As we near the end of this alphabetic tour, it's a perfect time to think about those Guinness World Records.

This chapter will be about the -ests. The biggest, smallest, smartest, dumbest, earliest, and so on. We might enthusiastically begin with the weirdest. This is *Deinocheirus*—*deino* (dreadful/terrible) + *cheirus* (hand)—pronounced dy-no-KY-rus. Or D.K., he might say.

Fig 73. *Deinocheirus* had thick arms ending in long, sharp claws. He also had a duck bill, a long tail, and a hump-shaped back. There's no proof that he had a turkey-style skin wattle but, why not? He had everything else.

He was named "dreadful hand" because in 1965, only the eight-foot-long arms with their giant-clawed hands were found. Fifty years passed until other, more complete skeletons were found in 2015. Upon assembly, the resulting animal was absurd and surprising. But fossil hunters had found more than one skeleton.

D.K. had the longest arms of any biped—remember, the big predators had short arms—plus the duck bill, long tail, and a hump on its back. It was not an artist's view of a "conceptual" hump of fat, either. That is the way the bones fit together and were found with the skeleton. We have to trust that paleontologists, with their two found skeletons, were able to put this jigsaw puzzle together correctly. There have been plenty of cases where so many bones are mixed together, the head was put on the tail end and so forth. But this, apparently, is not one of them.

Deinocheirus was an omnivore, capable of eating plants as well as other small animals. Do you suppose they died laughing before he swallowed them whole? Did I mention… no teeth?

Size Matters

The hallmark of dinosaurs from the beginning was their size. They were discovered *because* they were huge. It was only later that paleontologist could even distinguish between bone fragments from the big boys and entire bones of their smaller cousins.

The biggest among the titanosaurs was either *Argentinosaurus* (from Arg—oh, you can figure that out?) or *Patagotitan* (also from you-know-where). Both weighed around 70 to 90 tons, which might be metric tons or regular tons depending on who wrote the study, but it doesn't matter. They were realllly big, ranging in length from 40 to 45 m (45 to 50 yds).

As soon as you get measurements, of course, you start wondering, well, how much is that? Football fields are handy just because many people have seen them. For reference, a 757 aircraft weighs around 100 tons and is about 40 m, so visualize a living, stalking creature that looks like a giant airplane. Not a small, light plane like *Quetzalcoatlus*, but a jumbo jet. Imagine it, walking around on a football field, waving its intensely long neck around and wondering where all the veggies went. Forty meters is also the world record (officially Guinness WR) for flinging a Frisbee, so imagine throwing a Frisbee as long as a dinosaur!

Of course, there are other ways to define big. The tallest dinosaur was 60 feet off the ground, *Sauroposeidon proteles*. That's Godzilla territory—the first Godzilla, that is ("G"). *S. proteles* was even bigger than the *Brachiosaurus*, which once was thought to be the tallest. The longest tail, already mentioned, is *Diplodocus*—he got his own entire chapter. The longest end-to-end was *Supersaurus*, perhaps 45 m. That's the one nearly half a football field.

Fig 74. Relative sizes of biggest (titanosaur) and smallest (parvicursor) dinosaur types, with human "twins" for comparison.

Just the femur, the top leg bone, of these titanosaurs could reach seven feet. Figure 74 compares a titanosaur with a human, though it's not even the biggest dinosaur, just one that helps us compare big dinosaur to humans to small dinosaurs.

One question for the titanosaurs is how did they "get" so big? To be more precise, how and why did they adapt to their environment to become 50 m tall? Remember that much of the environment where these guys lived was swampy and humid, ideal for lots of plants. Having a lot of plants would not make dinosaurs grow physically giant, but a tall-plant environment could provide an opportunity for a plant-eating population as a whole to thrive.

Think about the "natural selection" point of view for both the plants and dinosaurs. Plants competed for carbon dioxide, for space, and for sunlight. One way for a plant to compete with other plants is to grow taller and closer to the sun. That means more tall plants, which would mean animals who grew taller—like *Brachiosaurus* or *Argentinosaurus*—could gain an advantage in being the only ones tall enough to nibble the tasty treetops.

The other type of growth to consider is maturity. Kristi Rogers spent years studying sauropods, focusing on their maturity rate. Their eggs were the size of "soccer balls."[62] They were large but not propeller-sized. How can you get from a soccer ball to covering half a soccer field? (No, it's not by kicking it hard.) The conventional wisdom, before Rogers and her ilk started looking in microscopes, was that sauropods were long-lived and might take 70 to 100 years to grow that big. Rogers discovered that's not the case.

Paleontologists can look at shavings off bone and analyze these things called osteoblasts, bone-forming cells (*osteo*=bone), which have primary and secondary growth patterns. Think of tree rings and imagine the ability to see speed and pattern of growth in the bone. Scientists were able to look at the bone growth markers of dinosaurs and compare them with modern animals. Which modern animals had similar bone-growth markers? Not reptiles—birds.

The sauropods specifically had bone-growth markers closer to birds and even some mammals. Not every dinosaur grows the same way; not every sauropod grows the same way. Large sauropods, said Rogers, were closer to animals that grew quickly. They might put on 50 pounds a day when they were younger, and they could grow 40 times faster than modern reptiles. That's how something the size of a soccer ball would be hitting the three-story ceiling of the Museum of Natural History by the time it was 20 years old.

So much for the biggest of the big. Small dinosaurs, naturally, have been much harder to find. More have been found in recent times, for two reasons. First, opening up more fossil sites in places like southern Argentina and the Gobi desert made more sites available that were not viewed before. Who knows how many tiny dinosaurs Cope and Marsh blew up with dynamite in their Bone Wars? Second, new technology allows for more careful extraction. There are scanning tools that can see inside a few layers of soil to find smaller bones ("X").

Even so, small dinosaurs are hard to spot. The smallest of the non-bird dinosaurs, *Parvicursor remotus* ("small runner from far away") was only about 15 inches long. Let's go back to Figure 74. The

---

[62] Rogers, *Dinosaurs*, 118.

titanosaurs like *Rinconsaurus* could have a 20 m neck with some vertebrae individually as tall as our human Twin #1. *Parvicursor* might have a vertebrae that would be half the size of Twin #2s thumb. Talk about variation!

Brain Matters, Too

If you try to research the "dumbest" dinosaur, there is only one candidate and for only one reason. The *Stegosaurus* has long been described has having a tiny brain because it has only a small space in its itty-bitty skull. It carries the distinction for having the biggest contrast between brain case and body size of most any known creature. It's also the second- or third-most recognizable dinosaur in the world—go ahead, ask any five-year-old. Awfully famous, if it is dumb. Maybe not so dumb, really, huh?

In the 19th century, paleontologists like Marsh (of the Bone Wars) argued that *Stegosaurus* had a second brain because it had an open area above its hip cavity. He thought perhaps it led to an expansion of the spinal cord in the bones. Today, scientists think it was likely something else, perhaps a glycogen body. Birds have glycogen bodies in their lower parts to store extra energy. Once and for all, we should at least debunk the rumor: *Stegosaurus* did not have a second brain!

At the same time, all we have is the size of its skull. We don't know for sure how big the soft tissue of the brain was. Smaller animals do tend to have smaller brains, but there isn't a rule of thumb here. Animals have a brain that helps them adapt to the environment; if they have other useful features, they don't need a better brain. Moreover, it's not just brain size that matters, but how many wrinkles the brain has and how many different brain regions named after French and German Enlightenment biologists. Maybe stego actually had a very wrinkly brain! We don't know. Maybe he was shamming, and just pretending to be dumb.

Relative brain size has been what got *Stegosaurus* in the shame house. It's also what elevated a theropod named *Troodon*. (*Troodon*= wounding teeth). *Troodon* was thought to be the smartest dinosaur because, even though it was roughly human-sized, it had a large space for a brain. Apparently, that made *Troodon* the class nerd. Wonder if the *Allosaurus* used to give him wedgies? (Ha—just kidding. *Troodon* came from the late Cretaceous, way later than *Allosaurus*, so he was probably bullied by the *T. rexes*.)

Aging Gracefully

Our terrible lizard friends lasted for 185 million years. Across that span, it has been easier to find later period dinosaurs than earlier ones, simply because the later ones are buried closer to the surface. The one they had to dig for the deepest, the one dating back to the earliest time in the Triassic, was a little fellow called the *Eoraptor: eos* (dawn) + *raptor* (plunderer).

Eoraptor was a sauropod, but a very early one, not one of the giants. He was human-sized, perhaps five feet long and three feet tall. With his long legs, he was likely bipedal and had small, grasping hands. *Eoraptor* emerged during the early Triassic, a time period when the smallish mammals, early lizards, and crocodiles were all still pushing each other around. This was 230 million years under the earth, give or take a few hundred thousand.

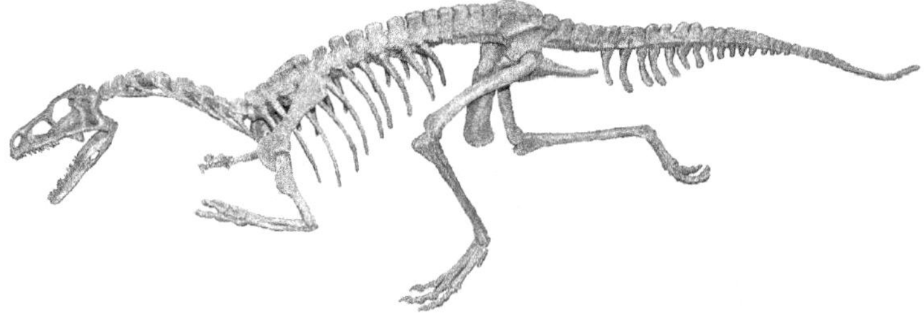

Fig 75. Skeleton of *Eoraptor*, perhaps the oldest known dinosaur, dating back to 230 my ago.

Which is the latest or most recent dinosaur to our time is a harder question to resolve. Remember that it's believed at the end of the Cretaceous that a big ball of dirt slammed into the earth. This happened near a time when most of the "extreme" dinosaurs had evolved. Natural selection by the late Cretaceous had created the tallest, fiercest, and weirdest dinosaurs. Adaptation gone wild!

Of the Cretaceous non-avians that went extinct, one of the last to appear before the K-Pg boundary was a well-known genus—*Triceratops*—our buddy with the three horns, the head frill, and beaked nose. He emerged some 65 my ago, which is very close to the K-Pg boundary. After the boundary, no more non-avian dinosaurs remained, or at least none have been found.

Even if you land in one of those camps that believes some non-avian dinosaurs were already disappearing before the Cretaceous ended or think that volcanoes might have had a bigger effect on extinction than the flaming giant in space, you still know that whatever killed off the non-birds killed them all. Notice my careful words here. Birds survived, and birds had existed before the Cretaceous ended, so birds—dinosaurs—technically survived.

Mammals survived as well, since those little *Morganucodons* (Figure 51) were around both before and after the you-know-what may or may not have done the deed. The only creatures that survived the boundary among the mammals and birds did so because: a) they were small; b) they lived in dark or with dim light; and c) they ate insects or seeds rather than plants or other animals. The ground-dwelling scavengers in their heyday! All the better to hide from the *T. rex* and the meteoric sword of death. Kind of clever. Might give that brainy *Troodon* a run for its money.

W is for Wings

The flying dinosaur is a tricky concept. If you research "flying dinosaur," you find links to a hundred sites that refer to pterosaurs. A few might bother to put "flying dinosaur" in quotes, but the big search sites (MSN, YouTube, Live Science, etc.) do not. Let's all join hands and say it together: *pterosaurs are not dinosaurs. There were no flying dinosaurs—oh, wait!*

Pterosaurs were on a branch of the family tree that split off before the dinosaurs developed. Different main branch. Now that we have that out of the way, they were also cool! Just look at the bones, the arms, the wings!!!! (Remember "Q")? Even if they weren't flying dinosaurs, we can still slip in a bit of information about the pterosaurs, just here near the end.

Plus, we still have to tiptoe around the words: non-avian and avian dinosaurs. Avian dinosaur is the paleontologist's way of saying birds. The *Avialea* branch on the clade emerged from the theropod, meat-eating dudes to become birds, i.e., flying dinosaurs. Every other kind of dinosaur was non-avian by definition. We know that some had feathers, but none of them could fly. But, oh, those feathers!

This chapter is going to take a closer look at all of the above: the pterosaurs, the wings, the feathers, the development of flight, and the missing link that changed the dinosaur family tree.

Pterrible Gliders

Pteron is Greek for wing, so pterosaurs were "winged lizards." Pterosaur is an Order, a clade of clades of clades. To get closer to the beasts, let's think about the genus of *Pteranodon,* "toothless" (*o-don*) and winged, or of pterodactyls, who were winged and "fingered" (*dactyl*). Like the dinosaurs, these flying lizards also came in a variety of shapes and sizes, although most of the skeletons found have been larger than modern birds. After all, *Quetzalcoatlus* had a 50-foot wingspan.

Don't forget, though, this means fossils found of pterosaurs were bigger than birds. Pterosaur bones were hollow, just like bird bones. If there were small hollow-boned flying reptiles, it is possible their fossils did not last. For instance, the ten-inch one, *Nemicolopterus,* was only found in China in the 2010s. It was only in 2023 that researchers were trying to determine where it fit on the clade. We could all be sitting a thousand feet up from a treasure trove of tiny pterosaur bones and never know it.

Nevertheless, most of the pterosaurs studied so far were bigger than birds. For most of them as well, their wingspans were longer than they were tall, which means they were primarily gliders. To understand why, we have to look at wing anatomy for a bit. Now that I think about it, I probably should have labeled this section Pterrific Gliders rather than Pterrible Gliders.

The Anatomy of Bats and Birds

Understanding flight, whether for pterosaurs or birds, should start with arm and wing anatomy. As we know, looking at living examples is a great way to understand body mechanics for extinct animals. To see how wings are designed, we can look at modern fliers for comparison. In fact, it can make sense for us to look at humans first, even though we don't fly. At least, we don't without a metal shell, a tray table, and an assigned seat.

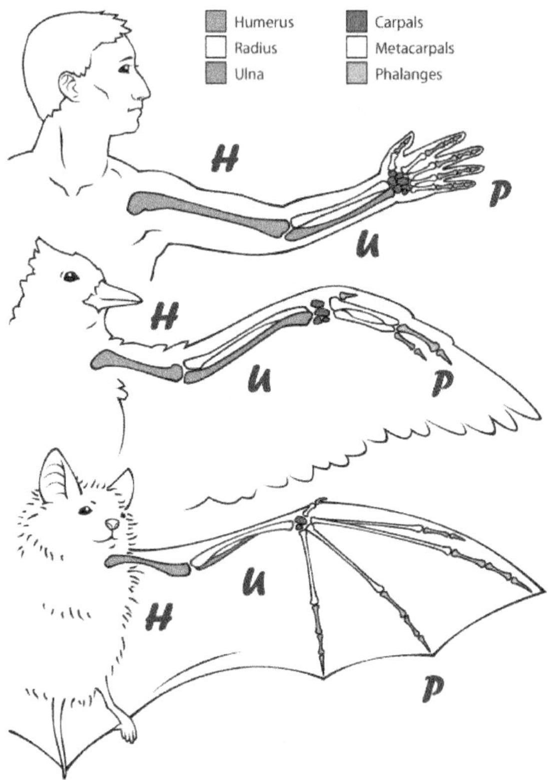

Fig 76. Comparative arm bones for humans, birds, and bats. Note the different length and placement of humerus (H), Ulna (U), and Phalanges (P).

Figure 76 compares the arm bones for modern "animals," including humans. The upper arm bone is the humerus, while the lower arm pieces include the radius (top bone) and the ulna (bottom). In birds and bats, the humerus is far shorter than that of humans. However, the ulna and radius are about the same in proportionate length. In all cases, the wrist bone, the carpal, is where the hand and finger bones attach (metacarpals and phalanges). This is where it gets really interesting.

In birds, the metacarpals, those bones humans see in the back of the hand, are reduced from five to two. Three of those metacarpals and their respective "fingers" are fused into a single little nub. The other two fingers, by themselves, support the end of the wing. The flight feathers of birds are then suspended from all of these key bones, the lower arm bones as well as the two finger bones.

In addition, the design of a bird's wing, including its layer of feathers, is thicker at the front and thinner at the back, like a plane's wing. This thick-and-thin combination creates their ability to lift through differentiated air pressure, which is that thing that some of us don't like to think about when on a plane, since it means we're flying on nothing but science. Also in birds, the wings attach with powerful muscles to a pronounced breastbone, one much pointier than ours. This allows birds to flap and lift practically straight upward.

Turning to bats, the story changes again. Bats have the same radius and ulna arm bones, but their metacarpals and phalanges, their fingers, extend considerably outward to become wing support. A skin membrane attaches from the outside of these fingers, which reaches down to their tail. Bats have evolved a different way to fly, even though bats are mammals and not reptiles.

The fact that three different creatures can all fly, though they emerge from very different branches on the tree, is called *convergent evolution*. Flight evolved as an adaptation for each of them in a completely different way. Flying is, thus, a behavioral adaptation, no more specialized than counter-shading or plant-eating. The reptilian bones of a pterosaur still have more in common with their lizard cousins than with bats or birds. Flight evolved to help different types of animals acquire food and survive. Humans only find it remarkable because we don't have wings.

The Anatomy of Ptero Wings

Because fossil hunters have discovered many complete pterosaur skeletons, they know how the bones attached. From the early days forward, based on the way the arms were constructed and because the bones were hollow, scientists knew they were fliers. But exactly how did the wings work?

The pterosaur skeletal anatomy has the same humerus, radius, ulna, and phalange bones as other animals. They have a large breastbone compared with other mammals, but a smaller one than that of birds, with fewer places for muscle attachments. Then, they have a shortened humerus, a long ulna, and a single, long metacarpal which ends in four phalanges (fingers). Three of those fingers sit on a wing "knuckle," while the fourth extends outward to hold the entire wing. Yep, the ring finger as humans would call it, held a pterosaur's wing. And, remember, 50-FOOT-LONG WINGS. That's some big finger!

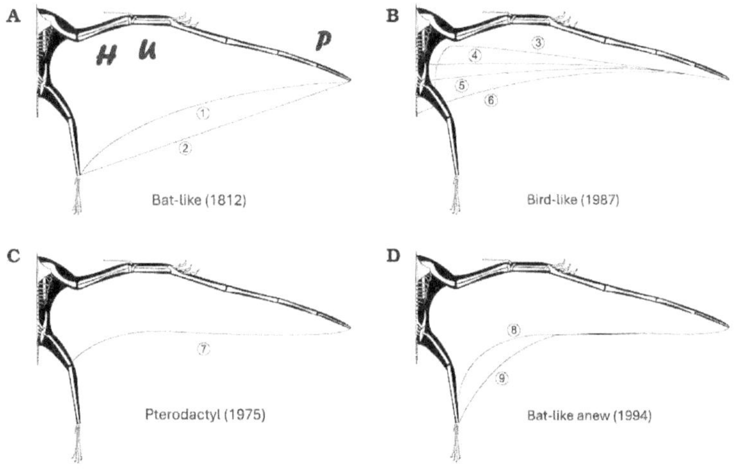

Fig 77. The pterosaur bones compared to the human arm (see previous Figure 76—H, U, P) with the fourth elongated finger holding the wing. But where did the membrane attach? Paleobiologist had at least four different points of view.

The big question was where the skin membrane attached. In the mid-19th century, the scientists looked at the bats and thought that the wing membrane attached to the knees. Others preferred the bird example and believed the wing membrane attached to the tail bone. During the 20th century, the pterosaurs were drawn with wings in between, with the attachment near the knees. The pterosaurs that many of us grew up seeing had that look, flying with their knees and feet swinging free. Most recently, the view has returned to the bat model. Without the preservation of soft tissue, this has so far been speculation. Perhaps different species on the pterosaur tree had different adaptations.

All of these structures, though, would have made pterosaurs excellent gliders because they provide a wide, horizontal frame skin that allow the animals to sit above the air currents. Pterosaurs were light-boned, so they likely stayed aloft for a long time. Because of their gliding abilities, most of them were thought to live near coastal regions and survive on fish or small animals. But if they dove into the water, it might be hard for them—as gliders—to get back aloft. They would have to skim the water and not dive. *Quetzalcoatlus* was not a skimmer, but other pterosaurs could have been.

Another big problem is: how did they get off the ground in the first place? While there was debate about whether *Qu* could fly at all, the current view is that he could. But the issue is similar for other pterosaurs because they did not appear to have a muscle structure, like birds, that allowed for a vertical lift. They could not spring into the air.

Those who study pterosaurs think they might have used the other three fingers (i.e., "a knuckle") as part of a walking and flying mechanism. Researcher Michael Habib ("Q") thinks a pterosaur would start walking with all four limbs on the ground, use its knuckles to push, then at speed open its wings, and push upward. This method means they did not have to live up in a tree or wind cave somewhere, but could start from the ground and go up, even if they did not burst directly upward as birds do.

A-R-C-H-....Bird-o-Saur

The logical ending to a discussion about flying reptiles and wings should be a close look at the dinosaur that started the whole bird discussion in the first place. This is the *Archaeopteryx*. He was discovered in a German limestone quarry around 1861. This smashed fossil looked like other dinosaurs, except that preserved in the limestone was the distinct impression of feathers.

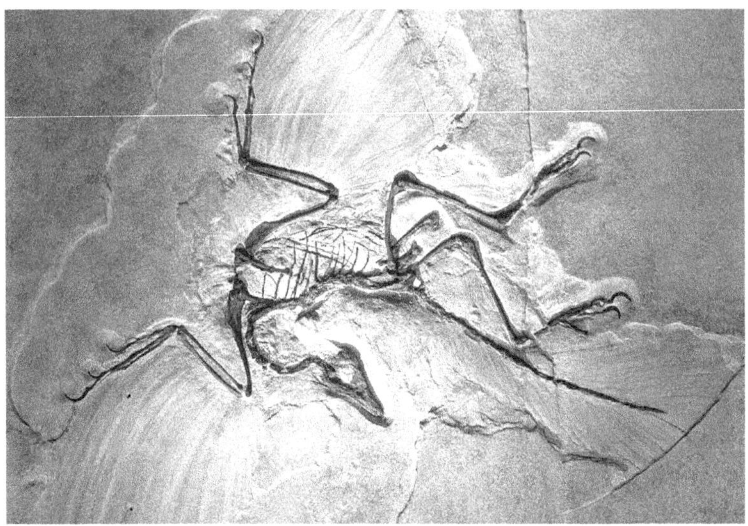

Fig 78. The 1861 *Archaeopteryx* fossil found in a German quarry. Note the impressions of feathers around the arms and down the tail.

Since the 1860s, more than a dozen sets of bones have been discovered in German quarries which have feathery impressions along their limbs. They named the genus *Archaeopteryx*, meaning *archae* (ancient) + *feneopteryx* (wing). It also means hard to spell. The Germans even had their own original name *Urvogel*, Primeval Bird, a.k.a. easier to spell.

At the time of discovery, naturalists believed this was the prototype of the first bird. They did not group it with the dinosaurs or reptiles, even though they knew from the soil that it was a late Jurassic creature. It was still early enough in fossil analysis that they did not immediately imagine anything feathered as a "reptile," but instead "early bird with weird skeleton."

Based on the fossil, *Archaeopteryx* was large for a bird, the size of a raven, perhaps a foot-and-a-half, beak to tail. As with other fliers, its bones were light but its upper arms likely supported wings. Unlike birds, this animal had teeth, three fingers plus claws, and a long tail. These were reptilian markers. You'd think they would have known.

Still, it took a full century until John Ostrom, a leader of that dinosaur renaissance, put *Archaeopteryx* back into the limelight. Some in the 1860s had noted that the small flier might have been a link between reptiles and birds, but the big-name biologists at the time paid no attention.

By 1961, Ostrom had two advantages. First, far more examples of feathered fossils had been found for him to examine. Second, he found how own new type, *Deinonychus*, and was able to match parts of *Deinonychus* with parts of *Archaeopteryx*. Thus, *Archaeopteryx* turned out to be a kind of missing link, but on the reptile branch not a separate bird branch. Once Ostrom could conclude that feathered dinosaurs were still dinosaurs, a cascading set of logic emerged. If chickens are close to *T. rexes*, then it changes both how we think about chickens and about *T. rex*.

Ostrom's also joined the debate about how *Archaeopteryx* might have used those feathers. Just as many had mulled over how pterosaurs could get off the ground, their scientist friends wondered how birds had learned to fly. They could see that *Archaeopteryx* was small, light-boned, with a long, feathered tail. O. C. Marsh, the Bone Wars guy, published a theory that birds began as tree dwellers who leapt downward and ended up improving their gliding. Those heavy-duty claws could have helped them climb trees, and being tree-borne might have offered protection from some predators.

Ostrom thought a "ground up" approach made more sense than "trees down."[63] The bipedal nature of the reptiles made them good runners. Over time—again, over many generations of dino-birds, not in a single lifetime—some might jump to catch prey, like insects. Those who grew feathers *and* had shorter tails *and* jumped up to catch insects would have an advantage. Over generations, those who could leap higher and higher could catch more insects. Eventually, their grandchildren might be floating for short spans. *Their* grandchildren would add more feathers, stronger muscles attached to bigger breastbones, and differentiated wing thickness. Ba-da-bing—they're flying!

In summary, just as not everything that swims is a fish, not everything that flies is a bird. Some of the ancient fliers had long hands, while others just one long finger. Some jumped up, some glided, and some flew down. All of them had to be light-boned. One thing is a certainty: More fossils are being found every day, especially

---

[63] John H. Ostrom, "The Origin of Birds," *Annual Review of Earth and Planetary Sciences,* 3:1 (May 1975): 55–77.

with better technology. Paleontologists are getting increasingly clever about digging out smashed little guys from their resting places in the deep underground. What we know about the fliers could still keep changing.

X is for X-ray

Cutting-edge X-ray technology is providing researchers with unprecedented insights into the ancient world of dinosaurs. On World Dinosaur Day, scientists are unveiling the hidden secrets of the Harbury Ichthyosaur, a marine reptile that inhabited Earth millions of years ago, using advanced X-ray imaging techniques and 3-D reconstruction.[64]

Scienceblog.com

They can X-ray—

—hold on!!! World Dinosaur Day? **Why isn't World Dinosaur Day a bigger holiday**?!?!?!? Mark your calendars, people, World Dinosaur Day is June 1st!

Meanwhile, guess what? They can X-ray 200-million-year-old fossils, oh yes, they can. Those paleontologists are so darned clever!

Figuring out where the nostrils go. Identifying the genus from a jumbled mix of squished bones. Embryos with teeth. Even, maybe, proteins which means…shhhh DNA. Maybe. X-rays, CT scanners,

---

[64] "Unveiling the Secrets of Ancient Dinosaurs: Cutting-Edge X-ray Technology Sheds Light on Prehistoric World," *Scienceblog.com*, University of Warwick, June 1, 2023.
https://scienceblog.com/538094/unveiling-the-secrets-of-ancient-dinosaurs-cutting-edge-x-ray-technology-sheds-light-on-prehistoric-world/

and particle accelerators are showing scientists a whole new world inside tiny, eroded bits of rock.

Paleo-snoutology

In the very first chapter, we noted that dinosaurs had a lot of holes in their head, even besides the eyes and the nose. Despite the big holes, though, they put the nostrils in the wrong place until X-rays came along. Early illustrations of dinosaurs placed those nostrils high, typically up where the eyes are. For example, take a look at the Charles Knight painting in Figure 9. If you think the dinosaurs need to submerge, then you put the nostrils up high.

But Lawrence Witmer, who runs the DinoNose project, used X-rays to sample a whole series of living animals to determine where their nostrils ended, relative to their nose holes.[65] In case after case, he found that the nostril openings in living animals were down in front, not up in back.

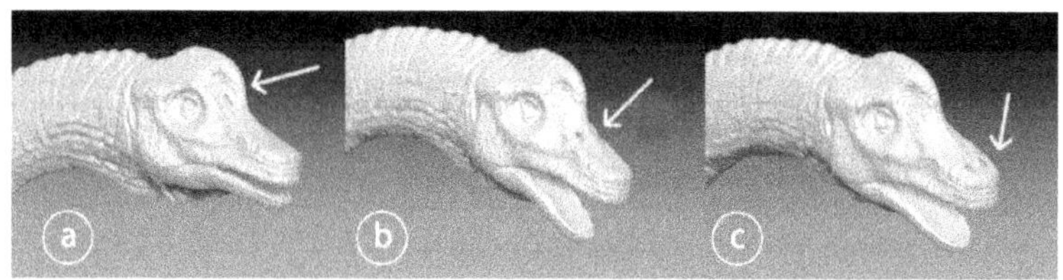

Fig 79. Graphic comparison of where brachiosaur nostrils might be placed: (a) near the eyes; (b) above the snout; (c) near the mouth. C is now thought to be most likely.

Nostrils near the mouth had several advantages. First, the nostrils would be closer to what's being smelled. The longer the snout, the more that's true. Second, having the smell occur near the mouth enhances the sense of taste. Finally, having the nostrils too far back would trap air into the nasal cavity rather than circulate into the lungs. Very inefficient.

---

[65] Erik Stokstad, "Dinosaur Nostrils Get a Hole New Look," *Science.org*, August 3, 2001. https://www.science.org/doi/10.1126/science.293.5531.779a

Why then, way back in the early dinosaur days, did paleontologists visualize the nostrils as much farther up in the skull? Remember that they believed the giant sauropods hung out in swamps. Scientists thought their bones would be too heavy to walk around, so they assumed they were primarily water animals. (But then why would they have long necks? And why would natural selection lead to an adaptation for an animal that limited them? Hmm…)

Marsh and Owen would probably respond that the long necks and high nostrils let them go into deeper water, so that they could hide from the bipeds with the big pointy teeth. That was the nature of the drawing from 1897. But if they were meant to swim, why not have fins? And if that big ol' body is all underwater, wouldn't they be eaten by the or mosasaurs or …oh, never mind. Darwin is just shaking his head at those high nostrils.

Nowadays, Witmer and his DinoNose superstar machines have produced a better argument. The nostrils should be lower, which frees them from the water and lets them wander off into the forest to smell the tops of trees.

More Fun with Jumbles of Bones

X-rays were used in another way to identify the pieces and parts of an ichthyosaur. Mary Anning probably could have told them it was an ichthyosaur, after extracting several of the giant reptiles painstakingly from the Lyme Regis rock. But even Mary might have been stumped here, when the fossil was barely a smear across a rock—frozen rock, to boot—found on the island of Svalbard near the Arctic. The rock was brought to an Oslo museum, but it sat there, unexamined, because other than recognizing its giant eye and naming it "Oda," little else could be analyzed.

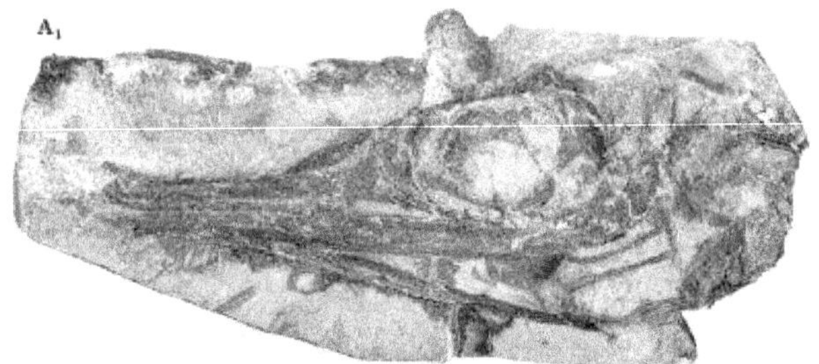

Oda, ichthyosaur fossil from Svalbard

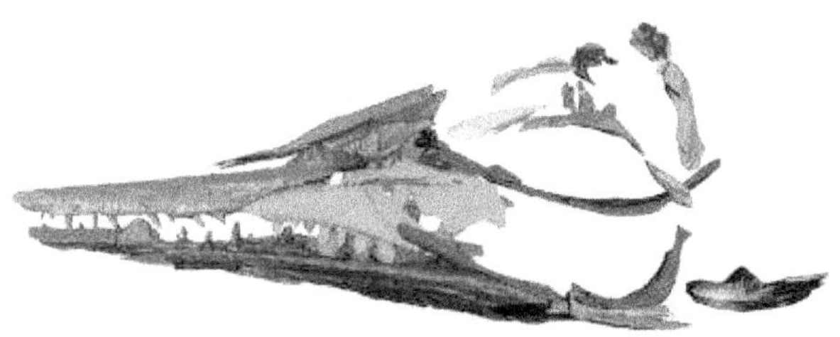

3-D imaging allows bones to be
separately identified

Fig 80. Three-dimensional imaging of this "smashed" ichthyosaur skull (ODA)
showed how the skull was constructed.

Using first a radiograph, then a CT scan, researchers in 2023 reconstructed the details of the skull and bits of vertebrae superimposed on it.[66] Part of the reason for the clarity is that the mineral which flowed in the water to turn it into a fossil was barite, which happens to be the thing most used to create contrasts in X-rays. Sometimes, you get lucky!

For this particular animal, they could even see different layers of skin and signs of melanin cells, which led to them to argue that it was

---

[66] Sarah Kuta, "Unraveling the Mysteries of Oda the Ichthyosaur," *Smithsonian Magazine,* June 2, 2023.
https://www.smithsonianmag.com/smart-news/unraveling-the-mysteries-of-oda-the-ichthyosaur-180982291/

(a) warm-blooded and (b) had counter-shading. Knowing that sharks also have counter-shading, and that ichthyosaurs were giant predators with pointy teeth, this was an example that proved predators also benefited from counter-shading.

However, counter-shading suggests that ichthyosaurs could see colors. Ichthyosaurs were massive, dolphin-like reptiles. If they were warm-blooded and able to see colors, that would be an interesting adaptation. On the other hand, dolphins are warm-blooded, so maybe having thermoregulation was not strange for ancient reptiles. Still, figuring that out from this smashed fossil is another thing entirely.

Teeny Little Dinosaurs

Giant modern machines can also reveal entire worlds in miniature. Such worlds might be visible even within the shells of dinosaur eggs, buried in fossilized rock. Although dinosaurs grew big, they started small. Some dinosaur eggs were no bigger than chicken eggs, and with very thin shells. Peering inside the egg to see the bones of a 200-million-year-old embryo is delicate work. Even though the fossil is a rock, scraping a five-inch embryo out would destroy it.

That's why it took forty years for a clutch of *Massospondylus carinatus* eggs found in 1976 to be analyzed. Eroded embryos were visible on the outside of the rock, but otherwise researchers were stuck. This was a golden opportunity to view an early Jurassic plant-eater in development, but they couldn't exactly open the eggs to see the rest. The insides remained tantalizingly out of reach.

Fig 81. Detailed view of *Massospondylus* embryo fossil. Without X-rays, nothing more is visible. X-rays show more embryos inside, sporting teeth inside the egg.

Particle physicists to the rescue! Cyclotrons were not exactly built to look at dinosaur embryos, but paleontologists went to the European Synchrotron Radiation Facility (ESRF) facility to peer inside the eggs. Synchrotrons have extra-powerful visualizing tools connected to 3-D imaging capabilities. Physicists use them to see particles smaller than atoms. But they can also "see" inside other solid objects, like fossils. In this case, the paleontologists could determine that there were teeth in the mouths of the growing dinosaur "chicks"–two sets of teeth, in fact.

Researchers could then compare the embryos to those of living relatives and see that this animal shared features with both chickens and crocodiles. They could tell that one embryo was 60% developed, another 17%, and another 90%. This difference in growth occurs in modern animals, too. After all, even if the mother lays several eggs, she does not do so simultaneously. They have to be popped out one at a time, which itself takes time. As paleontologist Jonah Choiniere put it, it's amazing that in 250 million years, embryo development inside of eggs has not really changed.[67] Choiniere's paleontology group calls themselves the Stormberg Giants, after dinosaurs discovered in South Africa. *DinoNose? The Stormberg Giants? These guys are so creative!!*

Giant Machines for Tiny Parts

Archaeopteryx also got the Cyclotron treatment. Because these "missing" bird-dino links had such thin, hollow bones, their smashed parts in the fossils are hard to separate (see Figure 78). Paleontologists have known for 150 years that these fossils had feathers but could not see much more.

However, once they ran those pancaked fossils through the ESRF, the fancy cyclotron-synchrotron in France, they could magnify and examine the fossil in fine detail. Even with small bones, the new images allowed paleontologists to reconstruct their bodies with far more accuracy. They concluded from the detailed measurements that *Archaeopteryx* could fly "like a pheasant," in small bursts. It was already on the road to transition that birds took, jumping upward to catch insects and sometimes achieving small bursts of flight. It might take a few tens of millions of years. Darwin can wait.

While some researchers are using giant machines to bombard particles at rock, others are working with increasingly sophisticated microscopes. One called an atomic force microscope (AFM) can see things that are a fraction of a nanometer, which is more than a 1000 times better than the optical diffraction limit. This means that the AFM creates an image with physical touch rather than with light, which can distort vision. The microscope has a super tiny probe, only a few atoms wide. The result can generate 3-D images of a surface with much more detail than a regular microscope.

Mary Higby Schweitzer used the AFM and other tools to invent an entire new wing of science called *paleoproteomics*. She used microviewing tools to do something that nobody believed was possible. She found living proteins in a dinosaur fossil.

---

[67] European Synchrotron Radiation Facility, "Dinosaur 'Eating Eggs' Reveal their Secrets in 3D Thanks to X-rays and High-Powered Computers," *SciTechDaily*, April 9, 2020. https://scitechdaily.com/dinosaur-easter-eggs-reveal-their-secrets-in-3d-thanks-to-x-rays-and-high-powered-computers/

Schweitzer's background was in communication, teaching, and biology, so studying fossils wasn't her first go-to subject. While working on her PhD in Paleontology at Montana State, she believed she saw evidence of proteins. The only problem was that others could not replicate her research. This claim was incredibly controversial, since the ability to extract 70-million-year-old living matter was science fiction. To paraphrase one scientist, if you're going to claim exceptional results, you better have exceptional evidence. [68]Other people have to be able to see it, too. Schweitzer was unable to convince the scientific community, until 2007.

While still working at the Montana State University lab, the director gave her a piece of a *T. rex* bone to study. In the decade since receiving her doctorate, the tools had advanced, and this particular piece of bone held promise. She fiddled with the chemistry of it, playing around with different solutions—chemistry solutions, get it?—until one of them made the sample stretchy. Fossil. Stretchy. Contradiction in terms. She saw red blood cells. She saw proteins. She saw proof that the *T. rex* was a pregnant female.

There were a unique set of circumstances for this specimen in the composition of chemicals that had held it since the end of the Cretaceous. That composition was key, both in allowing her to see "inside" dinosaur protein cells and in allowing others to finally replicate the work. Since then, dozens of studies have been able to look at extinct animal proteins. Not DNA, she is careful to say. There will be no cloning of dinosaurs.

In a recent 2019 study of birds in northwestern China, the scientists applied Schweitzer's molecular paleontology techniques to find an unlaid egg in an extinct bird, another cousin of *Archaeopteryx*. The paleontologists decided to thank Schweitzer for her work. They named the species *Avimaia schweitzerae: aves* (bird) + *maia* (mother) + *schwieitzerae* (mother of molecular paleontology).

---

[68] Barry Yeoman, "Schweitzer's Dangerous Discovery," *Discover Magazine.com*, May 17, 2019. https://www.discovermagazine.com/the-sciences/schweitzers-dangerous-discovery

Y is for Yucatan

BOOM! Or maybe it was thump…fshhhh..whap thumpa-thumpa…bubble boom glub glub BOOM!…boOM…boOM…

Which was it? Luis and Walter Alvarez had one story, and they were laughed out of the conference hall. Until they weren't. Gerta Keller, who disagreed with the Alvarezes, has been laughed out of the same rooms, despite also winning prizes for her research. The media has picked the asteroid over the volcanoes, although their vote shouldn't count. But if the more asteroids the merrier, then the Scots were happy to propose a second impact site, and an Indian scientist to suggest a third.

There are multiple stories still in play about how the dinosaurs ended. First, there is a story of a scientist who had a far-fetched idea outside his area of expertise and only a little data, which took decades for scientists to confirm. Then, there's a second story, of a scientist still fighting for her own version, one which would upend what is now conventional wisdom. There are stories of other voices chiming in, with their own versions.

The issue is that fame and fortune await those who can explain the Dinosaur Demise. Even if there is no Nobel Prize for Paleontology (and why isn't there?) there is scientific and public recognition. While people might scoff about media attention, positive stories about scientists create prestige for universities, which generates funding, tenure, and more resources to fly off to Italy, India, or the windiest parts of Montana.

It's been called "The Nastiest Feud in Science." The feud is still ongoing, even though now they have solved at least one mystery. They do know where the Big One hit.

They found the crater in the Yucatan.

Magnetic Anomalies in the Oil Industry

Two years before the paleontology bombshell lobbed by the Alvarezes, geophysicist Glen Penfield was flying over the Gulf of Mexico doing a survey for the Mexican oil company Pemex. Penfield was cataloging magnetic anomalies, and he noticed the anomalies formed a circular pattern. It was way too big for a volcano.

Penfield put his head together with colleague Antonio Camargo-Zanoguera, and they became convinced the saucer-shaped area had to have another cause. Penfield said he sent his data to the Alvarez team but never heard back. He and Camargo-Zanoguera then presented their findings at a 1981 geophysicist conference. Here the irony is overwhelming. The people who had the knowledge to connect the dots were not at the conference. Instead, they were at another conference, arguing against Alvarez's theory.

Penfield wasn't the only one who saw the anomalies, either. Other petroleum geologists working with Pemex had told the company about odd things at their site, too. More magnetic anomalies. Pieces of rock that looked like they had been fused by massive amounts of heat. The scientists gave the data to their bosses at the oil company in the 1960s and 1970s. Pemex stuck them in a drawer.

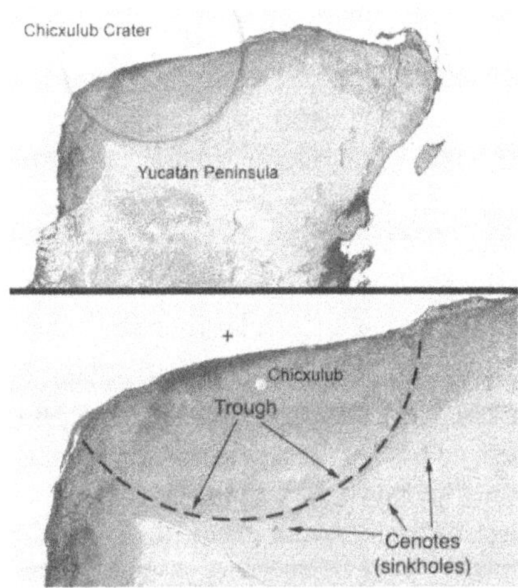

Fig 82. Survey map of the Yucatan by NASA/JPL, marking out both the circular magnetic anomalies and visible troughs in the landmass.

The oil company wasn't interested, and other scientists didn't seem to be. A warehouse burned down some of the records and core samples. The "search" for the crater continued, until a Canadian geologist, Alan Hildebrand, called them about a weird rock he found in Haiti, in the Gulf. The three put their heads together and, by 1991, they had the data to solve the puzzle. A sizable asteroid had slammed into the Gulf of Mexico and created a 100-mile-diameter crater. Iridium blew into the atmosphere as well as "shocked" rocks; both iridium and rocks had landed miles away. They had found Luis's crater from the asteroid that hit at the K-Pg boundary. Since then, it's been referred to as the Chicxulub crater.

Luis Alvarez passed away from cancer three years before the data was published. But he had been right.

You Get A Crater, He Gets A Crater...

Alvarez was right about an asteroid. But it turns out that it was not the only asteroid near the K-PG boundary. Were they multiple asteroids as part of a large-scale event? Or, was there one smaller asteroid a bit before the second, kind of like a John the Baptist warning—Repent All Ye Triceratops, the Big One's Coming! Or, if the smaller one came second, did it pile on the damage, like an anvil hitting Wile E. Coyote *after* he fell off the cliff?

For this next part, we need to know the word *palynological*, which might satisfy those with a Weird-Word-of-the-Month fetish. It means "the study of live and fossil spores, pollen grains, and similar plant structures," from the Greek *palunein*, which means "to scatter" as in dust or "pollen." Fern spores are very much in play here. And, for those of you with allergies, you now know that they are palynological.

Ukraine also had a crater, Boltysh, named for a nearby village. Discovered in 1975, scientists had not been able to estimate its date of impact. It was known to be "roughly" the same age as Chicxulub, but when it's 65 my ago, roughly could be mean +/- a million years, right?

Scientists in 2010 wanted to be more precise, to see whether Boltysh could be dated to *before* or *after* Chicxulub within a few thousand years. (I keep wanting to type "borscht," but that's a soup.

Of course, if an asteroid hit, a lot of things would turn to soup.) But was it *before* or *after* the soup course? If it was before, credit might need to be shared among the meteors.

Professor David Jonn of Aberdeen discovered that a bunch of fossilized fern pollen—*palynological matter*—was plentiful in the impact crater of Boltysh. But there was also a wee bit more pollen, a *second* spike, later on in the geological layers. Ferns are known to be among the first things to grow after an apocalypse, so Jolley theorized that there must have been two impacts. He also thought this meant that Chicxulub came after, which would put Boltysh at the head of the line.

Trying to tell time from rocks is tricky stuff. Geologists knew that the K-Pg boundary at the end of the dinosaur age was around 66 million years ago—66.04 ± 0.05/0.10 to be darned precise. In 1975, they looked at some fused rocks from Boltysh but could only date them to between 54 and 98 my ago, which was not specific enough. They got out the Geiger counter and stood far enough away, like in the 1950s' sci-fi movies, and using radioactive decay measured the impact at 65.17 million +/- 640,000 which is, guess when? Be-*fore* the *T. rex* went screaming and waving its tiny arms.

However, another canny lassie up in Glasgow named Annemarie Pickersgill, perhaps the best scientific name in this book, suspected there was more to it. She matched data from Ukraine with comparable data from Montana, using a technique that measures argon-argon, because every paleontologist knows that two argons are better than one.

Pickersgill and Friends used their argon-argon to date the Boltysh crater very precisely to "65.39 ± 0.14/0.16 million years or ~0.65 million years after the mass extinction."[69] A-Ha! It apparently was quite well done, because another scientist enthused: "The argon ages are absolutely beautiful."[70] This most accurate date confirms that Boltysh came after the K-Pg boundary. Based on Professor

---

[69] Annemarie E. Pickersgill *et al.* "The Boltysh impact structure: An early Danian impact event during recovery from the K-Pg mass extinction," *Sci. Adv.* no., 7(2021), 1.

[70] Philippe Claeys, a geologist at the Free University of Brussels, Belgium who didn't participate in the study, so could act as a referee. Shi En Kim, "New Research of Impact Crater Blows Away Previous Estimates of Its Age," *Smithsonian Magazine*, June 18, 2021. https://www.smithsonianmag.com/science-nature/new-research-impact-crater-blows-away-previous-estimates-its-age-180978023/

Pickersgill's work—I just love typing that name—the Boltysh crater must have followed Chicxulub.

Why do the two fern spikes matter? Imagine that the planet is already going crazy from the big daddy at Chicxulub. Volcanoes are spewing everywhere, the parasaurolophuses are writing their last will and testament, pterosaur divas are screeching, *The sky is falling!!!!…* And another asteroid hits. The first asteroid creates devastation and recovery (fern spike #1). The second creates another wave of doom and recovery (fern spike #2). What this helps scientists understand is that when climate change is triggered by *any* cause, it could lead to a chain of additional climate change spikes, triggers, and more recoveries. This is something we would all find useful right now.

The Scots found a crater, but so did a scientist in India. Naturally, once the Alvarez theory was first advanced, everyone began looking for craters. Professor Sankar Chatterjee thought he had found one in Southwest India, under the Indian Ocean. He called his crater Shiva, after the Hindu god that dances to destroy the world. Shiva is a much cooler name than Boltysh and easier to spell than Chicxulub, but he has had less success in getting air-time. This was partly because the Shiva crater he surmised would have been covered up with additional activity from the Deccan Traps.

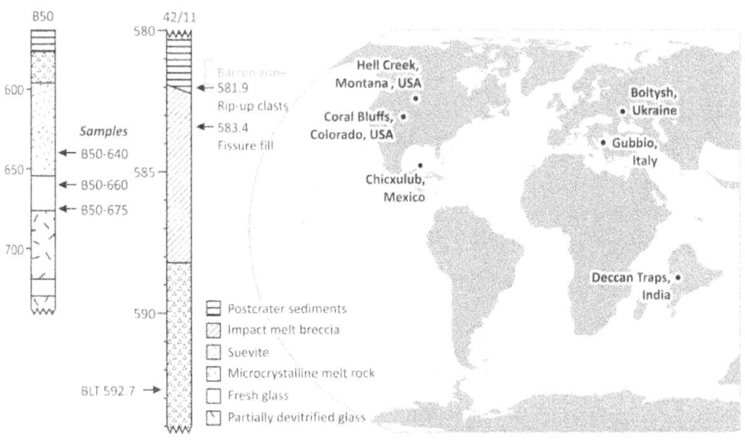

Fig 83. Graphic from Pickersgill et al. showing the various location of K-Pg boundary impact craters.

Chatterjee has been publishing papers on Shiva since 1997, but he has more skeptics than supporters. His crater has an odd shape, and his evidence is limited. Because of the volcanoes, the sea floor around the area shifts a lot, with lots of lava, so perhaps all his argon evidence has been just covered up, you know, from the lava. If it weren't for all that lava and floor-shifting, maybe he would have been able to prove that his asteroid got there first. So he claims. But even Gerta "Deccan Traps" Keller isn't buying it: "Unfortunately, we have found no evidence to support his claims. Sorry to say, this is all nonsense."[71]

Translated: Chatterjee's claim that Shiva was *the* crater is even less supportable than Chicxulub or Boltysh. Maybe Shiva happened, but it can't be included as contributing to the end of the Cretaceous.

Perhaps Keller's assessment of Chatterjee was a little harsh. But lots of harsh words have been thrown around on this topic.

Smart People Saying Dumb Things

Whether an asteroid did or did not hit Earth, whether multiple asteroids hit, or whether volcanoes poisoned the atmosphere is all speculation. Because of the stakes involved, hyperbole and rancor has spilled into the science, which is a shame.

Perhaps Luis Alvarez should have been prepared. He had won a Nobel Prize, so maybe he thought they'd cut him some slack. Instead, it appears the paleogeologists did the opposite. Being a Nobel Prize-winning physicist, Alvarez was smart. If you saw the movie *Oppenheimer* or know something about physicists, they are so smart, and they hear that so often, that some can get a little arrogant.

Alvarez fought back. In one published exchange, he responded to one of his critic's arguments by calling the paleontologists "stamp collectors." *ouch* In another case, a scientist making a case at a conference was told in the Q&A period that some of his data was erroneously labeled. Alvarez told the media later, "it took my son two

---

[71] Clara Moskowitz, "New Dino-Destroying Theory Fuels Hot Debate," *Space.com*, October 18, 2009. https://www.space.com/7413-dino-destroying-theory-fuels-hot-debate.html

minutes to demolish" the professor and that the audience "burst out laughing."[72] It seems like Alvarez himself had become thin-skinned enough to lob a few choice *nyaah nyaah nyaahs* back.

Keller, for her part, says she was called a troublemaker and a "bitch." Over several decades, she had authored and coauthored more than a hundred papers on the topic of this mass extinction and the Deccan Traps. She looked at mercury levels, the dispersal of iridium, the types of biotic material that existed before and after. Her work was intricate, sophisticated, peer-reviewed, and strongly supported with solid data. Still, it barely got any play once the asteroid hypothesis was proposed.

Consider, too, that Keller was a woman scientist growing up in the days when women were taught home economics, not science. She had to fight much harder, coming into the field, in order to get the position she obtained. Her work was probably always challenged, so she learned to make it as airtight as possible. Nevertheless, she was sometimes treated as "the most dangerous woman of the world" who should be burned at the stake.[73] More recently, some media outlets have started treating her like an underdog and advancing her "what really happened" theory.[74] But it should not be reported like a race or a contest. The data is the data.

At least in some staid conferences, son Walter seemed to play peacemaker. Alvarez the Younger has said in more than one venue that both volcanic activity and an asteroid might have been the one-two punch required to take down the sophisticated dinosaur reign, which had gone unchecked for so long. It's a curious offshoot of the topic that this scientific rivalry became so bitter. Luis had already died in 1988 after a bout with cancer. He lived long enough to see more data captured to support his theory, but not long enough to be vindicated.

In 2010, finally, an international group of 41 scientists—experts in paleontology, geology, and other fields—tried to end 30 years of arguing by ruling that an asteroid had indeed struck the earth 65 million years ago. Bad stuff happened after that. End of story.

---

[72] Malcolm W. Browne, "The Debate Over Dinosaur Extinctions Takes an Unusually Rancorous Turn," *The New York Times*, January 19, 1988, 49.

[73] Bianca Bosker, "The Nastiest Feud in Science," *Atlantic*, August 14, 2018.

[74] Simon, "Epic Fight."

Gerta Keller continues to gather data. The Deccan Trap volcanoes did wreak havoc near the end of the Cretaceous, whether they were the main cause for extinction or not. Textbooks today compromise and note that some species had been undergoing background extinction before 65 my. Many were not. But the asteroid may have delivered the final blow for all the dinosaurs.

Walter Alvarez, since 2010, has been working on a project called "Big History," giving lectures and producing technology to help people understand the significance of time scales. Some of those lectures are online and free. His reputation survived perhaps, in part, because he didn't lob insults at people. Frankly, being a scientist son of a Nobel Prize winner was probably not the easiest thing in the world.

But if his dad hadn't taken such an interest in his work, then we'd still think the dinosaurs were just wicked.

Why It's Hard to Be Certain

The reason for all this uncertainty and debate is complicated. In the first place, we all love dinosaurs, right? That's made it possible for me turn out 26 chapters on these magnificent creatures, barely scratching the surface of their complex world. We all want to know what happened to them.

Second, the idea of a world-influencing asteroid is really sexy science. It's why there was so much resistance to Alvarez's cockamamie notion in the first place. The paleontologists probably knew that if he was right, there would be no end to the *National Enquirer*-style headlines and graphics. He was right, and they get to continue churning them out.

When science gets this much attention, it's career-making. We're talking floods of money for lab equipment, international travel, press releases, and tenure, whether you're arguing that an asteroid killed all life or that it didn't. Even the Wikipedia entry that merely documents the discussion about the K-Pg boundary lists 289 papers alone.[75]

---

[75] "Cretaceous-Paleogene Boundary," *Wikipedia.org*, Last updated November 23, 2024.
https://en.wikipedia.org/wiki/Cretaceous%E2%80%93Paleogene_extinction_eve
nt. Accessed November 27, 2024.

Not being a scientist, I can't evaluate all the technical arguments. As a historian, though, I know that two things here will cause problems. The first is the idea of "precision." Sure, radiometric dating and other new technologies are giving scientists the ability to date more precisely. But plus or minus tens of thousands of years is still a long time. Mounds of evidence strung together, like chemical composition, site dispersal, and the prevalence of specific flora, can be convincing. Yet at the end of the day, it's still primarily suggestive, whether it's a giant asteroid or exploding volcanoes. Both would have undoubtedly had an impact for hundreds of years. Which came first would give the "discoverer" the popular opinion version of a Nobel Prize. But could we ever really know without a time machine?

Then there are the fossils. We're all sitting atop a K-Pg boundary that's not been dug up. Paleontologists know what they know based on what they've found, but it's partly because of where they were, in Utah, Mongolia, or Haiti. We can know that there were comparatively more *here* and comparatively less *there*, but it's educated guessing. We might be incredibly certain that the *T. rex* lived during a specific part of the Cretaceous. However, whether his massive jaws or strong powerful legs were *more* of a contributor to his success is hard to say.

Which invention was more important in your life, the telephone or the computer circuit? Or literacy? The plow? Once we get into the "most important" or "came first" or "most significant contribution" arguments for things which all occurred and all contributed, then it's guesswork. Forty-one people agreeing on Cause A doesn't mean it really was Cause A, no matter how smart those 41 people are.

The bad part of all this is that we still don't one hundred percent know how the dinosaurs died off, and people's careers have been tarnished by all the infighting. Yet it's not the first time scientists have fought over dinosaurs. Remember how Gideon Mantell ("I") was stabbed in the back by Richard Owen? Both of them downplayed the contributions by Mary Anning ("M"), not to mention their wives finding fossils, providing illustrations, and editing manuscripts, all while raising children. In the Bone Wars in the American West, Edwin Cope and O. C. Marsh stole each other's fossils and sabotaged each other's work ("U"). Paleontologists ever since have had to hire security guards to watch their discoveries while they sleep. Not to mention the uneasy alliance between amateur and commercial fossil hunters. The history of acrimonious fighting over dinosaurs is ongoing. The more we want to know, the more valuable the prize for being right.

It's not ultimately bad for scientists to disagree. Some, maybe even most, of this disagreement has been healthy for science. The crazy asteroid theory launched a whole new interest in paleo research, helping to turbo-charge the dinosaur renaissance. The Deccan Trap theory has kept it going and fueled interest. New technologies have been discovered along with new ways of proving a theory.

That is the essence of what science is supposed to be. It would just be nice if they'd leave the name-calling out of it.

Z is for Zuul

While Z is often a hard letter to write about for an alphabetic challenge, there were actually plenty of choices of Z dinosaurs to choose from.

- *Zalmoxes*—A strange-looking ornithopod from Romania.

- *Zanabazar*—Named after a Buddhist spiritual leader.

- *Zapalasaurus*—This "diplodocoid" sauropod lived in early Cretaceous South America.

- *Zby*—This dinosaur's name was inversely proportional to its size.

- *Zephyrosaurus*—Otherwise known as the Western Wind Lizard.

- *Zhanghenglong*—A transitional hadrosaur of late Cretaceous Asia.

- *Zhejiangosaurus*—The first identified nodosaur from Asia.

- *Zhenyuanlong*—Also known as the "fluffy feathered poodle from hell."

- *Zhongyuansaurus*—The only known ankylosaur to lack a tail club.

- *Zhuchengosaurus*—This hadrosaur was even bigger than *Shantungosaurus*.

- *Zhuchengtyrannus*—This Asian tyrannosaur was the size of *T. rex*.

- *Zhuchengceratops*—It probably figured on the lunch menu of *Zhuchengtyrannus*.

- *Zuniceratops*—This horned dinosaur was discovered by an eight-year-old boy.

- *Zuolong*—It was named after General Tso, of Chinese restaurant fame.

- *Zupaysaurus*—This "devil lizard" was one of the earliest theropods.[76]

- *Zuul crurivastator*.

That last one is, indeed, Zuul from the movie *Ghostbusters*. It's the Zuul who inhabits Sigourney Weaver's body in order to search for the Keymaster, schlubby Rick Moranis, so that their coupling will release the demon Gozer into the world. The movie is a nerdy fantasy written by nerds about nerds for nerds.

Frankly, I was a never fan of that movie, but when I was running down the list of "Z" dinosaurs to figure out which should front this last chapter, I said the word *Zuul* aloud. My spouse, who is also a writer, immediately said *Oh! The Gatekeeper of Gozer*. Paleontologists, I suppose, are as nerdy as romance writers, Olympic historians, and Hollywood directors, so, yes….

They did indeed name a dinosaur for Zuul.

---

[76] Bob Strauss, "A to Z List of Dinosaur Names," *ThoughtCo.com*, Last updated May 2, 2024.

Fig 84. *Zuul crurivastator* in the wild. In the movie, Zuul is more dog-like, but both creatures have horizontal horns.

Zuul's hold on popular culture—a dinosaur based on a mythical creature—is too hard to resist. For this last chapter on dinosaurs, it seems perfect to wrap up with our friend the shin-biter and mythical "gatekeeper." It's the ultimate example of the strong hold that dinosaurs have on us and our popular culture. Dinosaurs are increasingly named for fictional characters, much as fictional characters have been named for dinosaurs.

Destroyer of Shins

The discovery of *Zuul crurivastator* echoes many of the topics covered so far: for-profit fossil collectors, lucky finds, and skins of horned dinosaurs. Fossil collectors were using small pieces of construction equipment (Figure 85, left photo, top), digging down twelve meters, looking for a meat-eater named *Gorgosaurus*. As this excavating machine went *clunk*, they stopped digging, and *voila!* They found a beautiful thing, a tail club of an ankylosaur, those low-to-the-ground armadillo things. Forget the *Gorgosaurus!*

Fig 85. The discovery of the well-preserved remains of Zuul, uncovered while digging in Montana. Zuul's skull shows its bony side horns.

This ankylosaur was, to use those perfect fossil-collecting words, perfectly preserved. It also was upside down, like the one in Chapter "S." Do ankylosaurs die upside down for some reason?[77] It turns out Theropoda LLC—the fossil collectors in this case—were able to sell it to a museum, and in Canada! The Royal Ontario museum scientists laser-scanned it and were able to reconstruct the skull.

Why name it Zuul? The head, with its horizontal horns, made it a dead ringer for the dog in the movie. Clearly, someone on the research team was a fan of *Ghostbusters*. Feel free to poke the internet to see a picture of the Zuul from the movie. You may also find that many people have named their cats Zuul. It's ironic, since CGI artists who develop movie monster designs often use what for the models? Dinosaurs! Things come full circle.

Zuul's second name is even better. *Crurivastator* really does mean destroyer of shins:

crus (shank, shin) + *vastator* (destroyer)

Because ankylosaurs—Hmm, is that why they were named *ankle*osaurs? Anyway, they had a tail club, which they used to swish at the lower limbs of predators, so they could indeed be a destroyer of shin bones.

---

[77] Since fossilized animals are often preserved because they die in water, i.e. rivers, it's possible that ankylosaur bodies naturally flip over in water.

No Spielbergi

This naming of dinosaurs for movie characters brings up a question I've been wondering about since chapter "J." Steven Spielberg hired dinosaur experts like Jack Horner and Robert Bakker for his 1993 film. That film portrayed dinosaurs more accurately than had ever been seen before and, in turn, influenced and inspired future dinosaur enthusiasts. Did the dinosaur enthusiasts return the favor?

In 1993, the group that discovered an impressive dino called *Utahraptor* tried to give it the species name *spielbergi* in anticipatory honor of the director. This was before *Jurassic Park* had even appeared. At the time, the group said they were hoping for a funding source, perhaps from Spielberg or Universal Studios. When they didn't get funded, so one story goes, they changed the name.[78]

Fig 86. *Utahraptor ostrommyi* in full chomp mode at the Dinosaur Journey museum in Fruta, CO. A bit over-the-top gory, but as the dinosaur originally planned to be named *Utahraptor spielbergi*, the monstrous depiction seems fitting.

But that version doesn't really ring true, does it? Scientists usually aren't blackmailers. Instead, according to a more recent account, Universal was the one that screwed it up for Steven, or themselves,

---

[78] Brooke Adams, "Director Loses *Utahraptor* Name Game," *Deseret.com*, June 15, 1993.
https://www.deseret.com/1993/6/15/19051844/director-loses-utahraptor-name-game/

depending on your point of view.[79] The third party involved was a tiny Pennsylvania museum, created by a local scientific society, which planned to exhibit the *Utahraptor*. The Putnam Museum used the word *Jurassic* in their promotional materials. They had done so many times before. It's like using the word *Gondwanaland* or *Oligocene*—if you know what it means scientifically, you do, but other people don't. People don't usually get upset and start suing.

At the time, in late 1992, *Jurassic* was not a household word. But Universal was thinking about the trademark side of things when they heard of the exhibit. They threatened this poor little Erie Zoological Society with legal action. The Putnam Museum had printed up T-shirts with *Utahraptor spielbergi* already on them, but they had to take out the word *Jurassic*.

As a result, the *Utahraptor* scientists changed the proposed species name to *ostrommyi* since the Hollywood types were making such a fuss. This name was for John Ostrom, the guy who made *Deinonychus* famous and helped push forward the dinosaur renaissance, which had, in turn, influenced Spielberg's choices. It does seem a better name in the end.

Life Imitates Art Imitates Life

Lots of dinosaurs have been named for fictional creatures, just like Zuul. Some fictional creatures have also been named after dinosaurs, like *Gororosaurus* in the Godzilla movies or the Dinobots in the *Transformers* franchise. Since there are new animal species being discovered every day, they all need names. Many of those new names refer to fictional creatures, though the majority seem to be going to spiders, wasps, and beetles. If you want to see a whole menagerie named after H.P. Lovecraft characters, look in the insect section of the ICZN, the naming organization.

Every single species, whether dinosaur or otherwise, must walk a torturous path to its name. For example, the pterosaur (not a dinosaur!) named *Targaryendraco wiedenrothi* was originally named *Ornithocheirus wiedenrothi*, after the amateur fossil hunter who found it.

---

[79] Brian Vanhooker, "Spielberg's Raptor," *Inverse.com*, September 16, 2021. https://www.inverse.com/culture/spielberg-raptor-jurassic-park

After five more studies, though, the pterosaur clade was reorganized and the discovery was given its own tree branch. The genus was then renamed for the House Targaryen, the House of Dragons from *Game of Thrones*.

A list of dinosaurs recently dubbed with fictional names leans heavily into the meat-eaters. Throw them all together, and you get:

- *Pantydraco caducus*—after the Pant-y-ffynnon quarry in Wales, a thecodont

- *Hagryphus giganteus*—Egyptian god Ra + griffin + big, an oviraptor

- *Gojirasaurus quayi*—the Japanese Godzilla, a theropod

- *Bambiraptor feinbergi*—a theropod

- *Medusaceratops lokii*, because it has Loki-like horns, a ceratopsian

- *Thanos simonattoi*, a mean-looking theropod that must have seen *Infinity Wars*

- *Ozraptor subotaii*, a thief, egg-stealer, from Subotai of the Conan series

- *Bradycneme draculae*, found in Transylvania, another theropod

- *Irritator challengeri*, from Conan Doyle's *Lost World*, yet another theropod

- *Borogovia gracilicrus*, like Carroll's "borogoves," still another theropod

- *Lohuecotitan pandafilandi*, after Pandafilando, a giant in *Don Quixote*, a titanosaur

- *Dracorex hogwartsia*

The story about this last one is a bit sad. Paleontologists found pieces of a dinosaur in South Dakota. After the skeleton was assembled and acquired by an Indiana children's science museum, the museum had a naming contest. The Indiana patrons chose a name related to Harry Potter, which means Dragon King of Hogwarts in Greek.

However, the scientists apparently named it too quickly. It's now thought to be a juvenile version of *Pachycephalosaurus*, that widespread group of bony-headed vegetarians. It will probably get renamed and reclassified before ere long. Maybe *Pachycephalosaurus hogwartsia*???

Only time will tell. But that's what paleontology is pretty much all about, isn't it?

End Thoughts

Dreaming of Dinosaurs

It's curious that we have such a strong affinity for these creatures, who lived so long ago and have left us only some bones and the occasional piece of fossilized skin. We don't generally feel that way about trilobites, bacteria, or bark beetles, even though they, in various ways, also ruled their corner of the world. We don't even feel that way about our nearest cousins, the chimpanzees and gorillas. Instead, we write dystopian stories where we go to war with the apes.

But dinosaurs fill stories. Writing this, I was reminded of Guy Endore's short story, "Day of the Dragon." A scientist fixes a flaw in a crocodile's heart, and it becomes a dragon. Could it not also have become a dinosaur? Ah, but then the scientist would have had to fix the ankle bones, as we saw in "A."

There's also Ray Bradbury's "A Sound of Thunder," where time travelers use technology to hunt dinosaurs. One freaks out at seeing a *T. rex*, veers off the path, and crushes a Cretaceous butterfly. Upon returning, fascists have taken over America. Perhaps that explains it…

I still believe if we found enough bones, we would be certain that dragons have been dinosaurs all along. Dinosaurs are both real and the stuff of dreams: half-real and half-imagined. Even though we can draw flesh on their bones, they can be hard to see as real, even when we're looking at well-rendered, life-sized versions. At the same time, everyone aims to create their own versions. If you travel around the country—around the world—you can see how many of us imagine dinosaurs. Take a trip through the back roads in America, and you find sculpture after sculpture, museum after museum. So many others dream of dinosaurs.

Fig 87. Call them roadside attractions or just fanciful backyard artwork, but America is full of dinosaur sculptures, like this little display on a back road in Michigan. See the Dinosaur U. S. A.!

We'd like to think that we could tame the dinosaurs, even though it's hard to imagine actually doing that. As the *Jurassic* movies showed, it's dangerous to think about trying. Because they ruled the earth and succumbed to climate change, we want to understand what happened to them, as hard as that may be ("Y"). We want to know what these bones are trying to tell us, 200 million years later. Given that we've only been studying them ourselves for a couple of centuries, we've probably barely scratched the surface.

What Dinosaurs Can Teach Us

> Those who cannot remember the past are condemned to repeat it.
>
> *Santayana*

Dinosaurs do matter to our future. Of course, I am not suggesting that there will be a time machine where a bespectacled

Parasaurolophus jumps out and yells, "You must plant okra, before it's too late!" … although that would be cool. Kenneth Lacovara, who we met when discussing *T. rexes* ("T"), also believes that dinosaurs can teach us valuable lessons.

What lessons can dinosaurs teach us? Is it that, if you see an 8.5-mile-wide asteroid heading for your neighborhood, bend over and firmly place your head between your knees… or something a little less primitive?[80] Lacovara's compelling argument derives from the idea that dinosaurs were an incredibly successful branch on the tree of life. That's what paleontologists have been trying to tell us all along.

Across 185 million years, dinosaurs proliferated into thousands of species, and we've barely found a fraction of them. They might be smaller than a chicken or bigger than a Boeing 737. Their reign covered nearly a third of the span of time that multi-celled life has been on Earth—three times as long as us mammals. The biggest irony, in fact, is that the word "dinosaur" is used as a metaphor for being outmoded or incapable of change, given that the dinosaur kingdom's capacity to diversify and adapt is still unparalleled. They didn't really "go extinct" as much as being extinguished by an extraterrestrial bolt of lightning. Besides, technically, they're not extinct.

Here's the payoff. This incredibly diverse, widespread, long-lived group of creatures were killed off by a freak event, an extraterrestrial rock that refused to deviate from Earth's path. It wasn't about lack of adaptation; they couldn't see what was coming. Even if it was volcanoes, the dinosaurs couldn't adapt around that, didn't cause the extinction event, and did not know what was happening. At least we can adapt. At least we know. We're at the beginning of a mass extinction event. Let's not even debate who or what caused it; we know we're there. Given this, we can learn two things by looking back at the past.

First, we can learn humility. *T. rex,* as one of the most powerful predators in 600 million years, still couldn't survive massive change, despite his superior adaptations. Being a superior creature on the planet isn't enough to outlast everything.

---

[80] In case you never heard the joke, during the Cold War, they used to say, "In case of a nuclear war, bend over, firmly place your head between your knees, and kiss your ass goodbye." That's a bit of a rude way to end a book, so perhaps just think of saying goodbye.

Second, the mini-turkeys and mole-like shrews that made it past the K-Pg event were funny-looking and small, with very few of what we would deem superior adaptations. They just had the adaptation that worked for the time.

If the *Morganucodons* can figure this out, surely we can as well. The faster we do it, the less suffering and damage for future generations. Because, although *T. rex* did have those huge, efficient jaws, he did have a tiny brain. That's where *H. sapiens* has an advantage.

If only we can use it.

Acknowledgments

It's not easy to write about a topic that you are not an expert on. There is that gremlin that never leaves your shoulder, whispering sweet negatives. Fortunately, I have an excellent ongoing support team of friends and family who never once asked, "Why *are* you doing that?" I am particularly blessed by those who read the online posts or work-in-process and provided encouragement and feedback. All it takes is one person saying, "I never thought I would find this topic interesting until I read your post…" to fuel another few thousand words out of me.

I especially appreciated the questions and comments from Jac Hills, whose description of being a youngster, constantly visiting Dippy at the British Museum, was repeatedly inspiring. Thanks to MJ and Bea, who followed me while I wandered around Colorado, looking at every dinosaur footprint and bone that crossed my path.

I also wish to thank the folks who dreamed up this blogging challenge of "A to Z," Arlee Bird and J. Lenni Dorner. The A to Z event doesn't get the play of NaNoWriMo, but it's been a big help to me.

Thanks again to my supremo editor Heather Flournoy, who said "Sure," and fit this in with somewhat short notice. My work has continued to improve because of her wise pair of eyes, and she must be the best editor on the earth, um, I mean on Earth. Thanks also to my mentor, Dr. Nancy Park from the CSU East Bay History department, who taught me to "feed the baby" and helped me reduce some of my worst meandering down rabbit holes.

I did not realize, until I started putting this work together, how many dinosaur museums I had visited, how many dinosaur roadside sculpture photos fill my files, and how often I had hijacked a road trip to see one more set of footprints or bones. For someone not into science, I just can't get enough about dinosaurs.

Fig 88. While I seem calm, I was mentally dancing the mambo while touching this 200-million-year-old dinosaur fossil at the Quarry Exhibit in Dinosaur National Park in Utah.

My immense gratitude, therefore, goes to all the folks who put together the dinosaur museums, exhibits, and national parks. We are blessed in the United States to have more than a dozen dinosaur-themed National Parks, multiple Dinosaur Ridge Trails, and at least a half-dozen Dinosaur Museums—that's just the ones I know about. Thanks for feeding my dinosaur passion.

Most of all, I also extend my biggest appreciation to my wife and family, who endured my addiction during all our vacations. Thank goodness that the tiny town of Blandings, Utah, famous for its own Dinosaur Museum, also has an excellent milkshake shop across from its coin laundry.

Appendix

Maps of the Earth Over Time

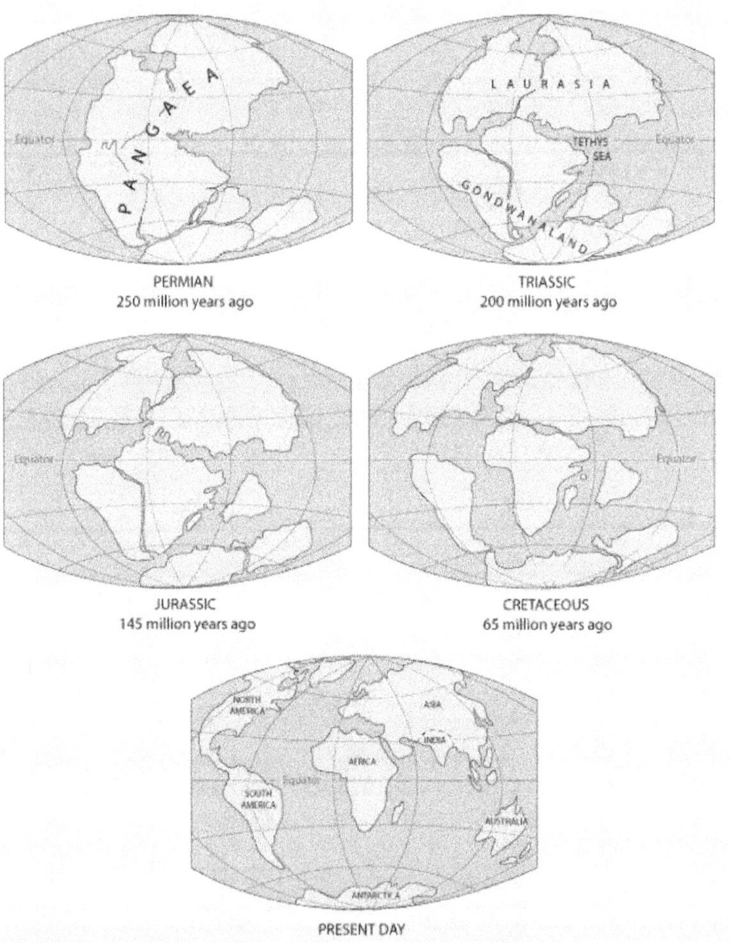

Fig 89. Map of the continents from before the three Mesozoic periods, during the three periods (Triassic, Jurassic and Cretaceous), and today.

Geological Divisions

Fig 90. The Age of Reptiles—the Mesozoic Era—encompassed the birth of dinosaurs in the Triassic, their expansion in the Jurassic, and their extinction at the end of the Cretaceous.

ERA	PERIOD	AGE	Million Years Ago
CENOZOIC Age of Mammals	Quaternary	Holocene	today-0.01
		Pleistocene	0.01-1.6
	Tertiary	Pliocene	1.6-5.3
		Miocene	5.3-23.7
		Oligocene	23.7-36.6
		Eocene	36.6-58
		Paleocene	58-66
MESOZOIC-- Age of Reptiles	Cretaceous	Diversity/Extinction of Dinosaurs	66-144
	Jurassic	Expansion of Dinosaurs	144-208
	Triassic	First Dinosaurs/ Mammals	208-245
PALEOZOIC	Permian		245-286
	Carboniferous		286-360
	Devonian	Age of Fish	360-408
	Silurian		408-438
	Ordovician	Age of Invertebrates	438-505
	Cambrian		505-570
PreCambrian			570-4600
FORMATION OF EARTH			

Dinosaur Family Tree in Brief

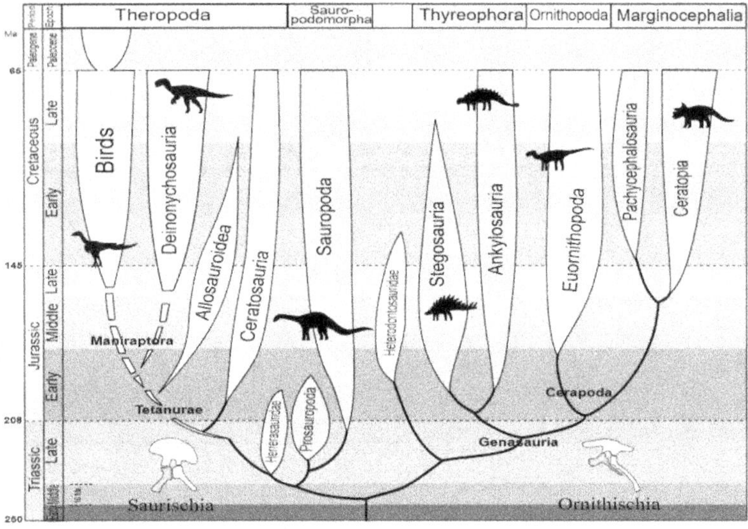

Fig 91. Abbreviated version of dinosaur clades (branches) based on Saurischia and Ornithischia divisions.

Key Sources

Books/Courses:

Bakker, Robert T. *The Dinosaur Heresies: New Theories Unlocking the Mystery of the Dinosaurs and Their Extinction.* New York: Zebra Books, 1986.

Brusatte, Steve. *The Rise and Fall of the Dinosaurs: A New History of their Lost World.* New York: Harper Collins, 2018.

Cadbury, Deborah. *Terrible Lizard: The First Dinosaur Hunters and the Birth of a New Science.* New York: Henry Holt & Co., 2000.

Fastovsky, David E., and David B. Weishampel. *Dinosaurs: A Concise Natural History.* 3rd ed. Cambridge: Cambridge University Press, 2016.

Lacovara, Kenneth. *Why Dinosaurs Matter.* New York: Simon & Schuster/TED Books, 2017.

Powell, James Lawrence. *Night Comes to the Cretaceous: Dinosaur Extinction and the Transformation of Modern Geology.* New York: W. H. Freeman, 1998.

Rogers, Kristi Curry. *Rediscovering the Age of Dinosaurs.* Twenty-four lectures and guidebook. Chantilly, VA: The Teaching Company, 2022.

Wallace, David Rains. *The Bonehunters' Revenge: Dinosaurs, Greek, and the Greatest Scientific Feud of the Gilded Age.* New York: Houghton Mifflin, 1999.

Williams, Paige. *The Dinosaur Artist: Obsession, Betrayal, and the Global Quest for Fossils.* New York: Hachette Books, 2018.

Articles/Websites:

Allmon, Warren D. "The Pre-Modern History of the Post-Modern Dinosaur: Phases and Causes in Post-Darwining Dinosaur Art." *Earth Sciences History* 25, no. 1 (2006): 5-35.

Alvarez, Luis W., Walter Alvarez, Frank Asaro, and Helen V. Michel. "Extraterrestrial Cause for the Cretaceous-Tertiary Extinction." *Science* 208, no. 4448 (1980): 1095-1108.

Baron, M., D. Norman, and P. Barrett. "A New Hypothesis of Dinosaur Relationships and Early Dinosaur Evolution." *Nature* 543 (2017): 501-506.

Carpenter, Kenneth. "A Dinosaur Paleontologist's View of Godzilla." In *The Official Godzilla Compendium*, edited by J. D. Lees and M. Cerasini, 102-106. New York: Random House, 1998.

Clemens, W. A., J. David Archibald, and Leo J. Hickey. "Out with a Whimper Not a Bang." *Paleobiology* 7, no. 3 (1981): 293-98.

Evans, David C. "Nasal Cavity Homologies and Cranial Crest Function in Lambeosaurine Dinosaurs." *Paleobiology* 32, no. 1 (2006): 109-25. Gorvett, Zaria. "The Polar Dinosaurs Revealing Ancient Secrets." BBC.com, November 30, 2022. https://www.bbc.com/future/article/20221130-the-polar-dinosaurs-revealing-ancient-secrets.

Keller, Gerta, Paula Mateo, Johannes Monkenbusch, Nicolas Thibault, Jahnavi Punekar, Jorge E. Spangenberg, Sigal Abramovich, et al. "Mercury Linked to Deccan Traps Volcanism, Climate Change and the End-Cretaceous Mass Extinction." *Global and Planetary Change* 194 (2020): 2-17.

Marx, Jean L. "Warm-Blooded Dinosaurs: Evidence Pro and Con." *Science* 199, no. 4336 (1978): 1424-26.

Nabavizadeh, Ali. "Did Plant-Eating Dinosaurs Have Cheeks?" *Science Connected Magazine*, February 14, 2019. https://magazine.scienceconnected.org/2019/02/did-plant-eating-dinosaurs-have-cheeks/.

Nesbitt, Sterling J. "The Early Evolution of Archosaurs: Relationships and the Origin of Major Clades." *Bulletin of the American Museum of Natural History* 352 (April 2011): 1-292.

Renne, Paul R., Alan L. Deino, Frederik J. Hilgen, Klaudia F. Kuiper, Darren F. Mark, William S. Mitchell, Leah E. Morgan, Roland Mundil, and Jan Smit. "Time Scales of Critical Events Around the Cretaceous-Paleogene Boundary." *Science* 339, no. 6120 (2013): 684-87.

Schulte, Peter, Laia Alegret, Ignacio Arenillas, José A. Arz, Penny J. Barton, Paul R. Bown, Timothy J. Bralower, et al. "The Chicxulub Asteroid Impact and Mass Extinction at the Cretaceous-Paleogene Boundary." *Science* 327, no. 5970 (2010): 1214-18.

Seymour, Roger S., Sarah L. Smith, Craig R. White, Donald M. Henderson, and Daniela Schwarz-Wings. "Blood Flow to Long Bones Indicates Activity Metabolism in Mammals, Reptiles and Dinosaurs." *Proceedings: Biological Sciences* 279, no. 1728 (2012): 451-56.

Weishampel, David B. "Acoustic Analyses of Potential Vocalization in Lambeosaurine Dinosaurs (Reptilia: Ornithischia)." *Paleobiology* 7, no. 2 (1981): 252-61.

Winick, Stephen. "She Sells Seashells and Mary Anning: Metafolklore with a Twist." *Folklife Today: American Folkslife and Veterans History Project* (blog), July 26, 2017. https://blogs.loc.gov/folklife/2017/07/she-sells-seashells-and-mary-anning-metafolklore-with-a-twist/.

Witmer, Lawrence M. "The Evolution of the Antorbital Cavity of

Archosaurs: A Study in Soft-Tissue Reconstruction in the Fossil Record with an Analysis of the Function of Pneumaticity." *Memoir (Society of Vertebrate Paleontology)* 3 (1997): 1-73.

Figure Credits

Figure 1   Author photo, Dinosaur Ridge Museum, Morrison, Colorado.
Figure 2   Author photo, Dinosaur Museum, Fruta, CO.
Figure 3   Author photo, Dinosaur Ridge Trail, Morrison, CO.
Figure 4   Author photo, Albuquerque Natural History Museum, NM.
Figure 5   Author graphic from originals via Wikimedia and Ohio State University Museum of Zoology, Cambridge Natural History Museum, Amsterdam Iconographia Zoologic.
Figure 6   Wikimedia drawing by Steveoc86.
Figure 7   Wikimedia drawing by Philcha.
Figure 8   Wikimedia, shared by Petter Bøckman, public domain.
Figure 9   Wikimedia, Charles R. Knight, public domain.
Figure 10   Wikimedia, Charles R. Knight, public domain.
Figure 11   Wikimedia, shared by Cervical 67, CC 3.0 license.
Figure 12   Wikimedia, shared by Annina Breen, CC 4.0 license.
Figure 13   Author graphic.
Figure 14   Author graphic.
Figure 15   Wikimedia, shared by Kiwi Rex, Amélie Pataud, CC 4.0.
Figure 16   Author photo.
Figure 17   Wikimedia, shared by Ballista, GNU license.
Figure 18   Wikimedia, from Library of Congress, public domain.
Figure 19   Wikimedia, Pearson Scott Foreman, public domain.
Figure 20   Wikimedia, shared by Smith609, arrows added.
Figure 21   Author table.
Figure 22   Wikimedia, photo by Bukvoed, CC 4.0.
Figure 23   Author photo.
Figure 24   Author photo
Figure 25   Wikimedia, photo by Poozeum, CC 4.0
Figure 26   Flickr, shared by Tom, CC 2.0 license, originally from Trans World Pictures.
Figure 27   Wikimedia, graphics shared by Ken Carpenter, Conty, and James A. Headden, cropped/rearranged by author.
Figure 28   Wikimedia, graphic from Ken Carpenter, CC 3.0.
Figure 29   Wikimedia, shared by Noger Chen, CC 2.0.
Figure 30   Author graphic.
Figure 31   Wikimedia, Nile crocodile skeleton shared by Paul Williams via Flickr, cropped and labeled by the author.
Figure 32   Author photo.

Hurum, J.H. , "First three-dimensional skull of the Middle Triassic mixosaurid ichthyosaur *Phalarodon fraasi* from Svalbard, Norway." Acta Palaeontologica Polonica 67 (1): 51–62.

Figure 82   NASA photo with graphics by NASA/JPL-Caltech, modified, public domain.

Figure 83   Image © Pickersgill, Mark, Lee, Kelley, and Jolley, exclusive licensee American Association for the Advancement of Science, CC 4.0.

Figure 84   Graphic created by ABelov2014 (https://abelov2014.deviantart.com/), CC 3.0.

Figure 85   Photo courtesy of Royal Publishing Society, by Victoria M. Arbour and David C. Evans (cropped by author), CC 4.0.

Figure 86   Author photo.

Figure 87   Author photo.

Figure 88   Author photo

Figure 89   Wikimedia, from US Geological Survey, public domain.

Figure 90   Author table.

Figure 91   Wikimedia, created by Zureks, CC 3.0.

Index of Ancient Reptiles

The following list of ancient reptiles are referenced in *The A to Z of Dinosaurs*. (D) refers to a dinosaur. (A) refers to an archosaur that is not a dinosaur. A letter in quotes ("X") refers to a chapter.

Index of People, Places, and Ideas

The following list excludes dinosaurs and other ancient reptiles, which are listed in the Index of Ancient Reptiles. A letter in quotes ("X") refers to a topic covered across an entire chapter.

About the Author

Maria Kaj is a historian and the author of three books on the Olympics, including *The A to Z Olympics*, the first of the *A to Z Essential Guides*. She also authored *Women and the Olympic Dream: The Continuing Struggle for Equality, 1896-2021*, published in 2022 by McFarland Publishing.

Along with the Olympics and dinosaurs, she has presented and written on diverse subjects from modern art to the history of the Mongols. In 2024, she received her master's degree in history, where her study of medieval accounting and culture won the university award for best thesis.

She began her sojourn into writing through her blog, "The Page Turns" at kajmeister.com. After decades working as a senior finance manager for a large corporate bank, she now enjoys digging through other kinds of data to help explain the world at large.

Her passion is nonfiction storytelling: everything has a story, which can be told equally with compassion and statistics.

When not obsessing about dinosaurs, the Olympics, or the Middle Ages, she mentors students in online business and economic classes for Stanley Kaplan, an education company, as well as volunteering as a free income tax preparer through the United Way. She is married to a romance writer, and, together, they are thrilled to be the parents of two gainfully employed college graduates. She lives in northern California.

She is working on a new book project which will focus on the untold stories of women in paleontology and archeology.

Read the blog: kajmeister.com
Contact the author: mariakajcv@gmail.com